TRAUMA-INFORMED EARLY EDUCATION

Helping Pre-School & Elementary Students Thrive!

MATTHEW S. BENNETT | SARAH BENNETT

Copyright © 2019 by Matthew S. Bennett and Sarah Bennett

All rights reserved.

First Printing, 2019.

Paperback ISBN: 978-1-6956-8103-3

Bennett Innovation Group, L3C

Denver, Colorado

www.traumasensitiveschoolsbook.com

Books may be purchased in quantity and/or special sales by contacting the publisher by email at matt@bigl3c.org.

To all those who dedicate their lives to the service and education of children: We thank you!

Contents

FOREWORD	11
INTRODUCTION	16
PART 1: What Is Wrong with These Kids?	21
Another Year, Another Bad Kid	23
CHAPTER 1: Why Won't They Behave?	24
How Behaviors Evolve from the Environment	33
Brain Development & Behaviors	37
States and Traits	43
Why Traditional Approaches Fail Students with Trauma	44
What Happened to You?	46
CHAPTER 2: Why Won't They Learn?	53
Trauma & Language Development	54
Trauma & Memory	56
Trauma & Future Thinking	58
Trauma & Cooperation	58
The Justification to Search for Answers	59
PART 2: The Trauma-Sensitive Classroom	65
What to Do with Caleb?	66

CHAPTER 3: Social-Emotional Learning: Strategies for Emotional Regulation — 71

    Calming the Body; Calming the Mind — 72
    Labeling Emotional States — 75
    Mindfulness and Emotional Regulation — 78
    Helping Students Establish a Positive View of Self — 82
    Shifting from a Fixed to a Growth Mindset — 83
    A New Goal: A Very Different Outcome — 85

CHAPTER 4: Social-Emotional Learning: Strategies for Relational Growth — 93

    Serve-and-Return Communication — 94
    A Different Approach to Behavioral Issues — 96
    OARS — 100
        Reflections — 101
        Affirmations — 102
        Open-Ended Questions and Statements — 103
        Summaries — 104
    Trust — 105
    Safety — 107
    A Different Approach — 109

CHAPTER 5: Positive Behavioral Supports for the Traumatized Child — 116

    Permission to Stop the Insanity! — 117
    A Skill-Based Approach — 119
    Trauma-Sensitive Restorative Justice — 121
    Values: What Are the Rules by Which You Live? — 122
    Finding a Starting Point — 123

CHAPTER 6: Positive Behavioral Supports for the Classroom — 136

   Shared Expectations & the Value of Repetition — 137
   Universal Expectations — 138
   Task-Specific Expectations — 140
   Rewards & Punishments — 142
   Trauma-Sensitive Positive Behavioral Support — 145
      Step 1: Regulate — 146
      Step 2: Relate — 146
      Step 3: Establishing Task-Specific Expectations — 146
      Step 4: Teach or Commence the Activity — 147
      Step 5: Monitoring Task-Specific Expectations — 148
      Step 6: Collective Review — 149
   A Whole New Classroom — 150

CHAPTER 7: Trauma-Sensitive Academic Instruction — 154

   One Size Fits One — 154
   Trauma-Sensitive Lesson Planning — 157
      Emotional Regulation — 157
      Attention Grabbers — 159
      Turn, Talk, Teach! — 160
      Mirror — 161
   Predicting and Preventing Retraumatization — 162
   A Different Classroom — 164

PART 3: Trauma-Sensitive Schools — 171

   An Uncomfortable Place — 173

CHAPTER 8: Engaging Families as Partners — 181

   Partners, not Scapegoats — 182

A Continuum of Family Engagement	183
Building Relationships	185
Team Approach to Academic Achievement	187
Addressing Trauma at Home	190
A Call	191

CHAPTER 9: Accessing Support & Resources — 196

Assessing for Trauma	196
Resources and Support	199
Trauma Treatment	203
When It Rains	207

CHAPTER 10: Transforming Schools One Practice at a Time — 216

Fueling the Transformative Journey	216
Finding the Sweet Spot	217
Development of a Trauma-Sensitive Transformation Team	221
Trauma-Sensitive Transformation Work Plan	222
Effective Review Process	225
Biting Off a Big Chunk!	226

PART 4: The Role of a Healthy School Environment and Self-Care in a Trauma-Sensitive School — 233

The Nature of Stress in Education	234
An Opportunity for Reflection	237

CHAPTER 11: Stress, Burnout, and Trauma of School Staff — 240

Empathetic Intensity	240
Are You at Risk?	244
Stages of Education Fatigue	246

Exhaustion	**247**
Guilt, Doubt, and Shame	**249**
Cynicism and Callousness	**250**
Crisis	**252**
What Happened to Us?	**253**

CHAPTER 12: Self-Care for Educational Excellence — **258**

Physical Health	**258**
Sleep	**259**
Exercise	**261**
Diet	**263**
Mind Health	**264**
Mindfulness	**264**
Purpose and Passion	**266**
Optimistic Mindset	**267**
Therapy	**269**
Improving Cognitive Functioning	**270**
Social Health	**272**
Personal Social Health	**272**
Professional Social Health	**273**
A Huge Step Forward	**274**

CHAPTER 13: Trauma-Sensitive School Culture and Climate — **279**

Toxic Cycles	**280**
Healthy Cycles	**282**
Honesty	**282**
Trust	**283**
Safety	**283**
Universal Expectations and Accountability	**284**

Recognition	**285**
Trauma-Sensitive Coaching	**286**
Concern for Connection	**287**
Concern for Consciousness	**288**
Concern for Competence	**288**
Concern for Contribution	**288**
Concern for Creativity	**288**
Trauma-Sensitive Leadership	**289**
The Last Meeting of a Transformative Year	**293**
CONCLUSION	**299**
Educational Assistants	**299**
Trauma-Sensitive Coach and Mental-Health Professional Support	**300**
The Fuel for the Brain	**302**
Specialize Specials	**302**
Physical Space	**303**
Leadership and Teams	**304**
Back to Reality	**304**
A New Year	**305**
ACKNOWLEDGMENTS	**309**
BIBLIOGRAPHY	**311**
INDEX	**320**

Foreword

The significant problems we face cannot be solved at the same level of thinking we were at when we created them.
Albert Einstein

Trauma-Sensitive Early Education: Helping Pre-School & Elementary Students Thrive creatively presents practical applications of research-based strategies to guide educators in their efforts to creating a trauma-sensitive school. After reading this book, educators will have a better understanding of what is meant by a "trauma lens." The trauma lens facilitates a school's ability to look beyond student disruption as a problem and see behaviors as a form of communication.

Matt and Sarah give the reader a methodology to decode the verbal and non-verbal messages behind disruptive behaviors and academic struggles. Their book offers practical strategies to respond to students' unmet needs or underdeveloped skills. Trauma-sensitive schools become a place for healing, recovering, learning, and growing for all students, not just a place that reinforces old beliefs and behavioral responses.

Traditional education models have focused on providing students with the content knowledge and skills they need for a specific grade or course. With about six decades of combined experience in education, this philosophy dominated most of our careers. Many conversations focused on the assessment results received by our school, followed by how we were going to improve our performance as teachers.

Behavior was a separate thing to consider and only came up when teachers faced a student who was not compliant to a teacher's style of behavioral management and teaching. The prevailing belief was that if this student were just more motivated, they would stop their misbehaving, and all would be well. As teachers and administrators, we would brainstorm possible ways to motivate the students with a stick and carrot approach.

Teachers split up each part of the day into chunks to give students regular feedback on their behavior. They would get a sticker or star if they behaved during the check-in times. If a student got so many predetermined stickers at the end of the day, they would get a reward.

If not, there was always tomorrow. If a student continued to exhibit problematic behavior that disrupted the class, they were removed and sent to someone else for additional discipline, including possible suspensions or expulsions. The underlying belief was that these rewards and consequences would motivate our students to comply with grade-level expectations.

Unfortunately, educators and administrators fail to understand why a student was misbehaving, falling behind their peers, and how to improve their abilities to succeed. Our jobs were to impart academic content, not teach behavioral capabilities. Students were just expected to come to school with the capacity to manage their behavior and focus their attention on what we as teachers were presenting.

Trauma-Sensitive Early Education: Helping Pre-School & Elementary Students Thrive skillfully challenges these traditional ways of seeing a child's behavior as either "good" or "bad" or "motivated" or "unmotivated." It raises the question of what has happened in this child's life that is affecting how this child's brain reacts to environmental stressors and what skills does this child have to effectively meet this situational demand? Like us, after reading this book, you will possess such a better understanding of why teachers with a "trauma lens" don't ask "what is wrong with a child?" but "what has happened to this child and how can we help?" Matt and Sarah provide a road map for teachers and administrators to help support each and every students' success in their role as a learner.

As our understanding of the importance of trauma-sensitive schools grew, it helped bring to the surface the challenges the educational system as a whole was experiencing. High levels of chronic stress have an impact on organizations, as well as individuals. Under pressure, individuals and organizations have a tendency to make decisions quickly, and the process of decision-making is characterized by extremist thinking and a deterioration of complex processes into oversimplified choices.

An excellent example of this reactionary decision making to real and perceived threats is the zero-tolerance discipline policies that got implemented across the country. These policies originally focused on expelling any student who brought a weapon onto campus. The practice of zero-tolerance was intended to increase safety for schools across the country.

Unfortunately, zero-tolerance quickly became a tool to deal with the increasing number of behaviorally and emotionally dysregulated students who do not respond to traditional behavior-management programs. Teachers began to feel overwhelmed with the expectations of meet these students' needs while meeting increasing demands for high academic achievement scores on standardized assessments. This dilemma generated high levels of stress for teachers and administrators, resulting in feelings of helplessness and frustration.

To cope with the distress, schools began to rely on exclusionary zero-tolerance disciplinary policies. These policies started to creep down into even minor violations. The underlying belief was that strong disciplinary action in response to minor offenses would result in the prevention of more severe violations.

Nipping the problem at the bud was viewed as the best strategy for decreasing escalating aggression in our schools. Students started getting expelled or suspended for wide ranges of conduct, not all related to violence. These practices were well-intended but misinformed.

In practice, there was no evidence that these disciplinary actions decreased behavioral disruptions. Besides a lack of concrete evidence of positive impact, these policies disproportionately affected minority and students with disabilities. Minority students were four times as likely to be suspended as white students. Those with disabilities were more than twice as likely to be suspended than students without disabilities.

Punitive actions had the perceived impact of temporarily managing behavior but did not lead to significant long-term change. In many situations they actually led to escalation of the problematic, aggressive, and impulsive behaviors policies were designed to manage. Underlying these disciplinary policies was a belief that students who did not meet behavioral expectations were making choices and were not motivated to comply (American Psychological Association, 2008).

In 1992, Jerry had the opportunity to attend a conference in La Jolla, California, at which the leading experts in the field of trauma presented. Each presenter shared convincing clinical findings suggesting that exposure to chronic stress, especially interpersonal trauma, has long-term effects on a child's developing brain and body. Leaving the conference, Jerry could not stop thinking how this information explains why the children in his residential-care facility and in schools were so reactive.

Later in that decade, we began to read about the ACEs study and how multiple exposures increase the risk for negative psychological, social, and physical outcomes. Repeated exposure to multiple adverse events, as opposed to single events, robs a child of a sense of security. Instead of being curious and open to their social-emotional environment, they begin to prioritize defensive strategies. We were left thinking that now that we had a better understanding of what has happened to the children, we must figure out ways to integrate this information into our work with children.

It was not until the last ten years that research, and application of that early research, really began to emerge. Science began to not only educate us about how negative experiences can alter the developmental trajectory of our biology, but informed us as to how positive experiences create health, restoration, and growth.

Trauma-sensitive schools are the practice of applying the evolving neurobiological science of traumatic stresses and how it impacts learning. The research has found that to optimize learning, it is more useful to provide developmentally appropriate experiences to children and teach social-emotional skills within a safe relational environment than it is to rely on harsh disciplinary policies. The information shared with the readers of this book is a framework for applying the foundational principles for creating an optimal learning environment based on relational connectedness; physical, psychological, and social safety; and teaching social-emotional skills.

Trauma-Sensitive Early Education: Helping Pre-School & Elementary Students Thrive is a book that outlines the why and the how-to for implementing trauma-sensitive practices. A trauma-sensitive school is a learning environment in which all students feel safe, welcomed, and resourced. Through a real-life scenario, Matt and Sarah share a trauma-sensitive framework that will change not only your students, but impact you, whether you are a teacher, administrator, policymaker, or anyone that works in or cares about schools and children.

In a world in which change is happening so rapidly, with such an abundance of information available through new books and social media, this book creates a foundation for understanding, integrating, and applying not only what we know about trauma, the brain, and the learning today, but what might be available tomorrow.

Dr. Jerry & Lauren Yager, 2019

Colorado, USA

Introduction

When substantial clumps of my hair started falling out in the shower, I began to worry. Just the week prior, my doctor told me I needed to change my diet and eat more iron-rich foods because I had developed anemia. I hadn't had a full night's sleep in months.

I was only in my early twenties and I seemed to be in a physical and emotional downward spiral. My hair loss was my body's reaction to my first two years of teaching in a public school in Harlem. It was my first experience teaching children who were traumatized and I felt powerless to help.

I can't remember precisely when the sleepless nights began. It might have been when my first-grade student came to school with a burn on his cheek the exact shape of a scalding hot clothing iron. Or maybe when an irate parent was dragged out of the building by security because someone at the school had contacted Child Protective Services and she wanted to confront the teacher she suspected of the deed. Or maybe it was when one of our students shoved his second-grade teacher down a flight of stairs.

What I wished I had known then was that I was not helpless in assisting those kids and families. I was actually in a perfect position to do so. Nearly two decades later, I am older and wiser. I am also married to Matt, who teaches others about creating trauma-sensitive schools and classrooms. Matt and I are writing the book I wish I would have had access to all those years ago. It's a guide for school staff in working with students suffering from psychological trauma.

As Matt's career as a school administrator, therapist, nonprofit leader, and trainer progressed, the focus of his work became increasingly related to the growing body of research on trauma-informed care. This ongoing research clearly demonstrates trauma's impact on mental, social, and physical health. In 2017, he left his job to pursue independent projects that focused on spreading the power of the trauma-sensitive paradigm through his writing, blogging, podcasting, and training. His first book, *Connecting Paradigms*, was released shortly thereafter. Around this time, his work started to include more trainings with school staff on the implications of the trauma research in school settings.

Matt's work as a school administrator and trainer give him a compelling perspective on the struggles of the current education system to effectively help children with traumatic histories. Besides his work in the educational system, he also conducts trainings for providers in the homelessness, mental-health, addiction, and criminal-justice systems. We know people in need of these services are much more likely to have experienced multiple traumas in their childhood. Due to the failure of our current educational system to identify and help kids struggling with trauma during the school years, too many students will grow up to experience poverty and homelessness, battle with addiction, or end up behind the bars of the criminal-justice system (Cole et al., 2009; Craig, 2016).

This book focuses primarily on how trauma leads to academic and behavioral issues and how innovative approaches help these students heal and thrive. Trauma is curable if it is recognized and treated, yet too many children in our communities carry the pain and suffering of trauma into their adult lives. It is crucial to take a moment to consider the consequences of not changing our current thinking and strategies for the children struggling in our schools.

Unresolved trauma increases the chances of experiencing any one or more of the following:

Social struggles:

- Incarceration
- Domestic violence
- Sexually transmitted infections, unintended pregnancies, and HIV
- Difficulty establishing healthy romantic relationships
- Attachment difficulties with children
- Social isolation

Personal struggles:

- Suicide
- Addiction
- Extreme poverty and homelessness
- Anxiety disorders including post-traumatic stress disorder (PTSD) and attention-deficit/hyperactivity disorder (ADHD)
- Depression
- Personality disorders
- Loss of positive view of world and self
- Anger control issues

Medical issues:

- Stroke
- Fetal death
- Somatic pain
- Cancer
- Heart attacks
- Chronic fatigue
- Autoimmune disease
- Asthma
- Obesity
- Constipation or diarrhea
- Diabetes
- Liver disease (Herman, 1997; Mate & Levine, 2010; Nakazawa, 2016).

The list could go on for pages, but the choice is clear: we either figure out how to help these children or let them continue to fall into pipelines to prison, poverty, and lives filled with suffering.

As Matt was traveling the country for his work, I was back in Colorado in the classroom teaching first graders. As a teacher, I bring a unique background of experiences into my classroom. My first teaching assignment was as a Peace Corps volunteer in Turkmenistan, educating communities on health and infectious diseases. After being evacuated due to the 9-11 attacks, I worked at an alternative special education school in Colorado before going to graduate school at Teachers College, Columbia University, and teaching English Language Acquisition (ELA) in Harlem. Upon my return to Colorado, I continued teaching in 4th, 2nd, and 1st grades, and worked as an ELA teacher.

As anyone married to a teacher knows, you spend a great deal of your after-work time talking about students, parents, co-workers, and administrators! My conversations with Matt increasingly centered around how trauma impacted the behaviors and struggles of students, their parents, and many of the school staff. The seeds of this book grew from these nightly conversations and our frustrations of how the current educational system fails these students and their families.

While this book was a natural progression for us as a continuation of our nightly conversations, its real inspiration comes from all the kids we worked with over the years. Call us crazy. We both love working with the kids who struggle. Unfortunately, while we appreciate working with them, we fear for their future in an educational system so focused on test results and conformity of behaviors. We worry about what will happen to these kids when they continue to live in traumatizing homes and dangerous neighborhoods. Then they graduate into higher grades where teachers often do not have the time to get to know the good kid behind all the behaviors and low test scores.

These kids inspire our work and passion for education. However, this book is not about them; it is about you! Many good books dedicate hundreds of pages talking about trauma and its effects on the psychological, cognitive, and social health of the child. We will take a brief dive into this exploding body of research, but only in a practical way that applies to your classroom and school setting.

A trauma-informed school trains its staff on the effects of trauma on children. A trauma-sensitive school integrates this knowledge into its classrooms, school culture, and school-wide approaches to behavioral management. This book is a practical implementation guide for teachers and those who care about schools and the kids who too often struggle due to current and past traumas.

PART 1

What Is Wrong with These Kids?

Something tragic will happen to a child in your community today, something so powerful that it threatens to destroy their ability to succeed in school. If untreated, this same event increases their chances to struggle with poverty, self-harm, prison, addiction, and terminal and chronic diseases, and has the potential to steal 20 years off their life expectancy (Nakazawa, 2016).

This child will walk into school tomorrow carrying the emotional and physical scars of this event. How the school responds will echo throughout the rest of the child's life.

In recent years, research by the Centers for Disease Control and Prevention (CDC) (2016) demonstrates that the prevalence of trauma is widespread. The Adverse Childhood Experience Study found that by the time middle- and upper-class children turn 18, nearly two out of three children experienced trauma. In areas with high rates of poverty and violence, these numbers are dramatically higher (Cole et al., 2009).

Next time you attend a high school graduation ceremony, think about this: The majority of students walking across that stage have already experienced at least one traumatic event in their lives (CDC, 2016). We cannot continue to shrug off trauma as something that happens in third-world countries or on the "bad side" of town. A child born today is more apt to experience trauma by the age of 18 than to go through childhood trauma-free.

Trauma is a little tricky to define. The child's reaction to trauma is as key as the event itself. Even trickier is that fact that children experiencing similar stressful events, even in the same household, will react very differently. What one child experiences as stressful might traumatize another. Also, a trauma that haunts one child throughout the rest of their life may serve only as a minor setback to another.

What we want you to know about trauma at the beginning of our journey is that it overwhelms the child's ability to cope. Trauma elicits a fear-based survival response that stays with the child long after the event ends and the danger subsides. Examples of traumatic events that might trigger this response are physical, emotional, and sexual abuse; a parental separation such as an arrest, military deployment, divorce, or death; a natural disaster; an illness or accident; and other events experienced as overwhelming and threatening to the child (CDC, 2016).

A less-recognized form of trauma occurs with constant exposure to intense stress over an extended period. This type of trauma is not as visible when it shows up in your classroom. Unfortunately, we now know that repeated exposure to prolonged stress is just as damaging as the stress associated with a traumatic event. Extended stress can result from poverty, neglectful parents, or parents struggling with mental illness or addiction. Additional significant prolonged trauma might come from having a loved one with a severe medical condition, living in a dangerous neighborhood, bullying, homelessness, and habitually changing schools (Nakazawa, 2016).

While every child's response to trauma is unique, substantial evidence shows that the increasing number and intensity of traumatic experiences adversely impact social, cognitive, medical, and mental health. When we use the word "trauma" or "traumatized" throughout this book, we are talking about someone who still carries the pain and suffering of the experience with them (CDC, 2016; Craig, 2016).

Fortunately, trauma is not a life sentence if help arrives in a timely and appropriate manner. Schools are ideally positioned to identify children who are experiencing trauma. As we will show, trauma recovery increases resiliency, strength, and wisdom. The tragedy is that often trauma in children remains unidentified, robbing them of opportunities to receive the support and services they need to succeed academically and socially during the school years and beyond. Schools can help these kids get the support they need to recover.

Throughout this book, we will use a narrative to bring the concepts we present to life. While the story is fictional, it is illustrative of many of the students we have worked with and our own professional struggles in helping them succeed.

Another Year, Another Bad Kid

Mrs. Carey Vaughn was feeling that familiar knot in her stomach as she drove to work for her first day of the new school year. Even as a veteran teacher, that first day back brought out feelings of excitement and nervousness.

Her first commute of this school year found Mrs. Vaughn driving through a neighborhood in flux and to a school that reflected this transition. Recent economic growth in the downtown area led to several new development projects close to the school. She took in all the trendy coffee shops, bars, and restaurants within a short walk from her school building. Surrounding these expensive establishments were cranes building high-end apartments where abandoned houses once stood.

Having grown up in this neighborhood, Mrs. Vaughn had witnessed many transitions in her 44 years. Initially built by working-class Polish immigrants, most homes were the small post-World War II bungalow style. Over the years, many of the Polish families were joined by middle-class African-American families who found high wages at the local manufacturing plants. This diverse setting was the neighborhood Mrs. Vaughn knew as a child.

When Mrs. Vaughn was in high school, the large manufacturing plants closed, collapsing the economy of the community. The mix of economic desperation and the heightened drug epidemic devastated many of the families who sent their kids to her school. In a matter of a few years, her peaceful community found itself plagued by gangs, poverty, homelessness, addiction, and violence.

Mrs. Vaughn's mother was one of a small group of middle-class people who stayed and fought for the survival of the neighborhood and its schools. Part of her mom's social justice efforts was to keep her daughter in the neighborhood school and work to make it better. Unfortunately, her mother was the exception, as most families moved out or sent their children to private religious schools outside the neighborhood. Just as the community hit its low point, so did school funding and the community's investment in its schools.

After graduating from high school with honors, Mrs. Vaughn went to the local state college to get her bachelor's and master's degrees in education. By going into teaching, she hoped to come back to her neighborhood and continue the work of her mother. She started at her current elementary school as a student teacher. She was then hired on as a kindergarten teacher and moved into second grade a decade ago.

At that time, the neighborhood was going through another transition as immigrants, many of them undocumented, were moving in to take advantage of low rent. The number of students who spoke limited or no English increased dramatically. The school, under the leadership of Mrs. Vaughn's principal Dr. Griffin, transformed into a magnet school. Students from Latin America, as well as Africa and the Middle East, started filling the seats of the school's classrooms. While the level of poverty of her students was appalling at times, Mrs. Vaughn loved teaching in a diverse and vibrant school where multiple languages echoed throughout its hallways.

To this diverse mix, a new middle class recently started moving in. Unlike most of the migrant parents who were working long hours and multiple jobs to make ends meet, these parents had the flexibility to volunteer during the school day. Initially, Mrs. Vaughn and the other teachers welcomed the increase in parent participation.

However, they soon learned that some of the parents could get a little over-involved, believing that they knew better than the teachers how to manage a classroom and run a school. The school was already facing challenges like adopting new state standards, improving test scores, which left little time for the creative teaching that Mrs. Vaughn loved. These new parents took over the parent-teacher organization (PTO) with the hope of creating a model school for other similar communities. While Mrs. Vaughn shared their passion for social justice and education, she found that effectively managing these parents was a full-time job in itself.

As she pulled into the parking lot, one name echoed through her mind like a loud thunderclap: Caleb. Caleb is "that kid!" The kid whose former teacher, when class placements came out, advised his new teacher to start attending church on a regular basis and maybe consider getting on medication. Caleb left a path of destruction everywhere he went: a fight every recess, tearing classmate's paintings in art, throwing his milk at lunch, putting gum in a classmate's hair, and dropping a few choice F-bombs along the way. His exceptional talent was pulling all of this off in one day!

As she closed her car door, the reality of her school year hit her hard. Mrs. Vaughn knew Caleb's family well. She went to high school with his mother, and his siblings had been in the school through the years.

Caleb's home is unstable and, at times, a dangerous place. His mother has struggled with an addiction to alcohol and opioids even before Caleb's conception. Her occasional boyfriends seconded as her dealers and often got physically and verbally abusive with Caleb. His mother does nothing to stop the abuse and occasionally participates. She never attends any school events or parent-teacher conferences, and almost lost Caleb to Child Protective Services after Caleb showed up in the same soiled clothes three days in a row. No one is sure the whereabouts of Caleb's father.

A couple of his cousins fill in as surrogate parents. On the surface, this seems like a terrible reality, as his cousins dropped out of school in their late teens, are heavily involved in a gang, and spend their days and nights on the street selling drugs. Dig a little deeper, and you find that these two cousins, Jeremiah and Zion, love Caleb profoundly and serve as a combination of brothers and father figures. While no one would mistake them for positive role models, Caleb feels safer with them on their street corner while they sell drugs than at home with his mother.

Caleb's academic level is somewhat of a mystery due to his inability to sit still long enough to complete any of the tests. Everyone assumes Caleb is far behind his classmates. However, his learning, as well as the learning of all the other students in his class, is secondary, because his behavior requires the full-time attention of any adults in his proximity.

As a veteran teacher, Mrs. Vaughn's mix of "tough love" and kindness led her to get the reputation of being the best fit for the "bad kids." Few teachers would use the term "bad kid," but no matter what politically correct label is in vogue, all labels translated into the knowledge that this kid would make your life miserable for the next nine months. Mrs. Vaughn and her co-teacher for the last five years, Mr. Kevin Anderson, talked long and hard about the class assignments for the upcoming year.

The temptation was to give Caleb to the new teacher. Due to an increasing number of children coming into their grade, a new teacher, Ms. Emma Smith, is joining their team this year. Fresh out of college, Ms. Smith is excited about her first teaching job and being part of a team of experienced teachers. Mr. Anderson and Mrs. Vaughn, who over time have established a nice rhythm of shared responsibilities and efficient work, were a little hesitant to bring a first-year teacher into their challenging school setting. After much discussion, they agreed that some new energy and fresh approaches could help them improve their team. Mrs. Vaughn volunteered to take Caleb, keeping their teacher karma intact.

As the school year began, Mrs. Vaughn worked to manage Caleb's behaviors, keep everyone safe, and teach something in between all the behavior management. Caleb was living up to his reputation. His outbursts could happen at any time, usually the most inopportune ones! This unpredictability made lesson planning and classroom management nearly impossible. Mrs. Vaughn's best preventive approaches were unsuccessful. Her threats of potential consequences were also ineffective and too often seemed to trigger the next outburst.

Unlike some past students with behavioral struggles, Mrs. Vaughn's attempts to create a "motherly" relationship with Caleb were also unsuccessful. For some reason, every positive interaction seemed to precede an outburst where Caleb expressed his dislike of Mrs. Vaughn in his creative vocabulary. Most kids, even the tough ones, usually enjoyed the teacher's attention. Not Caleb.

One strategy that often worked in the past was putting kids like Caleb at a table with students who were better behaved and better able to tolerate Caleb's constant fidgeting and outbursts. Malik and Emilia were the right students for this role.

Except for the smile on Malik's face, it appears he just got hit by a train. Malik is starting the school year confined to a wheelchair; his right leg is in a cast and his right arm cradled in a sling. At a family reunion at the end of the summer, Malik was jumping on a trampoline with his larger uncle. He mistimed his landing and flew off the trampoline onto the hard ground. Malik dislocated his right shoulder and broke a bone in his right leg.

Malik's parents and all his family rushed to his side as he screamed in agony. Through the comfort and reassurance of his entire family and a growing excitement when he learned that an ambulance ride was in his future, he was able to smile through the tears. After all the drama, Malik's physical condition and reliance on a wheelchair changed his life at school in the short term. His long-term prognosis is good for a full recovery.

Malik's family is one Mrs. Vaughn wishes for every child. Malik's dad works at the local post office and his mom is the head supervisor at one of the new high-end restaurants. Since both work a variety of shifts, they find time to volunteer at Malik's school and someone is usually home for dinner each night. Malik is a joy in the classroom and his parents are highly active in the school's PTO and volunteer on several committees.

Meet Emilia, wait a minute, where is Emilia? The answer is usually in the corner with her nose deep in a book or head down, playing with whatever toys help her to avoid interaction and conversations with others. We do not know a lot about Emilia, as she always blends into the background of any setting or group.

Here is the little that Mrs. Vaughn pieced together early in the year. Emilia's family is from Maturin, Nicaragua, one of the most violent cities in Central America. Over the last six years, much of her extended family immigrated to the United States seeking asylum from the gang violence in their home country. Her family's eligibility for asylum is shaky, which leaves most of her extended family living with the label of "undocumented." While Emilia left Maturin when she was four, some of her earliest memories surround the death and funerals of family members and friends.

Emilia currently lives in a rented three-bedroom bungalow with ten family members. A year ago, Immigration and Customs Enforcement (ICE) did a sweep at the meat processing plant where her father was employed. He is currently in ICE custody awaiting trial and possible deportation. She lives with her mom, sister, brother, and a mix of cousins and uncles who do day labor or work as the cleaning crew at a local hotel. Her home life is a mix of chaos and love, as her mom tries her best to raise Emilia while pulling as many double shifts as she can to pay for legal representation for Emilia's father.

The Emilia, Malik, and Caleb seating arrangement seemed mildly successful three weeks into the school year. Emilia was always in her own world, ignoring Caleb. Malik was preoccupied with this physical condition and getting classmates to sign his leg cast. Then yesterday it all changed.

Malik's mom was volunteering in the classroom and with Malik's physical limitations and his mom's rapport with the other kids, Mrs. Vaughn welcomed the extra helping hand. Everyone was coming in from afternoon recess. Malik's mom helped him to his desk and, having to go to work, kissed him goodbye and said she loved him. As Malik's mom gathered her things, Caleb stood up, went straight over to Malik and punched him in the face, knocking over his wheelchair and forcing him to fall painfully on his right side.

Simultaneous screams erupted from Malik, his mom, Mrs. Vaughn, and some students who witnessed the assault. Immediately, Mrs. Vaughn directed one student to get the principal and another child to get the nurse. Malik's mom rushed over to him, instinctually pushing back Caleb, who recovered from the push to charge this time at Malik's mom. Fortunately, Mrs. Vaughn's hand intercepted Caleb's punch, but a struggle ensued. In the chaos, Malik's mom tried to comfort her son while ensuring Caleb did no further harm.

The struggle ended a few moments later as Dr. Griffin ran into the classroom and grabbed Caleb's other arm, helping Mrs. Vaughn gain the upper hand. At that moment, Caleb seemingly collapsed into their grip and walked like a zombie with Dr. Griffin to her office. In all the chaos, Mr. Anderson peaked his head in the door. Momentarily shocked at the scene, he saw the helpless expression on Mrs. Vaughn's face and asked her class to follow him to his room to enjoy a video. Slowly and quietly, the students rose, following Mr. Anderson out of the room. The nurse arrived, and everyone could now focus on Malik.

Malik's mom said she could take him home since his dad would get home from work soon. She strongly demanded a meeting with Dr. Griffin the next morning to figure out how to ensure that her child was safe in Mrs. Vaughn's class. Mrs. Vaughn managed to nod her head, knowing she lacked any answers as she already had exhausted her best approaches with Caleb.

Leaving to go to Mrs. Griffin's office, Mrs. Vaughn noticed Emilia still sitting at her table with a vacant stare on her face. In the quietest voice she could manage through her anxiety, Mrs. Vaughn whispered, "Emilia." The whisper startled Emilia back to consciousness and the vacant look transformed into one of the saddest expressions of grief Mrs. Vaughn ever remembered seeing.

An almost inaudible voice came out, "Will Malik be okay?"

"Come here dear," is all Mrs. Vaughn could muster as she started to tear up for Malik, Emilia, Malik's parents, and the students who witnessed the assault. Mrs. Vaughn hugged Emilia as much for her own grief as for Emilia's.

After walking silently to drop Emilia off at Mr. Anderson's room, Mrs. Vaughn headed to Dr. Griffin's office. She saw that Caleb was sitting in the central area of the office and was too disgusted with him to acknowledge or look directly at him. Dr. Griffin summoned her into her office and shut the door.

"Well, you made it three weeks before anything like this happened, not bad," said Dr. Griffin with a smile. She knew that Mrs. Vaughn was one of her best teachers and that every year she took on the toughest kids. This incident was a "Caleb thing" not a teacher performance issue. Even this reassurance could not prevent Mrs. Vaughn from breaking down.

Dr. Griffin knew that problem-solving could wait and spent the next several minutes just sitting with Mrs. Vaughn and letting her vent her frustration through her tears on how Caleb picked the most physically vulnerable kid in her class to attack. Dr. Griffin listened while Mrs. Vaughn spoke about how terrible it was that Malik's mother witnessed it all. She wondered aloud if she would let her own children go into a classroom where this sort of violence occurred.

After about half an hour, they started talking about strategy. Dr. Griffin said that due to the violent nature of the action, Caleb would receive a full week out-of-school suspension. Dr. Griffin called Caleb's mom, but she refused to come get that "son of a bitch." The ironic choice of words prompted Mrs. Vaughn and Dr. Griffin to give an uncomfortable glance at each other. Caleb would hang out in the office until he could walk home at the end of the school day. This time allowed Mrs. Vaughn to gather up some work to send home with him.

Back in her classroom getting some worksheets together for Caleb, Mrs. Vaughn was struck by the irony that her student with the lowest academic performance would now miss an entire week of instruction. All the interventions tried with Caleb over his time at the school had no positive impact.

After dropping off the homework at the office, Mrs. Vaughn saw a sight she was not ready for yet. Malik's dad entered the school pushing Malik in his wheelchair with a swollen nose and red eyes.

"Any chance we could chat?" Malik's dad said with a smile that seemed to communicate that he was not there to seek retribution against Caleb or Mrs. Vaughn.

"I'm so sorry," was all Mrs. Vaughn could muster. Realizing that the bell and ensuing rush of school dismissal was coming, she managed, "Why don't you two go down to the classroom, and I'll get Dr. Griffin."

Malik's dad apologized for showing up unannounced. His concern was that Malik was swearing that he would never go back to the school, and his wife was unlikely to calm down enough to meet the next morning. Right about that time, Ms. Smith, the new teacher, peeked her head in the door to check in on Mrs. Vaughn after hearing the story from Mr. Anderson.

Seeing that Malik, his dad, and Dr. Griffin were all in the room, Ms. Smith realized that Mrs. Vaughn's terrible day was still playing out. She asked Malik if he wanted to help her staple some assignments she was preparing for tomorrow. Malik smiled, happy to find a way to help and delighted to get rare one-on-one time with a teacher.

Seeing a smile come across his son's face as he was pushed out of the classroom by Ms. Smith, Malik's dad started with a controlled yet firm voice, "I'm not too old to remember that things like this happen, and as far as my wife and I are concerned, we are impressed with Mrs. Vaughn. However, I think you probably understand. I need to have some assurance that my child is safe in your classroom."

Dr. Griffin jumped right into explaining that she was not permitted to detail the disciplinary action taken. She went on to ensure them that she would inform all parties involved of a new safety plan that would be developed prior to Caleb returning to the classroom. Both Dr. Griffin and Mrs. Vaughn followed this up by reassuring Malik's dad that safety was the top priority at the school. Everyone would work hard to prevent this type of violence from ever reoccurring.

Malik's dad seemed to get what he needed and scheduled a meeting with Mrs. Vaughn and Dr. Griffin the following Monday, once everything calmed down. While happy with the response, he and Malik's mom needed to see tangible actions to ensure that Caleb would not have the opportunity to inflict harm on their child again. All agreed and left the meeting with handshakes and smiles.

CHAPTER 1
Why Won't They Behave?

What do you think differentiates children you adore from those who drive you crazy?

Students' behaviors stand as barriers between them and academic achievement. Unfortunately, many behavior management systems fail to help these students in ways that result in meaningful behavioral changes. In this chapter, we will make the argument that it is not the students' fault these systems fail. Instead, our current approaches are unsuccessful because they come from an outdated understanding of the nature of behavioral struggles.

Throughout this book, we attempt to present complex science in ways you can integrate into classrooms and schools. It is important to note that the knowledge around trauma has increased dramatically in the last two decades, thanks to technological advancements that allow us to watch the brain in action. When neuroscientists started viewing the brains of people with trauma, they found something mind-blowing. The actively traumatized brains operate differently than those with healed trauma or no trauma in their past.

How Behaviors Evolve from the Environment

Our brains are beautifully designed to adapt to our environments. As we confront changes or challenges in life, our brains evolve their structure and functioning to survive or even thrive in the face of hardships. Trauma, especially repeated traumatic experiences, create such an overwhelming environmental factor that the brain must adjust rapidly. Unfortunately, the brain has only limited capacity. If it overdevelops the areas needed to survive in a traumatic environment, the brain will do so at the expense of areas central to emotional regulation and intellectual ability.

To understand how the brain adapts to environmental changes, we need to explore the science of epigenetics. Epigenetics is the study of how the environment leads to the expression or suppression of specific genes. Most of us learned in school that the deoxyribonucleic acid, or DNA, we get from our parents determines our eye color, height, and the color of our skin. This type of DNA is chromosomal DNA and only accounts for around 2% of our total DNA (Wolynn, 2016).

Much of the remaining DNA is called noncoding DNA, or ncDNA. Our ncDNA expresses itself differently depending on environmental demands. When the environment needs a particular part of the brain to strengthen, the ncDNA releases proteins called ribonucleic acid (RNA). The RNA directs cell behavior, ultimately allowing the person to develop specific characteristics or traits. These traits can lead to changes in personality that support survival or success in the environment (Lipton, 2006; Wolynn, 2016).

If a student grows up in a dysfunctional, neglectful, or abusive environment, ncDNA releases RNA that promotes the development of the traits needed to survive these adverse situations. While the person remains in such settings, traits such as hyperalertness, being quick-tempered, or having the ability to shut down emotionally will help them to survive. An understanding of trauma and epigenetics helps us to identify why some students develop traits that are maladaptive in a school setting, while serving them well in their home or community (Cozolino, 2010; Shenk, 2010).

The most influential environmental factors in a child's early life are their attachment relationships or the dynamics of their relationship with their parent or primary caregiver. This initial relationship sets a template for how the child views all other relationships in their life. Young students walk into the school expecting their teachers and peers to relate with them in ways that reflect what they learn about relationships at home.

A healthy relationship with their parents creates a secure attachment, allowing the child to begin a lifelong process of exploring the world appropriate to their developmental stage (Ainsworth, Blehar, Waters, & Wall, 2015). A secure attachment develops when there exists enough safety and love between caregiver and child to allow for the natural development of the brain's ability to regulate emotions and optimize cognitive and social functioning.

Typical characteristics of a secure attachment include:

- Ability to reach intellectual potential
- Development of healthy relationships with peers and other adults
- Managing stress
- Exploring and being curious about the world
- Creation of healthy self-esteem
- Appropriately sharing feelings with others (Bloom & Farragher, 2011; Cozolino, 2010).

Students entering school with secure attachments come with the expectation that the teacher will treat them with a similar level of respect and support they get at home. This expectation elicits a sense of safety that allows the student to grow socially and intellectually with the teacher's guidance. These students are likely to succeed in any behavioral management structure used by the teacher and will respond well to most teaching methods.

Unfortunately, students abused and neglected by their parents or caregivers bring very different relationship templates into the classroom. Young children naturally reach out to parents for emotional and physical resources. Few things match the destructive consequences of when someone the child relies on for survival also becomes a source of uncertainty, confusion, or even fear. The resulting relationship templates used by the child become characterized by avoidance, anxiety, or disorganization. Just like trauma, negative attachment templates heal with the right treatment and experiences (Cozolino, 2010; Siegel, 2011).

Students with avoidant relational templates struggle with the empathy and vulnerability needed for healthy relationships. This template occurs when the attachment figure neglects their child's physical or emotional needs. Typical characteristics of those with avoidant templates include problems with establishing and maintaining close relationships with teachers and classmates, being aloof or controlling, having trouble connecting in relationships, and being unable or unwilling to share thoughts and feelings in appropriate ways (Ainsworth et al., 2015; Bloom & Farragher, 2011).

The anxious relational template is adapted when the caregiver is unpredictable, angry, or helpless in their role. The child experiences elevated levels of anxiety and a reluctance to become close to others. They constantly worry that their friends, families, and teachers do not love or care for them. In the classroom, students with anxious templates will struggle to regulate their emotions when they feel vulnerable emotionally or challenged academically (Ainsworth et al., 2015).

In family situations where trauma dominates the dynamics, parents demonstrate frightened, confusing, and erratic behavior in their interactions with their children. Too often the result of trauma in the home is a disorganized relationship template. This template results in contradictory behaviors that leave those working with the student confused and frustrated (Ainsworth et al., 2015; Bennett, 2017).

The first example of disorganized behaviors is dependency and neediness, mixed with disengagement or social isolation. The student feels a need for a secure attachment and will work hard to please their teachers. At the same time, they may have a fear of getting too close or trusting the teacher, because past relationships have been a source of harm and pain. They will often "act up" or push back with escalating behaviors to try and discourage displays of care and kindness because they don't know what to do with that. It is too hard to trust that a caring adult means what they say. Naturally, this doesn't lead to positive outcomes for the student and can be very frustrating, as it feels like the child is putting us in the role of either abuser or savior (Cozolino, 2010; Siegel, 2007).

The second disorganized behavior set is impulsiveness mixed with inhibition. Students know their behavior physically or emotionally hurts others, but struggle to access the internal resources needed to stop engaging in these behaviors. Without a great deal of help (usually intensive mental-health support), the student cannot stop themselves from continuing the harmful behavior. Unconsciously, these students are acting on the logic that it is better to hurt people than get close to them. Because of the experiences with their parents, they think all people will eventually let you down and harm you (Bennett, 2017).

The third disorganized behavior is a mix of submissiveness and aggression. This contradiction develops when a student acts submissively to survive a violent or abusive caregiver. Submissive behavior skills contradict the competing aggressive need to reestablish the power and sense of control that they never experience at home. Because these children fail to develop the skills to advocate assertively and constructively for themselves, they become verbally inappropriate or act aggressively. This aggressive behavior mirrors the behavior they witnessed from their attachment figure, which was how they learned to get what they needed (Cozolino, 2010; Siegel, 2007).

These behaviors alone will frustrate even the most empathetic teacher or school staff member. Unfortunately, there is one last finding about attachment that makes working with kids with avoidant, anxious, and disorganized attachment styles especially tricky. When they apply their relational templates to peers and teachers, they astutely get others to treat them in ways similar to what they experience at home. These behaviors exhibited by students toward adults and peers are not conscious actions, but traits developed to allow them to survive the violence and dysfunction in their home environments. Thus, school staff and the other students risk recreating these dynamics in the shool (Cozolino, 2006; Forbes, 2012; Hughes, 2017).

Brain Development & Behaviors

While the brain changes throughout life, it is incredibly adaptive during the school years. Tragically for many students, the challenge begins at conception in the form of intergenerational trauma. Recent epigenetic research demonstrates how a developing fetus's ncDNA is prepared to express traits that allow it to survive the trauma of its ancestors. The egg, which forms in our mothers when they are in our grandmother's womb, and sperm combine, ready to express the traits that allowed previous generations to survive or thrive in their environments. Studies demonstrate that some people with no trauma still show symptoms of trauma through this epigenetic expression (Hodge, 2014; Yehuda et al., 2005).

The hopeful news is that environmental conditions can override this preset expression. If a person's family has a history of trauma and suffering, they are born ready to express the genes that will give them the greatest possible chance to survive their family's historical experience. However, if that person grows up in a caring, safe, and secure environment, this preset expression will be minimized in favor of the traits necessary to thrive in a healthy situation.

In addition to intergenerational trauma, a mother's biological state also dramatically influences early brain development. Due to poverty, addiction, or highly stressful conditions, the student's mother might have ingested substances, been unable to afford healthy food and supplements, or released high levels of the stress hormone cortisol. Cortisol and other unhealthy substances in the mother's body then get passed on to the fetus. This unhealthy biological environment is highly detrimental to the formation of a healthy brain which has lifelong consequences.

Early brain development helps us understand why children are so vulnerable to trauma. On average, 250,000 neurons, or brain cells, form every minute throughout the pregnancy. At certain times during pregnancy, production can be as high as 500,000 neurons a minute. This process of creating new neurons is called neurogenesis. Typical neurogenesis results in a baby born with 100 billion neurons, with 90% of them generated midway through gestation. If the experience in the womb is healthy, the baby is born with a vast range of natural potential (Cozolino, 2010).

In the womb and during the first couple of years of life, genetics is the primary force structuring the physical brain. In a healthy environment, genetics create a brain with the ability to build expertise in a very diverse range of areas. With the right training and support, this healthy brain can develop into a world-class musician, a skilled athlete, or a professor at an Ivy League university.

In infancy, the number of neurons peaks at around 200 billion. During this time, the neurons are forming connections with other neurons; these links are called synaptic connections, or synapses for short. At their peak, between the 2nd month in utero up until two years old, synapses connect at a rate of 1.8 million per second. These connections help the young brain manage the infant's developing body (Schwartz & Begley, 2002).

Around age 2, the child's environment becomes the dominant factor in brain development. Driven by the epigenetic response to the environment, synapses that are effective in meeting situational demands strengthen. Those that are not effective weaken and eventually go away in a process called pruning. Through adolescence, pruning eliminates 20 billion synapses a day. The brain uses pruning to maximize limited brain capacity, thus creating a brain best equipped to survive or thrive in its unique situation. Unfortunately, for those experiencing high levels of stress, poverty, or trauma, the connections critical to surviving these situations are highly reinforced at the expense of those essential to emotional regulation and cognitive processes (Hebb, 1949; Schwartz & Begley, 2002).

Epigenetics, neurogenesis, and pruning combine to build a brain with a unique set of traits. This developing brain contains specific regions that are strengthened or weakened during development. To grasp the full impact of trauma, we need to learn about a few areas of the brain.

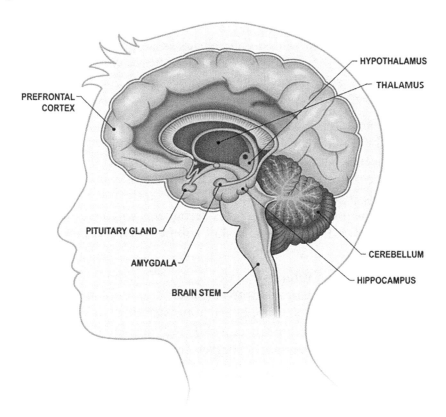

The thalamus sits in the center of the brain. It plays a critical role in facilitating an interactive process among the cognitive, emotional, and sensorimotor centers of the brain. It decides which systems are needed to address the current environmental demands. When living with stress and trauma, the thalamus starts to see danger everywhere. Students then begin to trigger a stress reaction in inappropriate situations. These behaviors are not intentional. Instead, their brain misinterprets variables in the environment. Unfortunately, these students often experience severe consequences because of these struggles, and that may lead them to a feeling that they are a "bad kid" or something is wrong with them (Cozolino, 2010).

If the thalamus does not recognize a threat in the environment, it activates the cortex or thinking part of the brain. The cortex provides meaning by processing the current situation through the lens of past experiences and related memories. If you have learned anything in the past about the brain or stress, your cortex is doing this right now. The information you are reading is being sent through your cortex and connecting to existing knowledge and experiences you have had in the past (Goleman, 2006; Siegel, 2011).

The cortex contains the prefrontal cortex, which is primarily responsible for making humans great thinkers and planners. The prefrontal cortex is central to executive functioning, meaning that it plays a significant role in managing the processes of the brain. These processes include reasoning, flexible problem-solving, planning, memory, and aspects of emotional regulation. A healthy prefrontal cortex recognizes when we are starting to get stressed out and which coping skill will best eliminate and minimize the stress.

Tragically, trauma inhibits the development of the prefrontal cortex. The very biology a student needs to pay attention, problem solve, manage stress, recall memories, and apply learning is smaller in size in children with repeated trauma. If unrecognized and untreated, this biological reality will result in years of struggles in school and into adulthood (Wolynn, 2016).

One of the lasting effects of trauma is the lingering memories associated with the traumatic experience. While modern mental-health interventions are highly effective in removing the power of these memories, students with these unresolved traumatic memories face continuing troubles. They risk becoming retraumatized by noises, visuals, situations, smells, or interactions with others that are similar to their traumatic event. Retraumatization releases the same intense emotions the person experienced during and after the traumatic event. One popular label for these reactions is post-traumatic stress reactions, which is a central symptom of the mental-health diagnosis of PTSD.

Many of the extreme behaviors that get students suspended from school are a result of retraumatization. Too many students are getting punished for unintentional reactions whose biological purpose is to keep them safe. If something traumatizes you, then you want to avoid experiencing that situation again. The extreme responses associated with retraumatization occur, so the student has the energy to either escape the situation or fight against it before they experience additional trauma. Staff in schools who have not received training in the science of trauma may misinterpret these behaviors. They believe that the student's behavior is intentional. These schools then punish students for a natural response that was triggered by an untreated traumatic past.

The amygdala is responsible for the emotions associated with retraumatization and other stress responses. When a student is engaged socially or intellectually, the amygdala, in collaboration with the hippocampus (see below), provides positive emotional responses. These positive responses lead to the establishment of friendships and the motivation to succeed in school. Our feelings for things and people create a more profound, positive emotional experience of the world around us.

The amygdala plays a leading role when the thalamus identifies a threat. Centrally positioned and highly connected, the amygdala is quick and decisive when danger is detected. When activated, it signals the hypothalamus, pituitary gland, and adrenal glands, also known as the HPA axis, to release the stress hormone cortisol. If the threat is significant, the stress hormone norepinephrine, also known as adrenaline, can also be released. Adrenaline increases the intensity of the stress reaction even further. Key indications of this include increased heart rate, increased blood pressure, shortness and quickening of breath, sweat and goosebumps on the skin (Goleman, 2006; Ogden, Minton, & Pain, 2006; Siegel, 2011).

As energy shifts from regular functions, such as digestion and executive functioning, into the muscles of the arms and legs, the student is then ready for action. In most situations, this amygdala response will continue until the threat has passed. The amygdala response creates elevated levels of strength and stamina. These reactions lack executive functioning. When systems such as the prefrontal cortex cease to receive energy, energy is redirected to the muscles and senses that are needed to take immediate action (Siegel, 2011).

Another unfortunate finding is that the amygdala is larger in students with unresolved trauma. The result of this increased size is that these students see more things as dangerous, causing them to exhibit a more extreme response to stress. Too often this response falls into one of three categories: flight, fight, or freeze (Wolynn, 2016).

The response that gets activated first in most situations is the flight response. The flight response directs energy into escaping the threat and putting as much distance as possible between the student and the stressor. The student in flight mode will try to get as far away from the situation as possible.

If it is not feasible to escape the stress, the student will mobilize energy to fight against whatever is causing the stress. The fight response manifests in verbal or even physical aggression. Like the flight response, the student has little or no ability to engage with the environment cognitively. In many cases, students realize they can't run out of the school making flight impossible. The student then strikes out verbally or physically at the person or thing causing them the stress (Ogden, Minton, & Pain, 2006).

The third response is the freeze response. Unlike the fight/flight response, which is triggered by the amygdala and HPA axis, the freeze response originates in the vagus nerve. The vagus nerve is responsible for heart rates and breathing. If the flight or fight responses fail, the last option is to shut down. In this response, blood pressure drops, heart rate and breathing slow, and sensations and emotions numb. The freeze response occurs when the student cannot flee or fight back.

Freeze often becomes the default response of students who experience repeated physical or sexual abuse. In these situations, they have little physical, social, or economic opportunity or power to flee or fight back. The only way they endure is by shutting down, and in extreme cases, dissociating from the situation to survive physically and psychologically (Ogden, Minton, & Pain, 2006).

The final part of the brain that we'll explore is the hippocampus. It plays a significant role in the creation of new memories. The hippocampus is essential to retention and learning. It also helps to quiet the amygdala once a threat no longer exists. A well-functioning hippocampus makes it possible to have a brief stress response, which might include fear or anger, but it doesn't allow these emotions to become a permanent state of being.

Trauma also impairs the hippocampus, but in the opposite way that it does the amygdala. Where the amygdala becomes overactive, the hippocampus weakens and often becomes physically smaller. Students with a weak hippocampus will find it more difficult to calm down after becoming stressed. Often their behavior escalates due to their inability to return to an emotionally regulated state. A smaller hippocampus makes memory formation and retention more difficult. Of course, this dramatically affects academic performance (Ogden, Minton, & Pain, 2006).

States and Traits

It is natural for emotions to become heightened when danger is present. If you are driving down the highway and a truck swerves over into your lane, your brain jumps into action, triggering a flight state and therefore preventing an accident. These states are temporary reactions to changes in the environment.

Life for students with trauma is comparable to the experience of driving down the highway and feeling like every vehicle is attempting to crash into you. You activate a flight state to escape danger. On the other hand, those living with trauma rely on the fight, flight, or freeze state so often that it becomes a trait or a part of their psychological and behavioral makeup. Unlike temporary states, traits transcend environments. The same traits needed to survive a traumatic home environment will show up in the classroom (Schwartz & Begley, 2002; Siegel, 2011).

Let's bring together all the science above to understand how a state becomes a trait:

1) A child is born into a dangerous and traumatic situation through no fault of their own.
2) The child utilizes fight, flight, or freeze states, which promote the most significant chance of survival.
3) Through epigenetic expression, the brain structures itself to support these states efficiently. After enough repetition, these states soon become traits.
4) These traits, which allow them to survive at home and in the community, are then brought into the classroom setting for the first time. They result in behaviors deemed highly inappropriate for the school environment.
5) Children are often labeled and punished as we try to extinguish the very behaviors and the way of thinking that they need to survive their day-to-day lives.

Why Traditional Approaches Fail Students with Trauma

There is an even darker picture of how our traditional approaches fail students with trauma. Research shows that they do not understand the concepts of cause and effect. For consequences to work, the student needs the ability to consider a future outcome and control their natural reaction in order to receive a reward or avoid a punishment. As shown above, the traumatized brain lacks the prefrontal cortex capacity to weigh all the options and make healthy choices (Cole et al., 2009).

In addition to the brain's inability to adequately consider the consequences of behavior, there is a lack of consistency in traumatic homes. Homes plagued by addiction or untreated severe mental illness are highly illogical places for a young brain to develop. A child, wanting praise and love from mom, might decide to do the dishes on Monday. Mom, who is sober at this moment, praises the child and rewards him with ice cream. Message to the brain: do the dishes, mom loves me, and I get ice cream! It is highly likely that the behavior gets repeated.

Tuesday, with fresh memories of hugs and ice cream, the child does the dishes again. This night, mom comes home drunk. Instead of love and ice cream, mom started yelling at the child and pointing out how terrible of a dishwashing job he did. This situation escalates further, and mom ends up spanking the child in a drunken rage. A child with consistent parents and a developed prefrontal cortex learns that following adult expectations keeps them safe and helps them learn about the world. Students from homes plagued by violence, addiction, and mental illness learn that they should not trust adults or their rules.

The above research paints a vivid picture of students who do not possess the ability to succeed in traditional educational settings. We should no longer view disruptive behavior as intentional or planned. Instead, most behaviors are hard-wired biological responses to stress in the environment. Students struggling with trauma are not "bad kids" waking up each morning only to plan out how to torture their teachers and classmates. These students lack the skills and have not developed the traits to thrive academically or manage their behaviors (Greene, 2008).

Our current education system works for students coming to our schools with the skills to succeed. These skills are the traits developed in healthy stable homes with secure parent-child relationships. Kids from these homes view teachers as caring adults, engage academically, and manage their emotions in an age-appropriate way. These students find things like good grades, treasure boxes, teacher praise, and novel projects like science fairs highly motivating. From a skills-based perspective, these children would succeed in just about any behavioral-management system a caring teacher implemented. They do not need these systems to motivate them to engage and behave appropriately.

Students who come from homes where the message is that you are not good enough won't believe they can earn these incentives, so they don't even try. Or, if they do, they often aren't rewarded because the level of their trying doesn't match the level of their "successfully behaved" classmates. We too often fail the children with trauma.

Those are the children suffering from pain inflicted on them at no fault of their own. Their only hope for a good life lies in the hands of a school system ill-prepared to help them succeed and get them the help they desperately need. These students do not enter school with the skills necessary for behavioral, social, and academic success. Historically, we viewed this skill deficit as a character flaw in an unmotivated child. The traditional view of these students is not only scientifically wrong, but it also labels them, medicates them, and punishes them without recognizing the need to help them build the skills they did not have an opportunity to develop at home.

What Happened to You?

Dr. Griffin volunteered to walk Malik's dad out after their meeting. Mrs. Vaughn collapsed into her chair. As tears of exhaustion, embarrassment, and worry streamed down her face, Ms. Smith peeked in her classroom. Immediately, Mrs. Vaughn sat up and attempted to go from exasperated teacher to mentor.

"How did it go today?" Mrs. Vaughn asked in a voice that gave away her actual emotional state.

"Seriously, Vaughn!" Ms. Smith said with an empathetic smile.

Dropping the façade, Mrs. Vaughn teared up and managed to say through her exhaustion and embarrassment, "Sometimes I can't understand how these kids become so malicious and mean at such a young age. What is in the soul of a kid who punches a boy in a wheelchair in front of his mother?"

Ms. Smith hesitated a second before saying, "I cannot imagine watching that play out, though I'm sure it is just a matter of time before it happens in my room."

Right then Mr. Anderson popped his head in, "Well the good news is you get a five-day vacation from Caleb!" Pulling up a chair next to Ms. Smith, "I'm not sure why we would ever let a kid like Caleb back into this school. How can the other kids learn when they might get attacked at any moment? How did it go with his dad?"

Mrs. Vaughn and Mr. Anderson were repeating a conversation they had several times each year about the "bad kids" who made teachers and other students miserable. "It went okay with his dad. Actually, it was better than I deserved, considering his little boy got brutally assaulted in my classroom today."

Mrs. Vaughn caught something in Ms. Smith's hesitation and posture.

Mrs. Vaughn's respect for Ms. Smith grew each day as she learned the ropes and realities of running her classroom. However, she had not yet found her voice in the team dynamic. Tired of the pity party the two were throwing for her she asked, "Emma, you seemed to want to add something a second ago. What were you thinking?"

Shyly, Ms. Smith said, "Oh, nothing much, maybe some thoughts for later."

Mr. Anderson stood up, "Well, I have basketball practice in a few minutes. You need anything, Carey?"

"I'm good. Thanks for the help today. Not sure what I would have done without it."

"Well, now I only owe you like a thousand more favors! Have that husband of yours take you out for some wine tonight. You earned it!" Mr. Anderson said as he left the room.

"Okay Emma, I want to hear what you were thinking." Mrs. Vaughn had built a great rapport with Ms. Smith and took her mentor role seriously. She knew that Mr. Anderson's directness made it hard for Ms. Smith to find her voice.

Ms. Smith could tell that Mrs. Vaughn no longer needed emotional support and she assumed that a "work" conversation would help get her mind off the day's events. Still a little hesitant, Ms. Smith asked, "I am interested in why you think Caleb hit Malik today."

"Because he's a bully." The words were coming out before she thought them through. Ms. Smith just sat in front of her with a concerned half-smile that communicated support but signaled that she was not going to accept that answer. Mrs. Vaughn paused for a second to consider the question on a deeper level.

"Sorry, it's funny. I rarely think about the 'why' behind the behavior. I usually jump to figuring out how we prevent it next time. I know Caleb is from a terrible home. His mom is addicted to God knows what. He has no positive role models. He lives in a constant state of chaos and they are very poor. While I understand that his home is less than ideal, he still made a conscious decision to get up and punch another child in the face."

"Why?" Ms. Smith repeated, as the concern on her face softened to reflect her enjoyment of this new dynamic with her mentor.

"I don't know," Mrs. Vaughn was shocked by the words coming out of her mouth. How could a veteran teacher of over twenty years not come up with a better answer? "Some mentor I am, huh?" She paused for a second and a look of disgust took over her face, "He is a bad kid and bad kids do terrible things." She hated her words, but she had no energy left to dress them up for Ms. Smith's sake.

"So, punishment, suspensions, and consequences should shame and motivate him to transform into a good kid who thrives academically." Ms. Smith's smile seemed almost sly at this point.

At this moment, all the students like Caleb that Mrs. Vaughn had over the years raced through her mind. She felt all the frustration she had in not finding the right mix of behavioral management and academic approaches to help them. She so wanted them to avoid their inevitable path to gang life, prison, or even worse. Just then, Dr. Griffin walked in.

"Dr. Griffin, why do you think Caleb hit Malik today?" Mrs. Vaughn said before even considering Dr. Griffin's answer might include poor classroom management by his teacher.

"Nice job, Emma; you've got her problem-solving already!" Dr. Griffin's answer came more quickly, "All the kids like Caleb come from homes with horrible and sometimes abusive parents who never taught them how to behave or even the difference between right and wrong. They get away with murder at home and they try the same at school. We do our best, but sometimes our best is focusing all our efforts on keeping the other kids safe."

Mrs. Vaughn shot Ms. Smith a look that seemed to communicate, 'your turn.' With her earlier hesitation, she said, "I agree that home life is hell for many of our students, but why would Caleb get up and hit another child at that particular moment?"

Dr. Griffin rarely lacked an answer to any question. Like Mrs. Vaughn, over the decades, she had developed theories and swift responses to challenges and criticism from parents. She felt confident in her ability to handle these situations, but did not have an answer ready for Ms. Smith's question. Uncomfortable with the momentary silence, especially in front of a new teacher, she said, "If it happened in another teacher's class, I would assume there was an issue with classroom management, but not in this room, not this teacher. I also assume that the other student did something to provoke the child, but from what I know, Malik did nothing."

They both turned to Ms. Smith, who was a little unprepared to challenge the philosophies of both her mentor and principal. She took a deep breath, "What if something happened to Caleb that forced his brain to develop differently than other children?"

"Like a traumatic brain injury?" Dr. Griffin asked.

"Sort of, but a psychological injury instead of a physical one. Think about Malik for a second. Over the summer, the poor kid broke his leg and can't use his right arm and needs a wheelchair. I assume Mrs. Vaughn made special accommodations for his physical injury."

"Of course! He gets a special place in line, his mom comes to school almost daily, and the nurse helps him out quite a bit. Since he can't write well with his left hand and can't physically use his right, I give him more time on tests. I let him use technology to type assignments when possible, and I do realize it is going to take a while for him to perform as efficiently as if he had no injury."

"Right," Ms. Smith continued, "you adjusted your expectations of Malik's performance and put in place special accommodations to help him succeed despite his biological injuries."

"Keep going," Dr. Griffin said, shooting Mrs. Vaughn a look that expressed pleasant surprise that this first-year teacher was challenging them both.

Ms. Smith turned to Mrs. Vaughn, "If you had to guess, what sort of trauma do you believe Caleb has experienced up to this point in his life?"

"Well. Dr. Griffin and I go back a long way with his mother and siblings. Tragically, I imagine he has experienced a great deal of physical and emotional abuse and neglect. Caleb lives with a mom struggling with multiple addictions and poverty. He witnesses violence in his community. He's failing at school and he doesn't know his own dad." She paused for a moment as a flood of emotions rushed over her. Her frustration with

Caleb turned quickly to pain, as her words painted a picture of a child in constant crisis and trauma.

"His life is a living hell," Dr. Griffin said filling the silence with contrite words that lacked Mrs. Vaughn's empathy. "Still that does not give him the right to punch another child in the face." Her words were sharp, but starting to lack the conviction that her words usually carried.

"Of course not," Ms. Smith said, her hesitation quickly turning to an enjoyment of her new role in this dynamic. "I took a course last year on mental health in the classroom. We learned how repeated and untreated traumatic events greatly impact brain development in children. Trauma damages the prefrontal cortex and other areas associated with academic performance. There is also damage to the areas of the brain that enable a child to regulate emotions and manage their behavioral responses when they get emotionally dysregulated."

Ms. Smith felt she was on a roll and not sure when she would get Dr. Griffin's time and attention again. She continued, "I highly doubt that Caleb got up this morning and thought 'Today is a great day to hit Malik and get suspended.' In fact, I had them both in math today, and they were getting along great. I would guess something happened in the environment that triggered Caleb, and before anyone, even Caleb, knew it, his fist struck Malik."

Ms. Smith continued, "We see Malik's broken leg and arm in a sling and immediately adjust our expectations and environment to accommodate for his biological injury. We don't judge him for his slowness on assignments; we don't call him lazy for needing more time for transitions or suspend him for not walking and needing a wheelchair."

This last statement about suspension shook something in Dr. Griffin. In a very assertive tone, she said, "His condition is not endangering the well-being of other children!"

Mrs. Vaughn knew Dr. Griffin's defensiveness was just her processing the conversation and jumped in to help her mentee, "Sure, but, if I understand Emma correctly, we set the environment and expectations in a way for Malik to still experience success." She paused to put the next sentence together correctly, "At the same time, we put Caleb's injury in an environment with expectations he is incapable of meeting." Another pause, "Then punish him for struggling behaviorally and label him as slow academically. His failure is a result of our failure to create an environment for him to succeed."

"Sure, but…" Before Dr. Griffin could jump in, Mrs. Vaughn continued.

"I agree with Emma that, relatively speaking, Caleb was having a pretty good day today. His behavior happened immediately after Malik's mom showed her son affection right in front of Caleb." Turning to Ms. Smith, "Emma, do you think that triggered the response?"

"Hold on, Carey, are you saying that I suspended a student for a week because he was triggered by seeing affection between a mother and child? Affection that he never gets in his home?"

Ms. Smith decided that answering Mrs. Vaughn's question was the best way forward. "Trauma is tricky and unpredictable. I doubt Caleb could tell you why he hit Malik today."

"He gave me the typical answer, 'I don't know,'" Dr. Griffin added.

"He is probably telling us the truth. I would guess that seeing the affection between Malik and his mother triggered deep psychological pain. His young brain could not tolerate this pain, and without the ability to recognize it, label it, and control it, he used violence to change the dynamics of his internal and external situation. We suspended a kid today because he hurt another child. That is our policy. It does not mean that Caleb made a conscious choice weighing all the potential consequences of his behavior."

"While we create safety for the other kids by suspending him, we do not address the underlying issue, do we?" asked Mrs. Vaughn.

"No. I also learned that kids with trauma do not understand the relationship between cause and effect. That makes behavioral consequences or rewards almost meaningless. Caleb will likely learn little from the suspension. In fact, having to stay at home may actually harm him."

Ms. Smith continued, "Our challenge goes beyond the delivery of consequences. How do we create an environment for children with trauma that enables them to experience success and learn the skills necessary to meet our rigid behavioral expectations? How do we help Caleb heal the biological injuries of his trauma so these behaviors do not happen again?"

"Okay, you've made your point, Emma. It's been a long day. You all have your team meeting tomorrow afternoon. If it is okay, I would love to join and continue this conversation. I want to see what Mr. Anderson says about all this trauma stuff. Let's go home!" Dr. Griffin could not get out of the classroom fast enough. Something about this concept was hitting her soul deeply and powerfully. It was not something she wanted to reflect upon in front of a first-year teacher.

Mrs. Vaughn went home a different way that night. Instead of her regular route, she drove past Caleb's house. As she made her way through her old neighborhood, she wondered what trauma Caleb and others would experience this night. How many kids would get hit, screamed at, sexually assaulted, hear gunshots, go to sleep starving, and witness violence between their parents? It was too much.

Ms. Smith's words resonated in her mind. "As teachers, it is in our power to help change the traumatic stories of these kids' lives, help them find hope, and change the health of our community."

CHAPTER 2
Why Won't They Learn?

Learning requires a calm, motivated, and curious learner. As we learned in Chapter 1, trauma limits the development of the parts of the brain needed for emotional regulation, behavior control, and learning. Instead, areas that support survival traits overdevelop. One day, the child walks into a pre-school or kindergarten classroom carrying all these traits with them.

As outsiders, we are horrified by the trauma these children have faced in their short lives. Tragically, for most young children growing up in traumatic environments, they view their situations as perfectly normal. Unless exposed to other healthy home environments, they only know abuse, addiction, untreated mental illness, poverty, and other household traumas.

Oblivious that anything is wrong, these students sit down in a classroom for the first time. Before long, they start getting the message that something is wrong with them. The same traits they unconsciously developed to survive at home become behaviorally maladaptive in the classroom. Shortly thereafter, they start receiving feedback on their academic work and get the first proof that they are somehow inferior to their classmates.

Unfortunately, our obsession with standardized testing and quantifying progress provides these students with ample opportunities to conclude that there is something wrong with them. Through these early struggles, learning and school become associated with feelings of stupidity and failure. How many failures does it take for a student to internalize that no matter how hard they try, they will never succeed? Eventually and unconsciously, they will stop putting forth effort. Not trying is less psychologically painful than exerting all one's energy and still failing.

Trauma's effects on the brain areas involved in cognitive functioning present numerous academic challenges that few classrooms today are designed to address. Just as the many students with trauma lack the skills to succeed behaviorally, most do not come into the school environment with a brain equipped for academic success. A child facing abuse at home, dangers in their neighborhood, a bully after school, or other traumas directs their energy toward safety and survival. Little energy is left over for the curiosity and patience needed to learn and apply new concepts.

It is important to note that some students with trauma do achieve academic success. They are highly perfectionistic with an almost obsessive drive for achievement and praise from their teachers. While these students perform near or above grade level, they do so at a cost. They try so hard to control their behaviors and focus intellectually that these efforts cause a great deal of distress. They are at risk for many medical and psychological issues due to high levels of cortisol in their systems (Cole et al., 2009).

Trauma & Language Development

One of the most devastating effects of trauma on the developing brain involves the underdevelopment of their receptive and expressive language. These skills are associated with the Wernicke's area and Broca's area of the brain (Casanueva et al., 2012). Take a moment to think about the role of language in academics. While spelling, reading, and grammar are the first subjects to come to mind, we would challenge you to think of a subject that does not require age-appropriate language ability for success.

Without the ability to process language, students living with trauma will struggle to comprehend even the most straightforward parts of a lesson. Unfortunately, many students go through their days without grasping much of the material. It is hard to measure, but many behavioral issues occur from this confusion. Try to imagine spending your day not comprehending much of anything happening around you. How would your frustration and humiliation manifest behaviorally?

The struggles with receptive language also explain certain puzzling behaviors that manifest in our schools. Students with an overactive amygdala exist on the edge of an outburst. The smallest thing might trigger a fight-or-flight response or retraumatize them. It only takes one misinterpreted word or statement to trigger an extreme reaction. You say "sit" and they hear "hit;" you say "great" and they hear "hate;" you say "fun," and they hear "run." The misinterpreted word easily triggers memories and traumas, and in an instant, you witness a child on the verge of a meltdown for no apparent reason at all.

Often with students struggling with trauma, expressive language deficits also manifest as academic and behavioral issues. Academically, literacy and other associated skill sets lag, sometimes drastically, behind their peers. These students will struggle with vocabulary and spelling words, grammar assignments, and word problems in math. Additionally, any written assignment that requires them to express their opinions, emotions, or beliefs is especially tricky (Cole et al., 2009).

Behaviorally, the struggle to express one's self hinders the child's ability to control their stress reaction. As we will examine in later chapters, labeling emotions and feelings is a critical step in self-regulation. Unfortunately, trauma's damage to the Broca's area of the brain makes labeling especially difficult for these students.

Finally, students experiencing complex trauma learn to use language as a barrier to keep themselves safe when they feel threatened. One of Matt's client stated this beautifully when he said, "When I act the fool, you all leave me alone!" While most kids lack this level of insight, this kid nailed it. Many outbursts and disruptive behaviors are unconscious attempts to get distance between the student and what is causing them stress, which is often the teacher, classmates, or the lesson itself.

In the moment, these students lack the prefrontal cortex capacity to think through the potential consequences of their behaviors. As stress and frustration increases, they become increasingly agitated. They lack the skills to manage the growing stress. The student then acts in a manner that will get them out of the situation. While being sent to the principal's office or removed from the classroom feels like a punishment to us, the student achieved their immediate unconscious goal of getting out of the situation and away from the cause of their distress.

Schools and classrooms provide students opportunities to grow as much socially and emotionally as they do intellectually. Deficits in expressive and receptive language mean that all the tasks associated with social, emotional, and cognitive growth are frustrating and challenging to master. Referrals to speech-language support are critical for these students. With every referral, schools need to ask the question, "What is happening to this child that might account for these language struggles?"

Trauma & Memory

The formation of long-term memory and memory recall is necessary to apply prior learning to a new topic. Students need to use previous information for creative thinking, problem-solving, and successful test taking. Unfortunately, trauma, especially repeated trauma, damages the hippocampus, prefrontal cortex, and other brain areas critical to memory creation and recall.

In the first several years of life, the memory systems are still forming. During that time, the baby and toddler rely mainly on episodic memory. Episodic memories form in chronological order. To recall an episodic memory, we must mentally return to the time and place the memory occurred to get the information. This method of memory retrieval is highly ineffective and one of the reasons we do not remember much from the first few years of life (Cole et al., 2009; Siegel, 2011).

As the young brain develops, it gains the ability to create sequential memories or memories stored with other like memories. To merely summarize a bunch of complex neuroscience, episodic memories function like an autobiography on an extended timeline. On the other hand, sequential memories work like a filing cabinet.

For example, if a teacher is presenting a new math concept that builds upon the material covered last week, a student relying on episodic memory would need to go back mentally and remember what was learned on Tuesday, then Monday, and then Friday to gather all the information required to learn the new material successfully. Unfortunately, without a great deal of prompting from the teacher, it is difficult, if not impossible, to pull in the necessary information in addition to focusing on the new material.

For memories stored sequentially, the student knows she is in math class, so her brain will open the math drawer of her memory filing cabinet and pull out the information needed to learn the new concept successfully.

The memories associated with the new idea will then go into the math drawer for later recall on a test (Cole et al., 2009; Van der Kolk, 2014).

Many students struggling with trauma rely heavily on episodic memory, due to damage to the memory centers of the brain. With biological struggles in memory creation and recall ability, these children will struggle to perform at grade level, explaining why students with trauma are 2.5 times more likely to fail a grade and much more likely to end up in special education. Unfortunately, holding these kids back or putting them in special education will do little good if the underlying trauma causing these delays is not also addressed (Cole, 2009).

Since we are on the topic of memory, we want to alert you to two other types of memories affected by trauma. Explicit memories are memories that we recall quickly on demand, for example, thinking about your last birthday. Implicit memories are memories that exist fragmented in the unconscious.

Due to the flooding of stress chemicals during trauma, memories of the event are not fully integrated as explicit memories in our memory systems. These fragmented memories haunt the trauma victim, as they retraumatize the person without the person knowing why they had such a strong reaction. These implicit memories may get stored in the body in areas associated with the traumatic event. Touching these areas, even with the kindest intentions, retraumatizes the student, leaving everyone dumbfounded by such an extreme reaction to an otherwise benign interaction (Cozolino, 2006; Siegel, 2011).

Trauma & Future Thinking

A traumatized brain becomes hardwired to survive the immediate moment. Traits associated with the fight, flight, and freeze responses help the student survive the threats present in their homes or neighborhoods. The overdevelopment of these systems comes at a cost. Besides struggling to understand cause and effect, there are academic issues that emerge when the student struggles to think beyond the present moment.

If we are honest, there is always something in the day a little more fun than even the most engaging academic lesson, such as recess, video games, playing with friends at home, lunch, music class, and the list goes on. One way to view education is as one long process of delaying gratification, whether the student is waiting for the next "fun" activity or, for older students, trying to graduate so they can make money with their diploma or college degree.

Most students with trauma are starving for immediate gratification. This trait is a survival response to trauma as well as to many aspects of poverty. The possibility that you might not eat dinner leads to eating everything in sight, even if the snack doesn't belong to you. Obsessively needing to finish a game started at recess even when told to put it away is about the gratification of winning in that moment. There is little thought of the time taken away at the next recess as a consequence for not following directions.

The short-term emotional rewards for the student outweigh any long-term benefit the child might consider. Unfortunately, research by Walter Mischel and others demonstrates how the inability to delay gratification in childhood carries grave long-term consequences. The children he studied who struggled with regulating the need for immediate gratification experienced worse life outcomes, as measured by academic achievement and overall health (Mischel et al., 2010).

Trauma & Cooperation

The picture of a class sitting in isolated silence at their desks is quickly becoming an artifact of education's past. Today's classrooms are alive with interactions, group activities, and project-based learning. As partner and group learning becomes more and more prevalent, students with trauma often struggle to manage the social components of these interactions in a way that allows them to learn or succeed.

As mentioned in the previous chapter, many students come from homes where they developed anxious, avoidant, or disorganized relationship templates. In activities with peers, whether on the playground or in the classroom, these students often lack the social ability to manage the growing complexities of cooperation and friend groups. Social interactions create a great deal of anxiety and often lead to behaviors that leave the student isolated and disliked by their peers and usually other parents as well (Cole et al., 2009).

A student experiencing abuse at home might start to bully their classmates. School staff should view the child doing the bullying as a child who learned this behavior from somewhere and not as a child who was born a bully. Other abused children who try to isolate themselves as a way to manage their stress often become the victims of bullying, a role that seems consistent with their experiences at home.

Very early on in their educational experience, too many students with trauma get bad reputations amongst their peers for being a lousy partner, a bully, or a bad influence. These labels make their trauma symptoms even worse and soon school becomes as hurtful a place as home. Any hope that school would provide a sanctuary from the pain and suffering of trauma is gone.

The Justification to Search for Answers

"The big boss is here? Did you all get in trouble?" Mr. Anderson said, walking into the team meeting the day after the Caleb-Malik incident.

"You know, if anyone on this team is in trouble, it would have to be you, Kevin." Dr. Griffin said with a smile on her face. "Sit down. We have a lot to catch you up on and new ground to cover today."

Looking suspiciously at the three of them, Mr. Anderson took a seat.

Dr. Griffin, Mrs. Vaughn, and Ms. Smith took turns reviewing their discussion from the previous day concerning the science of trauma and how it related to the Caleb situation. Mr. Anderson listened intently, as there were no two people he respected more in all of education than Dr. Griffin and Mrs. Vaughn. After they finished, he sat with the information for a moment before speaking.

"So, if I hear you right, we shouldn't hold kids like Caleb accountable for punching other students?"

Dr. Griffin replied thoughtfully, "Let's avoid talking about what we will do until we understand this issue much better. Trust me. Safety will remain my top priority."

"As it must be," chimed in Ms. Smith. "Safety is crucial for all children, especially those with trauma. If we better understand the reasons behind behaviors like what happened yesterday, the hope is that we'll implement strategies to prevent them and create a safer school environment."

Mr. Anderson wondered what brought on this transformation in Ms. Smith. Last week she was a sponge absorbing everything; today she seemed ready to run a meeting. "Okay, tell me more," he said with genuine interest.

"Let me jump in here with a couple of questions that I ruminated over in my head last night until the early hours of the morning," said Mrs. Vaughn, explaining the bags under her eyes today. "First, we discussed how Caleb's violent behavior yesterday is likely attributed to trauma at home. Are there other behaviors we might look for in our students? Second, you mentioned that kids with repeated trauma don't possess the same prefrontal cortex strength as other students. How would this manifest itself academically?"

"To respect everyone's time, let me try to answer both these at once," Ms. Smith jumped right in. "Our first task right now is to approach behavioral and academic issues with curiosity. Trauma will manifest differently depending on the child, their traumatic experience, and their relationships in the classroom. Any chaotic behavior, especially if a student displays this behavior on a regular basis, should make us question if they are struggling with trauma."

"You just described 80% of the students in my class," Mr. Anderson stated.

"You just described 80% of the kids in this school," followed Dr. Griffin.

Mrs. Vaughn sighed, "Think about it. With the level of crime, addiction, and poverty in our school community, does 80% of our students experiencing trauma sound out of the question? Even if they walk into our school trauma-free, one of their classmates might get up and punch them in the nose." One of the things that kept Mrs. Vaughn up late the night before was the guilt that Malik now was amongst the students living with trauma because of what happened to him in her classroom. Malik was absent from school with only a curt call from his mother stating he would stay home for the day due to his eyes swelling shut.

Seeing that Mrs. Vaughn was starting to tear up, Ms. Smith put her hand on her shoulder, "If Malik's family is as healthy as you say, and we help him feel safe again in the classroom, he is unlikely to carry any long-term consequences from the events of yesterday. If that child seemed unphased by a broken leg and arm, with the right support, he will likely gain something positive from the whole experience."

"Sorry, something positive from trauma?" Dr. Griffin asked puzzled.

"Yes!" Ms. Smith almost shouted. "Yesterday, we compared the trauma that Caleb has experienced as a biological injury of the brain that, roughly, compares to Malik's biological injured arm and leg. If both injuries receive timely and effective treatment, the pain and suffering of the trauma can turn into something my professor called post-traumatic growth."

Ms. Smith continued barely stopping for a breath, "Post-traumatic growth is a type of super resiliency. Think about a hard time you had in your own life, especially if it was traumatic."

"Yesterday!" Mrs. Vaughn said, rolling her eyes.

"Actually, a good example." Ms. Smith continued, "It is certainly possible that watching one of your children hitting another with his mother present in your classroom might traumatize you. Yet, think what happened next. Dr. Griffin rushed in to help out immediately, followed by Kevin's quick reaction to take over your class."

"Here I come to save the day," exclaimed Mr. Anderson in his best Mighty Mouse impression. Ms. Smith shot him a puzzled look to which he shook his head, saying only, "Millennials."

"Anyway," Ms. Smith resumed, "you received immediate support to reestablish safety, allowing you to regulate yourself emotionally. Shortly after that, you engaged in the intellectual activities of creating a homework packet for Caleb, followed by our conversation yesterday afternoon. I imagine if you think back to other, even more, intense situations or traumas in your own life, someone was there to help you through them."

"Yes," chimed in Dr. Griffin. "I look back on a few years in my life when I had some hard times personally and there were people there who always supported me."

"I wonder how you see those times now that you have some space and time to look back." Ms. Smith asked.

"I would never want to experience anything like those years again, especially the tough times. But, looking back, I feel I'm stronger today because I overcame those experiences. Life can throw things at me now and I respond, 'that's all you got?'"

"You gained wisdom and strength from those experiences?" inquired Ms. Smith.

"Yes. I'm assuming that is what you mean by post-traumatic growth?"

"Exactly," Ms. Smith added excitedly.

"But what about our kids?" Mrs. Vaughn paused, and a sad look came over her face. "They experience one trauma after another, and most have no one to help them get out of their realities or even help them heal and grow."

"They have us," said Dr. Griffin, before she considered all the challenges associated with her words.

"Okay, but I'm not a therapist or a social worker. Some days I barely feel like a teacher," said a now overwhelmed Mr. Anderson, looking back to Ms. Smith.

"Everyone is right," she said. "I'm sure we all agree that we won't blame a kid like Caleb for being born to a mother that abuses and neglects him."

"Right," agreed the group.

"Then we are left holding the other key fact about the lasting impact of trauma. If we find a way to become that positive person in his life, to help create a safe home situation, and to find ways for him to experience success, his life outcomes will likely be positive. If he continues to experience failure, we may lose him to prison, addictions, the streets, and even suicide."

"This stuff is fascinating," Mr. Anderson seemed all in. "I've got to run to practice in a few minutes. You mentioned chaotic behavior. I'm assuming this includes the fight-or-flight response we hear so much about?"

"Yes," said Ms. Smith, a little amazed at Mr. Anderson's sudden excitement.

"What else should we look for in considering if a child is being abused or traumatized?" he asked.

"Besides the chaotic behavior that can manifest in fight or flight, there is also the freeze response. Our freeze kids are harder to identify at times because they become good at being invisible. Freezing is a natural response if someone can't run away from danger or fight back. It often characterizes the behavior of kids experiencing repeated physical or sexual abuse where they can't physically fight back. Young children don't possess the ability to leave the abusive environment and often receive threats that terrible things will happen if they tell someone. Tragically, they can't run away either."

Oh God. Emilia! Mrs. Vaughn thought to herself. Another thing that kept her up last night was the frozen little girl in her class. The expression on Emilia's face haunted Mrs. Vaughn nearly as much as the punch.

Luckily Dr. Griffin spoke up, "But every behavior isn't related to trauma, right?"

Ms. Smith continued, "Of course not. Not all problems occurring in our school are related to trauma. However, if we don't ask the question, 'what is happening to cause such behaviors?' we miss the opportunities to help stop and heal the trauma and punish children for behaviors resulting from their traumatic experiences."

"The challenge I take from this statement is that when we identify kids with behavioral and academic issues which our typical interventions and strategies do not correct, we should be curious as to whether or not the student experienced trauma." Dr. Griffin added.

"So, if we are right, that 80% of our students might be traumatized, then what?" asked Mr. Anderson.

The question sat heavy on the group. Ms. Smith had some answers but was not yet sure if her newfound role of trauma expert gave her the authority to say, "We need a revolution in education!" So she held her tongue. She also knew that there was not a ton of great answers to this question. Just a small group of progressive school staff around the country were beginning to consider the issue of trauma-sensitive schools and classrooms. For today, she would leave the conversation satisfied that her school might have the right administrator and teacher champions to become a leader in the movement.

"Mr. Anderson, I think your question is a big one. I've got a meeting next week. Is it okay if I stop back in and continue this conversation in two weeks?"

Everyone agreed, and the team had many other issues to cover.

Mrs. Vaughn's commute that evening was one of silence. No music, just her thoughts about Caleb, Malik, Emilia, and the hundreds of other students she had taught over the years. How could she make any difference in the face of the poverty, abuse, neglect, and all the other problems her students faced daily? Teaching seemed to get more and more overwhelming each year, but through passion and hard work, she remained energetic and motivated. Facing down something as painful as trauma was a challenge unlike any she had taken on in her career. She knew she had to do something, but how would it ever be enough?

PART 2

The Trauma-Sensitive Classroom

Part 1 established how students with untreated trauma struggle both behaviorally and academically in school. Traditionally, failure to connect these problems to trauma led many schools to punish students, while not getting them the help that they need. The research on trauma challenges schools to work toward a new type of innovative classroom designed to help every student learn.

Traditional psychological thinking believed that personality and the brain were not flexible beyond the first years of life. Unfortunately, this way of thinking still permeates many aspects of our schools and society. The thinking goes this way: a "bad kid" is destined to become a "troubled adult."

Fortunately, advancements in neuroscience clearly show that this is not true. Instead, we now know that our brains are constantly evolving by adapting to changes in the environment, relationships, and new information. The ability of the brain to change is called neuroplasticity. If the brain can change and trauma can heal, then there is hope for reaching those children who seem unreachable. That hope resides in the trauma-sensitive classroom (Schwartz & Begley, 2002).

Every interaction, every lesson, and every day is an opportunity to help children with trauma heal and develop the skills necessary for success. In Part 2, we will delve deeper into the characteristics of a trauma-sensitive classroom and provide strategies to transform a traditional classroom into a trauma-sensitive one.

What to Do with Caleb?

Oh, the difference one child makes! With Caleb suspended, Mrs. Vaughn remembered why she loved teaching. She was not always holding her breath, waiting for the next altercation. Instead, she was able to spend time with students who often got sidelined as she dealt with Caleb's behaviors. There was a noticeable change in her energy and mood, and Mrs. Vaughn could see how her students shared her change in attitude as everyone seemed happier and more engaged.

While Mrs. Vaughn and the other students enjoyed their break from Caleb, she felt a dark cloud hanging over the positive atmosphere. Caleb was scheduled to come back in a couple of days and what had really changed? If Caleb's behaviors were a result of trauma, how would returning to the classroom where he would likely fail again help him when his family situation continued to be traumatic? What about the other kids? Mrs. Vaughn's tough-love approach with Caleb was obviously unable to keep Malik safe. Why would anything change due to the suspension?

Many questions and emotions rattled around Mrs. Vaughn's mind as she walked into Dr. Griffin's office to meet with Malik and his parents. After coming back to school with his dad, Malik only missed one day of school and seemed proud to show off his black eyes. As the days counted down to Caleb's return, Mrs. Vaughn did notice Malik getting easily frustrated and struggling to concentrate. Malik's mom was understandably a little more protective with Malik and not as friendly with Mrs. Vaughn when she volunteered. Even early in her learning about trauma, Mrs. Vaughn could understand why.

As usual, Malik's parents were early. Dr. Griffin started the meeting, "Thanks everyone for coming. I know that the events of last week left us all shaken. I hope that we will use our time today to make sure Malik continues to feel safe once Caleb returns."

Mrs. Vaughn did not wait, "I want to apologize to both of you." She tried not to get choked up again. "My number one priority is to create a safe learning environment for all of my students. The fact that Malik got hurt under my supervision disturbs me greatly. I am deeply sorry."

Malik's mom smiled, "I was distraught when it happened, but I was even closer than you were to Caleb and I couldn't predict it or keep my own child out of harm's way. How do you keep a child safe when a great teacher and a slightly overprotective parent couldn't prevent a child from assaulting another student?"

Malik's dad nodded his head in agreement. "I know kids from this neighborhood often come from impoverished and abusive homes. But how in the world do you prevent kids like Caleb from hurting other students or going after our son again?"

Mrs. Vaughn started in on her routine response to such questions, "Caleb would move from his table with Emilia and Malik to an isolated table. I will keep a special eye on him, so he does not have the opportunity to get close enough to harm the other children physically. He will hold my hand in lines and only play with one other child at recess within proximity to the supervising teacher. The special teachers are already familiar with Caleb's aggression, and similar structures are already in place."

While she did her best, she felt empty as she said these words. Sure, she might keep her other students physically safe, but nothing about this approach ever helped the student with the behavioral problem. Her understanding that Caleb's behaviors were a result of the trauma he experienced at home made this strategy seem like continuously punishing a student living with trauma for what he suffered at no fault of his own.

Dr. Griffin was going to give her regular school safety talk when Malik's mom interrupted, "I believe you will do everything you can to keep all your students and Malik safe. What about Caleb? Why would a child hurt Malik like that, especially in the condition he is in?"

Mrs. Vaughn and Dr. Griffin looked at each other for a moment. Neither was ready to talk about trauma, and confidentiality prevented them from going into what they knew about Caleb's home life. The best Dr. Griffin could muster was, "Ummm."

Malik's mom sensed she wasn't going to get a good answer, so she decided to move to problem-solving. "Dr. Griffin, I know Mrs. Vaughn is doing everything she can do. She needs help, and we cannot volunteer every day. Can the class get a teacher's assistant or some help? I'm worried that all this attention and energy on Caleb's behavior makes it nearly impossible for Mrs. Vaughn to teach the other students. Sure, my priority is the safety of my child. I also care deeply about his ability to get the great education that I know Mrs. Vaughn is capable of providing."

Mrs. Vaughn wanted to jump in and support the idea 100%. Every teacher in the school repeatedly asked for help in their classrooms. Each request received the same answer from Dr. Griffin.

Dr. Griffin answered the frequent request, "The idea is a good one, and I don't disagree that all my teachers could use the help."

Here it comes, thought Mrs. Vaughn.

"But the district doesn't have the funding right now to hire any more teachers or other classroom support. Our last five attempts at bond initiatives were voted down by the community. I'm afraid that isn't an option." Dr. Griffin communicated a sense of pain and fatigue for always giving the same answer to a legitimate question.

In the end, Mrs. Vaughn was happy that Malik's parents eventually agreed with the previously discussed strategies for Caleb's return and that everyone left the meeting feeling hopeful. After they left, Mrs. Vaughn collapsed back down into her chair.

Right then, Ms. Smith opened the door, "Perfect; you two got a second?"

"Sure," they both answered simultaneously.

"Dr. Griffin, Mrs. Vaughn, this is Dr. Lisa Rodriguez, my *Psychology in the Classroom* teacher, who I mentioned a few days ago." Ms. Smith did not hide her excitement.

Dr. Rodriguez shook everyone's hands and with a gentle smile said, "So, you got lucky enough to hire my star student?"

"I'm starting to think lucky is an understatement," said Dr. Griffin, beating Mrs. Vaughn to the punch. "I can't remember the last time a first-year teacher taught me half of what Emma has taught me over the last week."

Mrs. Vaughn took her turn, "We loved her energy in the interview, but she is…"

"Okay, you two, thanks, but I know I only get a few minutes of everyone's time, so let's stop praising me and get to work!" All nodded, and Ms. Smith continued. "I had coffee with Dr. Rodriguez this weekend and told her about our situation and our struggles with students like Caleb."

"Teaching in this city for many years, I'm familiar with the neighborhood, as many of my students did their student teaching in the area." Dr. Rodriguez added.

"Dr. Rodriguez said she was looking for a school to work with that is interested in becoming the first trauma-sensitive school in the area. While I have enjoyed my role as the expert in our initial conversations, I know Dr. Rodriguez is a much better person to help us if we are interested," Ms. Smith said, with an anticipatory excitement evident in every word.

"Please sit down, Dr. Rodriguez," Dr. Griffin motioned to a chair, as everyone took a seat. "Emma has taught us quite a bit the last couple of days. I have thought a lot about the importance of this information for both our current situation and the school. How would one go about creating a trauma-sensitive school?"

"I like to take one step at a time," Dr. Rodriguez started. "Since there is already an interested and motivated team, I would like to position myself as a resource to Mrs. Vaughn, Mr. Anderson, and Ms. Smith. Initially, our work would focus on the creation of trauma-sensitive classrooms. Once we have real-life success with kids like Caleb, we'll have data supporting our cause and some lead teachers to guide a school-wide process."

Mrs. Vaughn looked at Ms. Smith and smiled, "Dr. Rodriguez, it seems as though you know quite a bit about us already."

"Emma and I share a passion for the potentially life-saving benefits of trauma-sensitive approaches. You put us in a coffee shop with a strong latte and words fly at light speed! The good news is that the teacher's college at the university is also excited about the application of trauma research in schools. We already have a great deal of support to start implementing our research into the real world."

"Do I hear you offering free help?" Dr. Griffin said, knowing that the school had limited resources. Dr. Rodriguez nodded in confirmation. Dr. Griffin continued, "Well, it seems we all agree. Why don't you two get Mr. Anderson's buy-in and get me a brief proposal of what this would look like so I can work on getting district approval. I would also like to be as involved as possible. If we roll this out school-wide, I'll need to make sure I do everything in my power to set us up for success."

"Wonderful!" Ms. Smith jumped up. "I think we can catch Mr. Anderson before basketball practice."

Ms. Smith and Dr. Rodriguez left the office, followed by Mrs. Vaughn. Dr. Griffin in a half-whisper said, "Carey," Mrs. Vaughn turned around, "try to keep up!"

They shared a smile communicating their mutual enthusiasm for where this journey might lead them and their school.

CHAPTER 3
Social-Emotional Learning: Strategies for Emotional Regulation

Imagine for a moment that we lock you and your teammates in a meeting room. We hand out an IQ test and a team problem-solving task. We give you the allotted amount of time, collect, and score the assignments. Not surprisingly, your score is terrific!

The next day, we bring everyone back to the same room and pass out similar assignments. As you and your teammates begin the work, you hear something rattle that startles you into a primordial terror. Then you see it. A rattlesnake comes slithering from under the desk, and then another comes from behind a filing cabinet. You run to the door only to find it is locked.

After yelling and banging on the door in desperation, our voices come over an intercom with the harsh demand that if you do not finish the assignments, you will not get paid for the next three months. Knowing you must complete the task, you rush through the assignments, always keeping your eye on the snakes. What do you think happens to your scores on the IQ and team assignments?

You survive the rattlesnake encounter, but your scores drop dramatically. We also inform you that it is now part of your job to go back to the rattlesnake room once a quarter to see if your performance improves. However, we do offer you and your team the option to receive weekly training on how to manage snakes safely, treat any potential bites, and work together with tools to keep each other out of harm's way.

You take us up on the training. Your team reenters the room a few months later with hours of snake safety training. We allow you to take all your tools, antivenom, and safety clothing in with you. While your scores don't match the first time you took the test with no snakes, they drastically improve over the first time when the snakes made their surprising entrance.

For many students with trauma, their school experience is full of rattlesnakes. Teachers, classmates, assignments, social situations, recess, and other normal school activities carry with them a sense of imminent danger. An overactive amygdala that keeps the child safe in stressful or traumatic situations where they are required to locate possible threats and act quickly makes it nearly impossible to concentrate in the classroom.

We have good news. When teachers focus on creating a safe, healthy classroom community, everyone benefits. By teaching coping skills and building strong school staff/student relationships, teachers will not only help students with trauma, but will improve the performance of all students. Trauma-sensitive classrooms establish healthy environments where all students thrive!

Calming the Body; Calming the Mind

The better we understand the brain and nervous system, the more we see a strong connection between the mind and body. The concept of the "mind" is a controversial one in neuroscience. However, most agree that there is something about us as human beings that allows us to intentionally change our behavior, regulate our emotions, and consider different potential options and their consequences in the situations we face. For our purposes, think of the mind as a tool that allows us to act intentionally despite epigenetics, neurobiology, and traits that develop while we are trying to survive traumatic experiences (Siegel, 2016).

One of the best ways to help students regulate a mind dysregulated by trauma is to provide them with sensory strategies to calm their bodies. The first step in developing sensory strategies for students is to identify the sensory areas where dysregulation is occurring. These sensory areas include movement, temperature, and noises. The Wisconsin Department of Public Instruction (2017) worked to create a chart of specific observed sensory behaviors and strategies for school staff that promote regulation for students experiencing trauma.

Sensory Area	General Observations	Specific Observed Behaviours	Sensory Strategies
Movement	Students need gross motor movement to maintain regulation or become dysregulated when they do not have gross motor movement.	Rocking/swaying	Rocking chair/seat
			Wiggle seats
			Weighted blanket, vests, or lap covers
			Weighted neck pillows
			Fidget quilts or blankets
			Chew tools and chewelry (necklaces, pencil toppers, bite bands)
		Jumping	Stand up/sit down desk
			Pedal desk, ball chairs
			Hokki Stools
			Bouncy band for chairs
		Running/walking around	Movement breaks
			GoNoodle: free web-based short interactive movement activities
			Stand up/sit down desk
			Pedal desk, ball chairs
			Provide opportunities to deliver items around school building
			Assign classroom job of carrying heavy items such as library books or stacking chairs

Sensory Area	General Observations	Specific Observed Behaviours	Sensory Strategies
Movement	Students become dysregulated by too much movement or activity.	Chaotic or frenetic movement	Yoga, stretching Mindfulness, deep breathing GoNoodle: free web-based mindfulness activities Guided meditation or imagery
Movement	Students need fine-motor movement to maintain regulation or become dysregulated when they do not have fine motor movement.	Doodling, scribbling	Coloring book Free drawing Journaling Squiggle Story Write and wipe mobile student desk Privacy partitions you can draw on Hand fidgets and stress balls Sensory Putty
Temperature	Students report being uncomfortable	Too hot	Personal fans Flexible seating near window or door Hands-free ice pack with child-friendly designs
		Too cold	Blankets Hot therapy gel beads

Sensory Area	General Observations	Specific Observed Behaviours	Sensory Strategies
Auditory/Listening	Students become dysregulated when the room is loud; students seek quiet.	Too loud	Noise-canceling headphones Quiet corner Privacy partitions
	Students become dysregulated when room is quiet; students create noise when it is quiet.	Too quiet	White-noise machine Headphones to listen to music Auditory feedback phone

With our work in special education and with students living with trauma, you would be hard-pressed to find two bigger advocates for sensory strategies. We understand how valuable instruction time is in the classroom, and we do recognize that some sensory strategies do indeed take up time in your school day. However, if a child is unable to regulate their body and emotions, you will spend far more time managing the dysregulated child's behavior than teaching the lesson. Integrating sensory strategies into your daily routines will help your students struggling with trauma learn by promoting improved self-regulation.

Labeling Emotional States

Emotional regulation as an intentional act requires that the student possesses the ability to observe their emotions or thinking. Tragically, students in traumatic situations often do not develop the age-related mental strength to help them regulate emotions when compared to their peers. Because these students find it more difficult to make sense of their internal emotional states, often their behaviors seem immature to school staff. The child may throw tantrums when they do not get their way. They may have trouble focusing and staying on task. They may be unable to maintain friendships. If a child cannot identify their internal states, they will lack the ability to control their reactions and the behaviors that result from their thoughts and emotions (Nakazawa, 2016).

Emotions lose their power when people assign words to them. The act of labeling internal states provides space for conscious consideration. Labeling may initiate a more rational reaction to what is going on in the environment. Labeling is particularly challenging for students with an underdeveloped Broca's area, which limits their ability to express their emotional states to others and put their experiences into words.

Our work in special education demonstrated the powerful connection between labeling and behaviors. We worked with many nonverbal students with very limited vocabularies and traumatic histories. Their lesson to us: when a student cannot express to you their frustration or anger, their feelings come out in extreme and often violent behaviors.

Imagine if you were annoyed at someone but couldn't tell them that they were annoying you. Your frustration builds and builds until you do something extreme to change the situation. These students acted out because they were not able to verbally express their emotions. This response is often the same behavior we see in students with trauma who have poor expressive language skills. Once we found adaptive language strategies to help them communicate their frustration, we saw behavior improve dramatically.

In the classroom, strategic labeling practice helps the student develop this critical ability. In addition, it provides the teacher with helpful information about the student's current state. Young children, especially those impacted by trauma, will struggle to put complex emotional concepts such as anxiety, fear, or depression into words. The teacher needs to help. It is on us to provide a developmentally appropriate language to help students express their inner experiences.

While many educational programs aim to address social-emotional learning and sensory self-management, we have found the approaches used in Leah Kuypers' (2011) *The Zones of Regulation*® curriculum to be particularly impactful. *The Zones of Regulation*® teaches students how to recognize when they are in different states or zones, which are represented by four different colors. Students are taught cognitive-behavioral strategies, calming techniques, and sensory supports to help them move from one zone to another or to stay in a zone that fosters optimal learning.

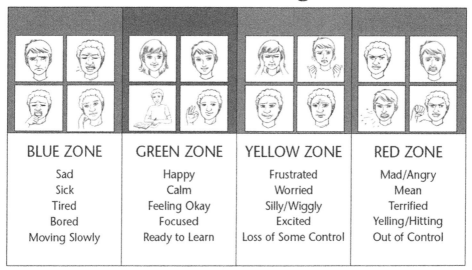

In constructing a trauma-sensitive classroom, we need to create brief intervals throughout the day to allow students to check in with themselves. During that time, they learn to observe and label their mental states. Even a minute to pause and connect with one's internal state activates the prefrontal cortex and calms the amygdala. In addition to helping regulate their brain, these check-ins also provide a chance for students to communicate with their teacher when they identify feelings of sadness, anxiety, fear, or anger.

One time that lends itself naturally to this type of check-in is during your morning meeting. It is incredibly helpful to know the state or zone a child is in when they first enter the classroom. Through this morning check-in, you may learn that a beloved pet has died or that a child is staying with a grandparent who lets them stay up all night playing video games. This information will help explain the state a child is in. It will help guide you in your decision-making throughout the day. For instance, you would not want to read aloud a story about dogs if one of your students is grieving the recent loss of their pet. A check-in may provide you with insight into your students that you would otherwise not have.

Another effective time for check-ins is before and after transitions.

Most transitions in the school day signal a need to change zones. The expectations in Physical Education (PE) that you can run and have a heightened voice level immediately change when it is time to line up and transition back to the classroom. Children are asked to change their zones quickly, regulate their body to walk in a line, and soften their voice level. Young children in general, but especially those with trauma and in special education, struggle to transition to different states needed for these radically different environments because of the changing social and cognitive demands. Unfortunately, we too often punish the resulting behaviors. We simply do not realize that their minds lack the ability to shift states in such short periods of time without adult assistance and support (Cole et al., 2009).

In a trauma-sensitive school, all staff understand that transitional struggles are biological struggles and not states that students can easily control. This knowledge calls on all staff to strategically support children during transitions. Support could include reviewing rules, taking a moment to check in, and adding some transitional activities like deep breathing. Letting a child know the appropriate zone for the next environment is essential. It is also powerful to ask the students what they need to help move them from one state to another. With practice, students become experts at knowing what they need to change their own states.

Establishing routines like line-up songs and body checks, and allotting adequate time to transitions gives students what they need to observe their zone and adjust accordingly. When we rush a transition, we are not providing students with trauma the time they need to transition successfully. When we are running late or rushing a transition, students feel our impatience and stress. Building in routines to support them during those times of transition will aid in promoting desired behaviors and self-regulation.

Mindfulness and Emotional Regulation

After you help your students learn how to label their emotional state, they are ready to learn how to control their thoughts and feelings. Mindfulness is a tool that strengthens the mind so that it gains the power to override and change the traits that would otherwise prevent it from succeeding socially and academically. The research on mindfulness has exploded in the last several years. It seems like for every social, emotional, or cognitive struggle, mindfulness is the solution! It helps the brain and body repair the negative impacts of stress and trauma. Mindfulness strengthens the prefrontal cortex and calms the amygdala, expanding the capacity for resilience. It also reduces the amount of the stress hormone cortisol in the body. In other words, a student in a mindful state is a student ready to engage, meet behavioral expectations, and learn (Siegel, 2011).

Mindfulness has also been shown to increase a person's ability to attune or connect on an emotional and intellectual level with others. Mindfulness enhances the quality of the educator/student relationship and their relationships with peers. These relationships become increasingly important as schools move toward collaboration and project-based learning. Students are encouraged to think critically. They learn to problem-solve and work with others. Mindfulness practice can support engagement in these types of school activities and academic lessons. When the student feels more connected and able to trust you and others wanting to help them succeed, significant changes happen. Mindfulness allows students to gain awareness of their stress levels and take positive actions to cope before negative behaviors occur (Burdick, 2013; Davidson et al., 2003; Langer, 2009; Rock, 2009).

That's not all! Mindfulness also improves immune functioning and facilitates faster healing from injuries. Students who practice mindfulness stay healthy in schools that battle seasonal flu, strep throat, and other illnesses. On top of that, it helps with many mental-health issues such as PTSD, ADHD, other anxiety disorders, and depression, among other conditions. Mindfulness might sound like a too-good-to-be-true miracle cure. Do not be misled; to realize these positive benefits, students must practice and develop the skills of mindfulness over time. The benefits help demonstrate why integrating mindfulness into classrooms is a journey worth taking (Burdick, 2013; Davidson et al., 2003; Langer, 2009; Rock, 2009).

To make mindfulness practical, view it as a skill. When we see mindfulness as a skill set, it takes away some of the mystery and stigma sometimes associated with the practice. For young children, quick opportunities for mindfulness practice throughout the day helps repair the biological injuries of trauma. All students develop better resiliency for future hardships, attention, cognitive ability, and emotional regulation. Let's review a couple of excellent short mindfulness practices for primary-age students (Siegel, 2011).

One of our favorites is a practice called belly breathing. Belly breathing occurs when students extend their stomachs outward on the inhale, filling the belly first with air before filling their chest. On the exhale, their stomachs go down as they contract their stomach muscles. To make this fun, give students a small stuffed animal or toy to place on their bellies. When they inhale, the toy goes up, and then it goes down on the exhale. This activity is a fun way to get students to focus on their breathing. Let's add one more concept to belly breathing. As you ask the student to breathe in and fill their belly, count to 4; then have them hold their breath for a count of 4, and then exhale to a count of 8 (please feel free to adjust these numbers; just keep the ratio of 1:1:2) (David, 2009).

Another mindfulness activity that focuses on breathing is called rainbow breathing. It can be done standing or seated on the ground. You may notice some students may naturally close their eyes during this activity; this is optional, but might seem scary for students with trauma, so don't force it. Students are asked to visualize creating a rainbow as they raise their arms upward at their sides with their palms facing up. They continue to inhale until their hands are touching above their heads. Then on the exhale, their hands will move slowly back down to their sides as if the rainbow is gradually disappearing. The exhale is intentionally slower paced than the inhale and their palms face downward until they touch their sides. The process is continued several times until the class has achieved the desired state of calmness.

There is some fascinating science behind these breathing techniques. Inhaling, we activate our sympathetic nervous system. The sympathetic nervous system prepares us for action, including the fight-or-flight response. On the exhale, we activate our parasympathetic nervous system, which brings on a sense of calm and relaxation. The longer exhale serves to strengthen the parasympathetic nervous system. Additionally, areas of the brain that support emotional regulation and cognitive focus come into play. Even if you only do the belly breathing with a toy once a day, you can use belly breathing without the toy to calm your students after recess or lunch, or at the beginning of the school day.

An additional practice that aids students in building their mindfulness is a technique called square breathing. Square breathing is done sitting in a chair or seated cross-legged on the ground. To begin, have your students point their finger in the air. Encourage them to visualize that they are drawing a box or square in the air. They will trace an imaginary line across their body as they inhale for 4 seconds. Once completing the inhale, they will now hold their breath for 4 seconds as they trace downward the second side of their square. From there, they exhale for 4 seconds as they draw the bottom of the square. Finally, they can complete the last side of their imaginary square by tracing their finger upward and holding their breath for 4 seconds. The process should be repeated several times as it takes some practice to get the hang of it.

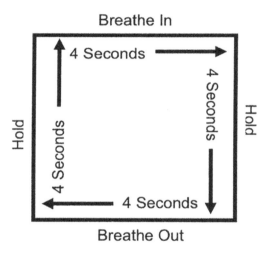

While square breathing does not utilize the longer exhale, the strategy balances the sympathetic and parasympathetic nervous systems. Balanced breathing exercises are great transitions for activities that require more energy and focus, but less relaxation, such as tests. It also has the added benefit of crossing the midline, the imaginary line that divides the body into right and left hemispheres. Activities that cross the midline are shown to improve fine motor skills and strengthen brain functioning (Parnell, 2008).

Other good mindfulness practices for students with trauma are yoga poses or stretching. Research demonstrates that yoga is an effective treatment for trauma. When doing a simple yoga stretch, have the students focus on both their breathing and how their body feels. Yoga poses named after animals, such as cobra pose, downward dog, and cat pose, are especially engaging. Yoga calms both the mind and body, and is also great for transitions and getting students up after sitting down for long periods of time (David, 2009; Van der Kolk, 2014).

Regardless of the practice you use, reassure your students that their random thoughts and feelings are natural. Each time one pops into their head, it gives them an excellent opportunity to refocus. This refocusing is where many of the early benefits of mindfulness practice occur. Challenge students to catch a wandering thought or feeling and redirect their attention back to the activity. Refocusing is a function of the prefrontal cortex and an excellent activity for strengthening the damage done by traumatic experiences (Siegel, 2016).

There is one cautionary note: keep the mindfulness activities short and focused on an activity, such as focusing on the breath or a yoga pose. For some students with trauma, calming the mind without focus opens up the opportunity for traumatic memories to come up into consciousness (Treleaven, 2018).

Helping Students Establish a Positive View of Self

The experience of repeated abuse, neglect, bullying, or ridicule sends a message to the student that they are unworthy of love and dignity. Eventually, repeated mistreatment leaves the student with a negative view of self, other people, and the world. As a result, too many students develop something called the fixed mindset (Bronson & Merryman, 2009; Dweck, 2006).

The fixed mindset, especially when resulting from trauma, often manifests as a type of victim mentality. It is a natural consequence of experiencing harm done by another human being. Everyone who is traumatized is a victim of something or someone. In the fixed mindset, the trauma or life situations continue to hold power over the student and keep them stuck in the pain and suffering associated with the trauma. While younger students struggle to verbalize the feelings of shame and self-loathing resulting from abuse, these unexpressed feelings dramatically influence their internal self-talk and self-esteem (Dweck, 2006).

This negative view of self steals aspirations of hope for the future and any sense of self-confidence. In this fixed mindset, students fail to find motivation when facing opportunities for improvement. Unfortunately, school, which is an opportunity for advancement and growth, presents challenges that elicit a sense of overwhelming anxiety instead of excitement. Fixed thinking, combined with the reality that many students' energy goes to surviving their current impoverished or dangerous situations, prevents them from seeing a brighter future on the horizon and how success and school could help them live a more fulfilled life (Bennett, 2017).

In young children, a fixed mindset can present itself in a variety of ways. A few examples are a child who will only write their name and sit quietly in hopes of not calling attention to themselves, the student who destroys their work or the work of others by scribbling all over it, or the student who uses avoidance behaviors like restroom breaks, water breaks, and repeatedly breaking their pencil to avoid independent work. Students with this type of anxiety and self-doubt might ask excessive amounts of questions because they are desperately afraid of doing something incorrectly. All these behaviors result from a fixed mindset.

One of the greatest gifts school staff give to students with trauma is to help them learn to be kind to themselves and stop the harsh self-judgment associated with trauma and the fixed mindset. Trauma-sensitive classrooms work to help the student understand that their past behaviors, thoughts, and feelings do not define them as a person. Most students will struggle with this at first. You should view it as a skill that needs reinforcement and practice.

Shifting from a Fixed to a Growth Mindset

When teaching students to adopt a growth mindset concerning their education and behaviors, school staff are setting them up to succeed in school and beyond (Gladwell 2005). Carol Dweck (2006) termed the concept of the growth mindset, the opposite of the fixed mindset described above, as:

In a growth mindset, people believe that their most basic abilities can be developed through dedication and hard work—brains and talent are just the starting point. This view creates a love of learning and a resilience that is essential for great accomplishment.

One of the critical components in transforming the pain and suffering of trauma into the strength and wisdom of post-traumatic growth entails the development of hope. Hope is a student's belief that their future is bright, lacking the pain and suffering of their past. Without the ability to see a better future, students will struggle to find the motivation to change behaviors or invest energy in their studies.

Due to past struggles and trauma, many students cannot see a future different than their current situation. For these students, we need to hold their hope in the short term. Holding hope requires patience, reframing, and helping the student appreciate even their smallest accomplishments. Over time, most students will slowly start to build a growth mindset and escape the "bad kid" label that threatens to follow them throughout their school years. The growth mindset provides the self-confidence the student needs to realize hope for a better future. Hope elicits the motivation to engage academically. Research by Blackwell, Trzesniewski, and Dweck (2007) demonstrates that students taught about growth mindset improved their growth percentiles and showed more resiliency after a setback on an academic task.

We want to help students transform their fixed mindsets into growth mindsets and view themselves as survivors who are no longer prisoners of their past pain. As confidence replaces pain and suffering, trauma's grip loosens, and a new person emerges. As this transformation occurs, school staff should hear more positive self-statements and see increasing levels of motivation.

School staff's language is critical to the student replacing a fixed mindset with a growth one. When staff use well-meaning statements like "You're a natural at science" or "You are so smart," they are unknowingly promoting fixed thinking. So, why is this important? If a child believes they're great in science and then gets a low grade on a science test, they'll internalize this as "I'm a failure."

Dweck found that this led to feelings of depression or anxiety when they faced future challenges. Believing they are now "bad" at science destroys their motivation to work harder. "I'm bad at science" stops motivation.

In contrast, growth-mindset statements like, "You worked so hard for that score on your history test" or "You've put a lot of effort into your homework this grading period and look how your grades have improved" equate success with student effort and determination. A student with a growth mindset realizes that success is a result of the effort put forth. If confronted with hardship or setbacks, the growth mindset motivates the student to work much harder and not give up. They recognize that their success in school and the hope for a better tomorrow is dependent on the effort and work invested in making it a reality. Internal thoughts such as "I need to work harder next time to get a better grade" set the student up for success.

Those with a fixed mindset believe that some people are born superior. Natural talent may help some people succeed in things like music and sports, but Dweck's research shows that successful people, even world-class musicians and athletes, work harder than their peers to develop their talents. Few geniuses are born. Instead, genius emerges from hours, days, years, and decades of dedication and practice. Those who believe their skills are a result of arduous work spend more time developing these skills and expertise (Dweck, 2006).

Helping shift a student's self-talk from a fixed mindset to a growth mindset takes time and repetition. The first step involves helping the student to hear their fixed mindset voice, then to observe and label it. It is essential to teach your students a little information about fixed and growth mindsets. You can talk to the student about the brain being like a muscle: the more you use the areas that promote thinking, calm behavior, and friendly behavior, the stronger their brains become at those tasks.

Thinking about the brain as a muscle is one of the best ways to teach the concept of growth mindset to primary-aged students. Find a video clip of a massive bodybuilder lifting weights. Ask the students how many hours of lifting weights they think this colossal person did to get that big.

Then help the students understand that, even though their brains are inside their heads, brains get strong the more we work them out. The more you study spelling, the larger the brain area gets that helps you succeed on a spelling test. You cannot integrate the "brain as a muscle" analogy too much in your teaching approaches. It is a great way to get students excited about more repetitive learning tasks. The message: the harder and longer you work, the stronger the brain becomes!

A New Goal: A Very Different Outcome

Mrs. Vaughn's anxiety rose as Caleb's return drew closer. Understanding that Caleb's issues were due to abuse, poverty, and a chaotic home life did nothing to alleviate her doubts that she could keep her class safe. The trauma-sensitive stuff sounded good in theory, but how would any of this stop Caleb from hurting another student?

Ms. Smith scheduled a meeting with the team and Dr. Rodriguez for the afternoon before Caleb's return. The meeting went well. Mrs. Vaughn felt terrible for Mr. Anderson, as she figured he had his doubts, but in the face of Ms. Smith's excitement, Dr. Griffin's growing determination, and the presence of Dr. Rodriguez, Mr. Anderson had zero opportunity to voice much concern. Ms. Smith was becoming a force of nature, and her passion was contagious. Mrs. Vaughn did wonder if her enthusiasm would lessen if Caleb were coming back to HER class tomorrow.

Dr. Rodriguez made the argument that academic achievement must remain the ultimate goal. However, if Caleb did not learn to regulate his emotions, not only would his academic achievement suffer, but his long-term social skills and eventual employment future were likely to resemble that of his mother.

The focus on the emotional and psychological health of her students was a different sort of pressure. Mrs. Vaughn was not a therapist, and it seemed like she needed that level of expertise to help students with trauma begin to heal and grow psychologically in addition to academically. While Caleb was the focus of everyone's attention, what about Emilia and the other kids who were also struggling with trauma?

Her hope rested on a set of emotional instructional approaches centered around the concept of mindfulness and the *Zones of Regulation*® that Dr. Rodriguez had provided. While she had a plan to create some isolation for Caleb in and out of the classroom, Mrs. Vaughn liked this approach, as it focused on the whole class and not just Caleb. Ms. Smith and Mr. Anderson were also introducing this approach in their classes; however; Dr. Griffin had decided to sit in on Mrs. Vaughn's class to see how it went and help keep an eye on Caleb.

As her class started coming in the next morning, she and Dr. Griffin pulled Caleb aside and let him know that he would sit at a "special" desk until Mrs. Vaughn thought his behavior was appropriate to join the rest of the class back at the tables. Caleb let out a huff but put up no further resistance.

As Caleb walked to his new desk, Malik and his mother came through the door. While Malik's mom usually came in later in the morning, both Mrs. Vaughn and Dr. Griffin were not surprised that she showed up early today. Mrs. Vaughn realized that she was about to teach mindfulness for the first time in front of a concerned parent and her principal.

Mrs. Vaughn's goal was to introduce mindfulness this morning and start practicing throughout the day. As the bell rang, she quickly got the class settled and began.

"Good morning class. Today we are going to try something new. We are going to learn a new routine for our morning meeting that will help us get our brains and bodies ready for learning. To do this exercise, I am going to pass out a breathing buddy for each of you. The buddy you get today may or may not be the same buddy you will get in the future." The eyes of the three adults followed Caleb like a hawk. Mrs. Vaughn kept close to him as he was handed a small stuffed bear for his breathing buddy.

"All right friends, I want you to find a nice spot on the floor, lie down on your back, and put your breathing buddy on your belly. I want everyone to take a deep breath and pay attention to how your body feels."

There were a few chuckles, but everyone followed the directions. After dimming the lights, she continued, "Okay friends, when we breathe in, I want you to push your buddy up as high as your belly can go. Let's give this a try." The class continued to follow her instructions.

"Great job, friends! Next, we are going to breathe out and see how low we can get our buddies." Again, everyone seemed highly focused on the task. Realizing that a few of her more competitive students were watching their peers trying to get their breathing buddy higher, she reminded the class, "To do this right, you must keep your eyes focused on YOUR buddy."

"All right, everyone got it?" A collective "Yes" came from the floor. "Class, do you think Dr. Griffin and Malik's mom should join us?" A loud "YES" answered this question.

"I'm going to give Dr. Griffin a dragon and Malik's mom a unicorn!" All the students chuckled. They had never seen their principal on the floor before! If the principal was doing this, it must be important.

Transitioning into a calm, quiet, and slow voice, Mrs. Vaughn began the exercise, "Okay friends, now it gets a little harder, but I know you can do it. I'm going to have you take a deep breath in, hold it, and then you will release a long breath out." Mrs. Vaughn had the class breathe in for a count of four, hold for four, and exhale for eight. She could tell that some of her students struggled at the end of the exhale, so for the second time, she reminded them, "Make sure you breathe in deeply so you have enough air to breathe out."

She continued having her class breathe for three minutes, and all the kids did a great job, even Caleb. "Okay, friends I want to take a moment to see how you feel now. Do you feel a little different than before our fun exercise?"

Most of the students answered, "Yes."

"Okay, let's put our breathing buddies up and work our way back to our seats."

Once settled, Mrs. Vaughn went over to the *Zones of Regulation*® poster she had prominently displayed on the whiteboard. "Okay, friends, besides our breathing, we are also going to do something else new today. I want to understand your feelings and how ready you are for learning activities. One way to help me understand your feelings is to tell me what zone you are experiencing. It is normal to feel lots of different ways throughout the school day. No zone is good or bad."

"If you feel angry, for example, you would tell me you are in the Red Zone. Can anyone tell me what it feels like to be angry?"

Caleb's hand shot up. Mrs. Vaughn thought it was his area of expertise. "Okay, Caleb, what does anger feel like?"

"It feels like you are ready to explode!" He jumped up a little in his seat, threw his arms backward, and then collapsed on the chair.

"Thanks, Caleb! Is that how everyone feels when they are angry?"

"Yes," was the answer from most, but Emilia seemed hesitant.

"Emilia, do you feel something different than Caleb? If so, it's fine, as everyone experiences emotions slightly differently," said Mrs. Vaughn

In her normal whisper voice, Emilia answered, "When I am in the Red Zone, I want to cry and hide from everyone."

"Emilia, thank you so much. You show us all how different people feel emotions in different ways. There is no right or wrong when it comes to how we feel, whether we are angry or happy. The important thing we are going to work on together is to identify when we feel certain emotions."

Mrs. Vaughn went through the other three zones and tried to emphasize that although no zone is good or bad, the Green Zone indicates that we are ready to learn, calm, and focused. If we are not in the Green Zone, we have the power to move ourselves from one zone to another by using calming strategies and other tools that they would learn over the next few weeks. The kids seemed excited to be learning about the zones and had lots of examples of times they felt different emotions.

"Great job, friends. Now I want you to take a deep breath and think about what zone you are in right now." Pointing to the poster, Mrs. Vaughn continued, "We learned the sign-language alphabet and are going to use it to help us share what zone we are in. First, I want everyone to create a cover with your other hand, so our zones are private." Mrs. Vaughn showed them how to make a little roof with one hand so that others couldn't see what letter they were signing. "When you show me your zone, you will only sign to me the first letter of that color. 'R' for red, 'G' for green, and so on."

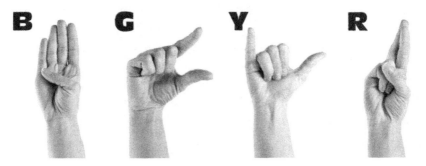

"Now, show me the color that represents what you are feeling right now." Since the activity went so well, Mrs. Vaughn was not surprised to see that many kids felt they were ready to learn and in the Green Zone. She also realized that the breathing probably calmed down a little of the fear that some students had concerning Caleb's return.

Mrs. Vaughn did not expect that some children would indicate that they felt they were in more than one zone at the same time. Some children said they were in Green Zone (ready to learn) and Blue Zone. When she dug a little further, she discovered that one child had a cold, so they were in Blue Zone too. Another student was also in Yellow Zone because her birthday was next week, and she was getting excited. Mrs. Vaughn was delighted that a simple check-in provided so much information about all her students, not just Caleb.

"All right class, it is time for art. Before we go, please stand up at your table and make sure there is plenty of space between you and your neighbor. I want us to take five deep breaths together while we practice a calming strategy called rainbow breathing. When you breathe in, your arms will raise up at your sides, and eventually your hands will be pointing to the ceiling. On the exhale, your hands will move slowly down back to your sides. If you go slowly, it will look as if you are creating a rainbow with your arms that slowly disappears. Remember, take a deep breath, because the exhale will be twice as long." The class practiced their rainbow breathing and went off to art with everyone in a good mood.

Coming back to her class, Mrs. Vaughn walked into a conversation between Malik's mom and Dr. Griffin, who was explaining some of the research on mindfulness and trauma. Malik's mom, seeing Mrs. Vaughn, said with a smile, "That was a fun start to the day."

"Yes, it was. I was a little nervous as it was my first time doing anything with mindfulness, but it seemed like the kids picked it up right away." Mrs. Vaughn said, feeling a mix of exhaustion and relief that Caleb's return was at least off to a good start.

"And I feel weirdly refreshed," Dr. Griffin added. "I'm not sure when was the last time that I felt this way at school. Maybe there is something to all this breathing stuff."

"Next time, I get the dragon!" Malik's mom said with a laugh as she left to join the class in the art room.

Mrs. Vaughn integrated what she termed "brain breaks" throughout the day: a yoga pose after recess, another belly breathing session after lunch, and even some square breathing before an important math test. After each, she had students share what zone they were in.

While most students were in the Green Zone, she did get some different zones throughout the day. She found some time to check in with these students shortly after and found that most of their emotions were due to smaller events that occurred throughout the day. Her favorite was one boy who said he was in Yellow, Blue, and Red Zone! When Mrs. Vaughn checked in, he stated he was frustrated, angry, and sad that his mom packed a banana and not Hot Cheetos in his lunch.

As she chuckled to herself, Mr. Anderson peeked his head in the door, "Got a second?" Mrs. Vaughn could tell something wasn't quite right in his tone.

"Sure, but first, what zone are you in?" She wondered if Mr. Anderson would really follow through and implement the routines Dr. Rodriguez taught them.

Walking in, Mr. Anderson held up a sign language letter 'B', indicating he was sad and in the Blue Zone.

"What's up?" Mrs. Vaughn said in a more empathetic voice.

"Well, I did the *Zones of Regulation*® chart today and check-ins. I was having fun with it, as you can imagine, until one of my girls held up a 'Y' for Yellow Zone. When I checked in with her before lunch, she said she was nervous because tonight she had a babysitter who sometimes touched her in ways that made her feel uncomfortable."

"Oh," was all Mrs. Vaughn could utter. All this emotional instruction got very real very quickly. Right at that moment, Ms. Smith popped in with the excitement of the day written all over her. Mrs. Vaughn needed to hold her young teammate's enthusiasm at bay so Mr. Anderson would feel okay to continue, "Kevin was just telling me about a concerning comment …" She was not sure what word to use next.

At that very moment, Dr. Griffin walked in. "Hey, I probably know what you all are talking about."

"I only told them the gist," Mr. Anderson replied.

"Yeah, well I spent the afternoon with parents and counseling staff, and then on the phone with Child Protective Services and the police." Dr. Griffin seemed on the brink of breaking down.

They all just sat there in silence for a full minute.

Finally, Mr. Anderson muttered, "All from a *Zones* poster."

"We asked the right questions today." Dr. Griffin regained the power of her voice.

"I've been going back and forth all day. By not doing these sort of simple check-ins, kids at this school were getting hurt, and we were unaware. On the other hand, by asking, we will hopefully stop abuse and prevent other children from getting hurt."

The weight of Dr. Griffin's statement fell heavy on the group. Mr. Anderson's head fell into his hands and through his attempt not to cry, said, "Who does that to a child?"

At seeing Mr. Anderson cry, Ms. Smith choked up as well. Mrs. Vaughn put her hands on their shoulders. The trauma-sensitive school thing became something more than just another educational initiative or flavor of the month.

Mrs. Vaughn's last thought as she left school that day was about Mr. Anderson and the other teachers whose students may be facing abusive situations. How do you go about your day normally, go to basketball practice, play with your kids, and listen to your spouse's day after learning what has happened to your students? They always found ways to make time for the kids' crises, but what about the trauma of the teachers and school staff?

CHAPTER 4
Social-Emotional Learning: Strategies for Relational Growth

Think about this: when you look at the vast number of adults who suffered traumatic experiences as children, what do you imagine is the most significant indicator of whether that child will heal or carry their trauma into adulthood?

The answer is whether or not that person was lucky enough to have someone in their life who cared about them, and believed in them and in their future (Bloom, 2000; Bloom & Farragher, 2013; Cole et al, 2009; Cozolino, 2010; Craig, 2016; Herman, 1997; Lipsky & Burk, 2009; Prochaska, DiClemente, & Norcross, 1992; Saxe, Ellis, & Kaplow, 2007; Van der Kolk, 2014). Think about that one great teacher who inspired you to go into education. What about them sparked your passion for teaching others? I imagine your answer is not one of the following:

"She really prepared me to perform well on standardized tests."

"His knowledge of the curriculum was better than my other teachers."

"She made sure to address every standard on the grade-level curriculum."

Instead, we are inspired by those teachers who pushed us academically, while simultaneously establishing special relationships with each of their students. They got to know us personally and found ways to spark our passion for learning. For students with trauma, their outcomes dramatically change if they are lucky enough to have people in their lives who care, challenge, and inspire them. If they do not get this from adults at home, those at school represent one of their last chances to connect and heal before carrying the pain of their trauma into their adult lives.

Serve-and-Return Communication

If you want a simple model of effective communication that develops the cognitive and emotional brain, imagine two professional tennis players warming up in a friendly serve-and-volley drill. One player, the student, serves the ball or initiates communication through a verbal statement or by paying attention to something in their environment. The second player, you, recognizes that the serve is coming your way, and you position yourself for an effective return. The goal of the game, or our interaction, is to identify the initial attempt at communication and engage in an active back-and-forth, or "serve-and-return" with the student.

Healthy parents engage in serve-and-return communication from their very first interactions with their baby. The baby smiles; her dad smiles back enthusiastically. The baby cries, and mom's face changes from a smile to an attentive look of concern and then back to a smile when she identifies her baby's need. These critical early interactions help form strong neuronal connections in the brain that serve as the foundation for cognitive ability and emotional self-regulation (Harvard National Scientific Council for the Developing Child, 2018).

Unfortunately, many of the students who struggle in our schools grew up in homes where parents were unable to provide this type of responsive communication. A parent might need to work multiple jobs to make ends meet. Addiction or untreated mental illness may prevent parents from providing appropriate responses. On the traumatic end of the spectrum, neglect or abuse are often the responses the young child gets in return.

Imagine trying to build a house without a foundation. Due to no fault of their own, many students enter pre-school or kindergarten without experiencing these critical early-development interactions. They have no foundations with which to begin building their education. The good news is if we can find the time and allocate attention, our serve-and-return communication style will help the student catch up cognitively, socially, and emotionally.

Serve-and-return communication is straightforward. First, notice what the student is doing or something they are focusing on: This is their serve. Your return involves noticing their serve, making eye contact, and showing interest, curiosity, or encouragement in what they are focusing on. Your curiosity and attention are powerful rewards in and of themselves.

Let's say you have a reluctant writer who develops a love of dinosaurs. One day they begin to draw a dinosaur during writing time. They may not be on the assigned writing task, but they are engaging their fine motor skills and attempting to do something on paper. You inquire about what type of dinosaur they are drawing, note the hard work they put into the details, and find other books the child may enjoy reading about their newfound passion.

You reward the child with your attention. You demonstrate that you care about what they care about. Establishing a shared focus shows that their interests are important. You strengthen the relationship. Encouragement supports behaviors that help the student succeed both at the task at hand and in future interactions with adults and peers.

Next, it is important to note that children with trauma can often lack the rich communication at home that develops the areas of the brain that support expressive and receptive language skills. As a result, these children often face the challenge of expressing their social and academic ideas coherently or in a socially appropriate way.

One strategy to help them strengthen their expressive language skills is to provide them with sentence stems or sentence starters. If they are given the initial language with which to respond to a question repeatedly, then that language becomes a part of their language toolbox, and they can draw from it in the future.

On the playground, a sentence starter may be an "I message." "I feel (emotion) when you (action)." In the classroom, it may be academic-based, such as, "I have a text-self connection. I also (name the connection)." The use of sentence starters allows the child a modicum of safety when expressing themselves, as they only need to fill in the blanks. The more comfortable a child is using these starters, the more their expressive language skills will develop.

Another critical component of a good return is matching the emotional intensity of the student. If the student is angry and yelling, your initial return should lie somewhere between their emotional state and the state to which you want them to transition. If the student yells, "I hate you!", don't yell back. Instead, state in a slightly exaggerated voice, "I know it is so hard when teachers tell you recess is over." When you communicate back in a similar state, the child is more likely to hear you and engage with your return. If they are more escalated than appropriate, lower your voice slightly under their level. Inversely, if you need them to get more energetic for an activity, the emotions of your communication should rise slightly above their current state.

The goal of the first couple of steps is to establish back and forth with the child. When you return the serve, practice patience. Some children will need time to construct their next return. Wait time is a term often used to describe this pause.

Wait time allows the student's brain to consider, think, and construct their response. By providing wait time, you are helping your student learn that it is okay to think before responding. Also, their response provides you with a better understanding of their needs, since they might need time to put their thoughts into words. An added benefit of this strategy is that you are modeling for all your students how to be a good listener. If they see you waiting for a response, then they are likely to mimic that behavior.

Finally, it is important to model how to transition successfully to the next task. Brief serve-and-return interactions are subtle yet strong reinforcers of positive behaviors. More meaningful and more extended interactions are also important. However, the reality of the classroom makes these opportunities rare. Teachers may juggle four, five, or more balls in the air at any given moment throughout their school day. As such, several small serve-and-returns throughout the day are wonderful tools to build strong relationships, develop brain areas crucial for cognitive and emotional focus, and help the student feel important and valuable.

A Different Approach to Behavioral Issues

"The kid is just a bully." "It is no coincidence that she is a mess. Have you met her parents?" "I have two students from THAT neighborhood this year. It's going to be a long year." Every teacher and school staff member at some point in their career has either heard or said such statements. Our attitudes, biases, and viewpoints become jaded when confronted year after year with the agonizingly frustrating behaviors of some of our students, especially those that seem irreversible.

School staff resort to punishments because all our teacher tricks and behavioral incentives are unsuccessful. They believe if they can just find the right consequence, the behaviors will stop. Over time, patience runs thin, as teachers exhaust every incentive chart, rearrange the seating chart a hundred times, and try every type of positive and negative consequence imaginable, but the behavior continues.

Most behavioral-management systems fail to make lasting changes that a child can generalize into other areas of their life due to two key factors. First, the student and school staff do not achieve any insight into the reasons behind behaviors. Typical interventions focus on the gain or loss of points, changing the color of their stoplight, or how close the class is to a group prize.

Cognitive-behavioral therapy and other best-practice psychological approaches demonstrate that real lasting change happens when the school staff gains enough insight to address the underlying causes of a student's struggles and helps them find internal motivation for change. For consequences to effectively help change behavior, the student needs to feel supported and understood by the school staff. As with most things concerning trauma, success and failure are highly dependent on the quality of the relationship. Unlike traditional behavioral management, these changes generalize into environments outside the classroom (Bailey, 2015; Miller & Rollnick, 2012).

Second, struggling students do not possess the coping skills necessary to succeed under the stressful conditions of the school environment. No child wakes up early to plan out their behavioral issues for that day. Instead, they find themselves in situations without the skills to manage their own stress and emotional reactions. If the student lacks skills to navigate the social, emotional, or cognitive situation successfully, they rely on chaotic behaviors that get them in trouble at school. Those are the very same skills that serve them well in an unsafe home environment or community. Instead of punishing students who lack the skills to succeed in our schools, we need to identify why they are struggling in the first place and help them build the skills they need to succeed.

In this section, we will present a simple, yet powerful tactic to gain insight and understanding into those unreachable children. When a student's behavior fails to meet our expectations, and we cannot figure out why they keep misbehaving, maybe we should ask the student what is going on! While asking the student sounds remarkably straightforward, we need a strategic communication approach. Because many of the reasons behind behaviors, especially those associated with trauma, go well beyond the current incident, they may take some time to identify.

Let's address a couple of crucial things here. First, it is much quicker in the short term to punish or give consequences to a misbehaving student than to explore the reasons behind the behavior. Meaningfully connecting with a student is an investment of time. Teachers and school staff have little spare time. However, if the staff and student identify the reason behind a student's behavioral difficulties and help them learn the skills to handle the situation differently, this investment will save you a great deal of time in the future.

Besides saving you time, if a student builds a skill, this new skill will transfer to other situations in their lives. The benefits are great for such a small investment. When you help a student identify the cause of their struggle and develop skills to eliminate the skill deficit, not only does that save you time in the long run, it helps the student well into the future.

The next thing we want to address is that few school staff outside social workers and mental-health professionals possess the training to explore the hidden reasons behind disruptive behavior, especially when these reasons are results of psychological struggles such as trauma. Just like a student who lacks the skills to succeed under certain circumstances, school staff rely on consequences and punishment because those are the skills we developed in the modern educational system to address disruptions in our schools and classrooms.

The contemporary classroom relies heavily on behavioral consequences. Punishments like suspensions and expulsions seem efficient and are immediate, visible, and socially expected. If a child brings a knife to school, a policy dictates that they get suspended. Problem solved?

The good news is that the communication that leads to insight is a skill that builds on the strengths most school staff already possess. Before we introduce you to a simple communication approach, we need first to establish a philosophical foundation to drive the intent behind our words. When school staff engage a student in a conversation concerning their behaviors, they want to do so from a place of acceptance, compassion, and partnership.

Punishment is a very familiar event for students with trauma. Acceptance challenges us to initially prioritize empathy over problem-solving. The cognitive behaviorists Miller and Rollnick (2012) define empathy not only as "an ability to understand another's frame of reference" but continue to make a critical point that it requires "the conviction that it is worthwhile to do so."

A trauma-sensitive approach to behavioral change involves a conversation where both the school staff and the student explore the issue without immediately jumping to judgment. To successfully fulfill this role, the school staff does their best to see the situation from the student's point of view. We will give you some skills to succeed in this challenging task. However, it is vital that empathy is viewed as a worthwhile endeavor. Nonjudgment does not mean the school will not act to ensure the safety of the student and others in the school environment. The goal is to balance safety with understanding the "why" behind the behavior.

Compassion challenges school staff to set aside their frustration and view the student as a valuable human being who is more than just the sum of their current behaviors. When adults come from a belief that every child wants to succeed and should have every opportunity to do so, they look beyond the problematic behavior. School staff provide help and support instead of eliciting shame through punishment.

Confronting students about their behaviors and shortcoming usually makes the student defensive. It is more likely that the problem will occur again. Counterintuitive to many traditional approaches, behaviors rarely change when someone else confronts us and gives us all the reasons we were wrong. Instead, change and healing occur when someone supports the student in exploring the reasons behind the action and collaboratively work toward finding solutions (Miller & Rollnick, 2012).

Acceptance and compassion set the stage for a partnership. For most students, the number one predictor of a successful behavior change is the quality of their relationship with their teacher or school staff. Traditionally, many believed that if the child wanted to change badly enough or if they found the right mix of rewards and punishment, that change would follow. Research demonstrates that the real predictor of change is whether the student has a strong relationship with an adult who approaches them with compassion and acceptance (Murphy, 2008).

Creating partnerships positions the student as an expert on themselves. Bringing the student into the problem-solving conversation helps them feel valued, which is a very different experience than being on the receiving end of a discussion about punishment. The truth is that the school staff do not have all the answers and solutions. If so, every classroom would resemble a utopia without any problems or disruptions.

The real and lasting answers lie within the student's experience. To explore their experiences, the school staff must work in partnership to identify the reasons behind the behavioral issues and the skills needed for success. They need this information so that the school can address broader issues such as trauma.

The partnership develops and strengthens through our communication style. There are three approaches to communication: *directing, following,* and *guiding*. *Directing* is when school staff tell the student what to do. Directing dominates traditional behavioral management approaches. *Following* involves staff passively listening, which does not move them or the student closer to a solution. Effective trauma-sensitive communication relies heavily on the third approach, termed *guiding*. As a partner in the process, the school staff's feedback and directions are central to problem-solving with young students. In the next section, we present a straightforward communication strategy that helps staff strategically implement the guiding style to help move from problem exploration to solutions.

OARS

OARS stands for open-ended questions/statements, affirmations, reflections, and summaries. The strategic use of OARS is central to a best-practice approach for helping people change that is called Motivational Interviewing or MI. While based in cognitive behavioral therapy, MI skills are useful regardless of training or previous experience. The goal of OARS is for school staff to be able to express empathy and collaboratively problem-solve with students (Miller & Rollnick, 2012).

We do not present the OARS concepts in the order of the acronym. Instead, we give them in order of suggested frequency of use. First, we'll examine the most frequently used skill, and the R in OARS: reflections.

Reflections

Reflections demonstrate to the student that the school staff are on the same page with them. They see that staff members are promoting empathy and collaborative problem-solving. Reflections show that this adult wishes to work with them as a partner. It is just as important that the staff member understand what the student is thinking and feeling as it is for the student to understand what the staff member is trying to communicate. When utilized as part of our serve-and-return communication, reflections work exceptionally well with younger children, as they help students who are still developing communication skills to label and gain insight into their emotional states.

There are two types of reflections, simple and complex. Simple reflections restate the student's words almost verbatim. If the student states, "I'm mad," the staff member simply reflects, "You're mad." It is that easy!

Using simple reflections communicates two things. First, it demonstrates that the staff member hears the student. Second, a simple reflection shows the student that the staff member wants them to continue to explore the topic more in depth. Just because simple reflections are, well, simple, don't underestimate their power to drastically improve communication with students.

The other type of reflections are complex reflections. Complex reflections strive to reflect the meaning and not just words spoken by the student. These reflections are perfect tools for when a school staff member wants a student to think more deeply about their behavior, their feelings, or a situation.

Younger students often have not developed the ability to gain insight into themselves or situations without your help. In the above example, the student states, "I'm mad." A good complex reflection would sound like, "It makes you angry when you can't figure out a math problem" or "You get frustrated with you are not picked first for kickball."

The beautiful thing about reflections is that it's okay if the staff member is wrong. If they reflect what they are hearing and the student means something else, it gives the student a chance to get them back on the same page. Not only does this help the student develop their expressive communication skills, but it also shows that they are a partner in the problem-solving process and the expert on themselves (Miller & Rollnick, 2012).

Affirmations

The next most useful strategy of OARS is affirmations. Affirmations promote growth mindsets by supporting and encouraging effort and positive accomplishments. With affirmations, school staff bring forth good and positive things in the student's life while speaking to the real challenges they face. For instance, they might say, "You shared your scissors with a friend, and I noticed they are smiling. Way to go!" Affirmations bring forth hope, promote self-confidence, and help to establish a positive working relationship with the student.

Affirmations help children know that the school staff see them. These small acts help build and maintain connections. For students who have a difficult time hearing personal affirmations, an observation goes a long way in developing trust. "Arriving on time helps get our day started smoothly." "Getting your workbook out and open really shows organization." These affirmations acknowledge that students are following directions and the school staff appreciates their efforts.

Students thrive in positive environments. Unfortunately, due to their behavior and the negativity at home, many students go through the entire day without hearing anything good about themselves. Trauma-sensitive classrooms are positive environments. Studies demonstrate that for people with similar skills, those who get 5.6 times more positive feedback than negative perform much higher on a range of activities than those with lower positive-to-negative ratios. Conversely, those who received 2.8 times more negative than positive feedback struggle the most. Remember, the type of positive feedback is essential to support the growth mindset (Achor, 2010; Wagner & Harter, 2006).

Because of all the negative feedback they receive and due to fixed mindsets, students with trauma struggle to separate themselves from their problems. Think about some of the labels and messages that get put on young children: ADHD, conduct disorder, the "bad kid," special ed, slow, and developmentally disabled, to list a few. Affirmations help students separate their struggles from their view of self by showing them that they possess value and strength.

School staff should practice this in their everyday language. We avoid using the term traumatized student throughout this book. Instead, describing them as students struggling or living with trauma shows that the student is more than just their trauma. It is a small change, but the more everyone practices separating the student or family from their issues, the more positive the climate of the school will become. Students are more than just the sum of their problems (Miller & Rollnick, 2012).

Finally, affirmations reduce defensiveness. When the student confronts negative behaviors and past setbacks, there is a high chance this will trigger an emotional reaction. They could experience retraumatization. Affirmations set a positive foundation in the conversation, making it less likely for the student to feel threatened by the discussion.

Open-Ended Questions and Statements

Most of us are great at asking questions. The structure of OARS helps to ensure that staff utilize questions in a way that communicates empathy while minimizing defensiveness. The first key to asking effective questions is to focus on open and not closed questions. Closed questions are those that can be answered with one or two words; for example, "Did you push Mollie at recess?"

The open-ended equivalent is: "What happened between you and Mollie at recess today?"

One of the easiest ways to improve communication is by limiting closed-ended questions. The nature of these questions often puts students on the defensive right from the start. Also, if school staff only ask the closed-ended question, they miss a potential windfall of information that is critical to the situation. Open-ended questions help identify which skill deficits contributed to the situation, and how the staff can help the student gain insight.

While questions seem like they are the best way to get information quickly, unfortunately, even open-ended questions elicit defensiveness. Asking question after question leads to feelings of being interrogated. Even if the school staff is practicing nonjudgment, the student naturally feels they did something wrong if questions become the primary method of communication (Miller & Rollnick, 2012).

Statements get the same information as questions, while decreasing the potential of defensiveness. Shifting from questions to statements is relatively simple, but does take practice.

Instead of asking, "What happened when you apologized to Mollie?", state, "I'm interested in how it went with Mollie." Starting a statement with "I wonder," "Tell me about," or "I'm interested" removes the question marks and improves the quality of the communication. Replacing questions with statements is a small change that actively encourages collaboration and partnership.

Summaries

The final OARS strategy is the use of summaries. Summaries are reflections that bring together several things the student has stated throughout your conversation. One of the most important roles of summaries is to help a student hear their voice and reasons for changing or thinking about something differently. Summaries are an effective method for ending conversations or transitioning to other topics. They are great ways to finish on the same page as students or to connect the current discussion to the next topic (Miller & Rollnick, 2012).

OARS offers a set of skills that take time to master and integrate into your regular communication style. We encourage you to pick a skill to practice every month. Here is a simple way to become a master at OARS:

1) Replace typical responses like head nods, "uh huh," or other short verbal and nonverbal communications of understanding with simple

reflections that state back the words of your students.
2) Find opportunities to increase the use of complex reflections by adding meaning or feeling into your statement.
3) Include at least one affirmation in every conversation with students (bonus points if you do it with your teammates and other school staff).
4) Try to decrease or eliminate closed-ended questions as much as possible.
5) Focus on replacing questions with statements. Instead of "Why," "What," or "How," start statements with "I'm interested," "Tell me about," or "I wonder about."
6) End or transition conversations with summaries.

Over time, OARS will become your natural mode and the default communication style with students. As you get comfortable with OARS, consider teaching it to your students at a basic level. Teaching effective communication builds the social intelligence that many students with trauma lack. It prevents them from forming healthy relationships with peers and adults.

Trust

In previous chapters, we discussed how abuse or chaos at home prevents healthy attachments between students and their parents. These students walk into a classroom assuming their relationships with teachers and other school staff will mirror their experience with their parents. Rarely do students with trauma enter the school environment with an open mind, ready to trust adults who treat them kindly, as most teachers do.

Instead of excitement and a healthy level of nerves about a new school year, students with trauma are probably releasing the chemical dihydrotestosterone or DHT. DHT, along with cortisol, is released when the student feels unsafe in the presence of others in their environment. This biological reaction, resulting from past maltreatment, increases the likelihood that the student will be anxious or fearful, making emotional regulation difficult.

Humans have a natural tendency to categorize people as friend or foe.

In other words, people see other people as trustworthy or as potential threats. Because of past abuse by others, the student, especially early on the relationship, may see teachers, school staff, and peers as foes, even if there is no justification for such an assumption (Restak, 2007).

DHT and cortisol can lead to retraumatization, making it impossible for them to focus on academic tasks, and making it difficult for them to see others as a resource. Serve-and-return communication and OARS provide two simple skills to counteract negative relational expectations and the anxiety resulting from DHT and cortisol. With enough repetition, the school staff's empathetic, accepting, and compassionate communication calms the student's nervous system, allowing for focus and learning.

Trauma-sensitive schools and classrooms are environments with high levels of trust. Trust is an assured reliance on the character, ability, and strength of the school staff working with the student. Every interaction provides teachers, administrators, bus drivers, custodians, cafeteria workers, and everyone else with a chance to communicate to the student that they are a valuable person in the school community. Let's further explore this definition of trust.

Establishing assured reliance is cultivated in an educational setting by predictability and routines. Can the students predict that their teacher will smile and greet them each day? Can they trust that they won't leave them behind in a fire drill? All the simple routines, visual schedules, and predictability of the classroom build trust and demonstrate to students from disorganized home environments that some adults can provide structure and consistency that they can depend on every day.

The school staff's abilities and strengths are also critical. Again, think about that great teacher who inspired you to become an educator. If you are like us, these role models possessed a strong sense of character. They were skilled at the art of teaching and had a personal strength that made us feel safe in their presence. A school staff member's ability to create trust with students starts with who they are as a person, their ability to manage their own stress, and their ability to bring their best self to work every day (Bennett, 2017).

As school staff establish trust with the student, the student's biology shifts from releasing cortisol and DHT to releasing oxytocin. Oxytocin is crucial to bonding in any relationship. It accounts for the good feeling experienced when we connect deeply with someone. It increases a student's ability to regulate their emotions, focus on a task, feel safe with peers, and feel like a valuable member of the class (Mate & Levine, 2010).

Richard Restak (2007) provides a perfect summary of his findings concerning the chemical effects of DHT and oxytocin as trust builds in relationships:

> Think of the experiments on trust as demonstrating the existence of two physiologic 'levers' in our brains (oxytocin and DHT) that activate in response to our interactions with other people. By creating an atmosphere of trust we enhance the oxytocin levels in the brains of those we come into contact with, and vice versa. Alternatively, if we signal distrustfulness, we activate the second 'lever' and increase DHT along with the accompanying likelihood of an aggressive response directed towards us.

Oxytocin elicits feelings of contentment, calm, and safety. These feelings build a secure base and promote a sense of safety in the classroom. Trusting relationships with school staff create opportunities for school staff to use serve-and-return and OARS for introspection and consideration about the harmful consequences of the student's current ways of thinking and behaving. Trust is a two-way street. If school staff want the student's trust, they must treat them with respect, believing that the student is doing their best in the face of past and present challenges.

Safety

Without trust, there is no safety, and without safety, there is almost no chance of learning, emotional regulation, and healing. For many students, safety is elusive, as the dangers at home, school, or in the community steal their ability to enjoy any real security in their lives. Without safety, the student will exist in survival mode.

Safety, in this context, is defined as freedom from hurt, injury, or loss. There are two types of safety that school staff should consider when helping set up a trauma-sensitive classroom. The first is physical safety. Future thinking, goal setting, introspection, and other prefrontal cortex activity become difficult when a student fears for their safety and security.

While possible, it is highly unlikely that a student living in fear of abuse, bullying, hunger, homelessness, or other trauma will focus on anything else outside surviving these traumatic threats.

Here lies one of the critical paradigm shifts with the adoption of trauma-sensitive schools. When a student fears for their safety outside the school environment, even the perfect school setting will struggle to help the student achieve academic success. In later chapters, we will put forth the argument that, if schools want what is best for their students, we must focus all available resources on ensuring all students are safe at school and in their homes and communities. Only then will academic success and healing be possible (Bloom, 2000).

The second type of safety is psychological safety. Each student will feel safe in their own way based on their past experiences. Psychological safety is the student's confidence that school staff and peers will respect their feelings and emotional well-being. This sense of safety emerges from the trust that school staff establish through their strength of character, consistent support, and empathetic communication.

In an early education classroom, regular caring community meetings and social-emotional activities need to be prioritized to provide the space for students to feel comfortable being their true selves. They need to be able to disclose fears, dreams, and struggles without worrying about being judged. This approach develops a secure base for the child and directly challenges their belief that all relationships are harmful. It builds a student's self-worth and gives them the confidence to dream about a better future (Bloom, 2006; Herman, 1997).

Establishing physical and psychological safety is a primary focus of trauma-sensitive schools. Without physical safety, there is little to no chance for academic success or behavioral change, as the student needs their brain and epigenetic expression to support survival functioning. Without psychological safety, students will struggle to see hope or have the energy for insight beyond survival thinking. While the school's resources and referrals improve physical safety, the spirit of partnership, compassion, and acceptance provides focus areas for building and maintaining psychological safety.

A Different Approach

The first week of Caleb's return went relatively smoothly. Mrs. Vaughn continued to integrate mindfulness and check-ins throughout the day. She continued to find that these approaches helped her proactively address student stress before it manifested in disruptive behaviors.

A few weeks after his suspension, Caleb came into school one day like a tornado. By 9 am, without any adults noticing, he had threated to beat up a child on the bus, pushed a boy in the restroom, and called another child a very inappropriate term in the hallway. Mrs. Vaughn always kept an eye out for Caleb in the morning in hopes of helping him transition into an appropriate classroom "state," a term Dr. Rodriguez taught them during a recent team meeting.

She could immediately see that Caleb was triggered as he walked into the classroom seemingly looking for a fight. Mrs. Vaughn tried to connect with him by asking him how he was doing and inquiring about what zone he felt like he was in right now. Caleb's face turned to pure disgust, and he held up what resembled a sign language 'R' for Red Zone except that he only used one finger, the middle one.

Mrs. Vaughn faced a situation that would challenge any veteran teacher. In addition to the usual chaos of students coming in and preparing for a new day, she now had a student who was potentially a danger to everyone in the class. Even with all her years of experience, she knew this was at least a two-person job.

Dr. Rodriguez taught them all these great communication strategies in their last meeting, but no one ever seems to answer the question, "How do we effectively manage one or more triggered children when we are responsible for an entire class of students?"

Luckily, the stories of Caleb's actions that morning reached Dr. Griffin. Just as Mrs. Vaughn was about to send her class to Mr. Anderson, Dr. Griffin stormed in the room looking for Caleb. Seeing Mrs. Vaughn already isolating Caleb physically from the other students gave Dr. Griffin a chance to take a breath. "Mrs. Vaughn, it seems like Caleb has had a very eventful morning. I'll need to speak to him in my office."

"Screw you!" screamed Caleb, "I'm not going anywhere with you."

Mrs. Vaughn had learned from Dr. Rodriguez that her return needed to match Caleb's verbal tone while refocusing his attention. Her suggestion was counter to what Mrs. Vaughn had practiced in the past, as she always thought that she should respond as calmly as possible when children were melting down. Giving it a shot, she summoned her best animated voice as she assertively stated, "Wow, Dr. Griffin, Caleb is mad right now. Yet, he was able to tell me he was in the Red Zone, so he is following directions this morning."

Dr. Griffin was taken back by Mrs. Vaughn's words. She also realized that the rest of the class and Caleb were either curious or taken off guard by a tone they had not heard from their teacher before. Dr. Griffin's anger with Caleb subsided a little, and since Mrs. Vaughn was implementing the trauma-sensitive communication approaches Dr. Rodriguez taught them, she decided to follow along.

Mrs. Vaughn was weighing whether to evacuate her class or if she could get Caleb calm enough to walk out. It seemed her return of his angry serve changed his state enough where she felt okay trying the second approach. A little less excited this time, but still with an exaggerated emotional emphasis, Mrs. Vaughn continued, "You know, Dr. Griffin, usually when Caleb screams at us, we send him down to your office, and he gets in BIG trouble."

"Yes, he does, Mrs. Vaughn!" Dr. Griffin felt silly trying to match Mrs. Vaughn's heightened voice level.

"Dr. Griffin, what if this time Caleb and I leave the classroom and chat for a little while?" Mrs. Vaughn decreased the excitement in her voice a little more. While her eyes were on Caleb most of the time, she shot Dr. Griffin a quick glance communicating her strong desire to handle this incident differently.

Dr. Griffin stopped herself. She wanted to explain right there that Caleb spent his morning bullying everyone in his orbit. She also felt pulled to say that consequences are coming Caleb's way. However, Mrs. Vaughn's glance carried enough strength to let her know Mrs. Vaughn was going forward regardless.

"Well, Mrs. Vaughn, I agree that usually Caleb would come with me, but I would love nothing more than to spend some time with your class this morning. Is there a worksheet I could help them with?"

"In fact, Dr. Griffin, there is a worksheet right there on my desk. Class, how lucky are you today? The principal is going to help you on a worksheet," Mrs. Vaughn said, while keeping an eye on Caleb, who seemed to calm down a little more now that he wasn't the center of attention.

Mrs. Vaughn then bent down to Caleb's level and said with a mix of compassion and excitement, "Hey kiddo, tough morning. Let's chat a little, as I would like to help you turn this day around."

Everyone in the class seemed very taken off guard by what was going on. Even at a young age, every student in the class knew how the teachers and the school handled kids like Caleb. They all knew Caleb would get punished and probably would not be in class for the rest of the week.

Caleb and Mrs. Vaughn left a silent classroom. She wondered who was more shocked by what just happened, Dr. Griffin or her students. Mrs. Vaughn took Caleb outside for a change of scenery. After sitting down on a bench, Mrs. Vaughn tried hard to follow Dr. Rodriguez's advice on limiting the use of questions, so in a calm voice, she stated, "I get the feeling something is going on today."

Caleb always had his go-to responses, "I don't know," "It wasn't my fault," and "Whatever." But without a question to respond to, these responses did not work as well. All he could muster was "Uh-huh."

Caleb's return of her serve was very neutral in tone, so she went down into a calmer and more empathetic tone. "We all have hard days."

Caleb returned a confused look, as if to communicate that Mrs. Vaughn surely had never had such a day.

"Yeah, sometimes I feel sad, frustrated, or even angry." Mrs. Vaughn made some funny faces exaggerating each emotion. "Usually, something happened to make me feel that way." She was proud of her return and of not using a question.

Caleb smiled a little at her tone and exaggerated faces. Mrs. Vaughn provided some wait time after her statement, and soon Caleb's smile seemed to turn to sadness. She waited, finding it hard not to fill the silence with a question.

After what seemed like a minute, Caleb uttered a quiet, "Yeah."

Mrs. Vaughn was not getting much of a return, but at least there was back and forth. She thought she might throw in an affirmation before digging deeper. "You know, kiddo, you did a pretty good job back there in the classroom. Many kids struggle to follow directions when they get angry."

Caleb's return was a look of surprise. His young mind couldn't really comprehend a compliment from a teacher he had just flipped the bird to a few minutes earlier.

"Sometimes, it is tough for me to control my actions when I get angry because something made me mad or sad. You did a much better job than I might have done, young man. I'm wondering if there was something that made you mad or sad." Again, she did not ask a question and she mixed in an affirmation; Dr. Rodriguez would be proud!

"Yeah, I was mad," Caleb said in a low voice.

Mrs. Vaughn returned a simple reflection in a low voice, "You were mad."

"Yeah."

"And, if you are like me, sometimes when I'm mad, I do things I wouldn't normally do." Mrs. Vaughn put some excitement in her voice, feeling like Caleb had calmed down enough to bring the tone up a little.

"Yeah, I'm in trouble, right?"

Mrs. Vaughn wasn't aware of the specifics of Caleb's actions before coming into class and was more interested in the "why" behind the behavior. "I wonder why you think you are in trouble, Caleb."

"Because I hurt kids by my words and actions," he responded, using some of the words he learned in the anti-bullying curriculum.

Mrs. Vaughn lowered her voice again and gave a simple reflection, "You hurt kids with words and actions."

"Yeah, I didn't mean to, but I just did it. Everyone makes me so mad."

"Yeah, and I bet thinking you are in trouble makes you even more mad and frustrated." Mrs. Vaughn thought she would try her first complex reflection.

"Yeah, I hate getting in trouble."

"It's hard," Mrs. Vaughn was getting the hang of the whole reflection thing. She wanted to give a more meaningful return though. "You know something, I hate it when kids get in trouble too. Giving consequences is my least favorite thing about being a teacher."

"Really?" Caleb gave a quick return this time.

"Yeah, I love teaching new stuff, and I love you kids. You know what I don't love?"

"Giving consequences?"

Mrs. Vaughn caught the closed-ended question, but figured getting a quick serve-and-return made it okay. "What a pair we make, Caleb; you hate consequences, and I hate giving them." She smiled as her tone expressed concern and empathy.

Caleb thought for a second about what Mrs. Vaughn said and seemed a little taken back by the fact his teacher hated giving consequences. After ten seconds, his face became sad again, "But because I hurt kids, you are going to kick me out of school again."

Wow, Mrs. Vaughn thought. Usually, kids like Caleb just said, "I didn't do anything wrong," or "I don't know." Mrs. Vaughn chose to get some good serve-and-return going before asking Caleb what happened to cause his behaviors.

"Caleb?"

"Yes, Mrs. Vaughn."

"Remember when I said that when I get mad and say or do things I wish I hadn't that something usually happened to make me upset beforehand?"

"Yes"

"You know what I'm wondering?"

"What?"

"I wonder if something happened this morning or last night that got you angry and you took that anger out on other kids." Mrs. Vaughn was getting used to turning questions into statements.

Caleb sat still for a second and weighed whether or not to reveal what happened. Mrs. Vaughn worked hard not to fill the silence as she knew Caleb's young brain might need time to process. After a good minute, Caleb spoke.

"This morning, one of my mom's boyfriends came by and started yelling at my mom about money or something. My mom yelled back, and he hit her so hard she fell asleep. Then he looked at me and said, 'Get the hell out of here.'"

"Oh, Caleb, that must have been hard for you to see," Mrs. Vaughn said with a hushed tone and trying a complex reflection through her sadness for her young vulnerable student.

"I guess; it isn't the first time one of my mom's boyfriends hit her. She always says they are good people and not to worry."

"I wonder how you felt when you got on the bus." Mrs. Vaughn was trying hard to keep using statements instead of questions, feeling somewhat amazed by how far this conversation had gone.

"Angry; I don't remember too much about this morning, but I know I hurt some kids. I'm sorry; I just did it without thinking."

Caleb started to cry but caught himself quickly, not wanting to seem weak. "Are you going to kick me out of school?"

Mrs. Vaughn felt herself choke up as well. "Honestly, Caleb, I don't know. There are consequences for hurting other children, but I'm more worried about you." Mrs. Vaughn ran out of words. She wanted to say, "NO." What would it say about us if we punished a young kid for acting in anger after witnessing his mother's boyfriend/drug dealer knocking her unconscious? Yet, every rule and policy would lead to another suspension.

Caleb's body slunk over, communicating a mixture of frustration and sadness.

"Caleb," Mrs. Vaughn put some excitement into her voice.

"Yes."

"I just realized Dr. Griffin isn't a teacher. Can you imagine a principal teaching our class?" Mrs. Vaughn said with a funny face.

"No!" Caleb shouted.

Mrs. Vaughn tried her first summary. "We covered a bunch, kiddo, and I want to thank you for sharing it with me. I know you are concerned about the consequences of your behavior and you are also worried about your mom. It's been a real tough day for you. While we both know some of your behaviors were not appropriate, you didn't mean to hurt anyone."

She continued, "We'd better rescue Dr. Griffin then. I wonder if you would feel comfortable telling her what you told me about your mom."

Caleb asked, "Could you be there? Sometimes Dr. Griffin gets mad at me, and I get nervous and say things that get me in more trouble."

"Of course."

CHAPTER 5
Positive Behavioral Supports for the Traumatized Child

Now we come to a critical point in our trauma-sensitive journey. It is great to gain the understanding that most severe academic and behavioral issues result from traumatic experiences. While this might increase our empathy and compassion, how do we manage a classroom where several students' behaviors draw all our attention? Many of us go into education to share our love of learning and shape future minds, not realizing that teaching all too often becomes secondary to managing behaviors and trying to maintain a safe classroom environment.

The real answer to this question is a systematic one. If we do not adequately fund schools to "right-size" classrooms and ensure proper capacity for special education, counseling, psychology, and social-work support, we will continue to struggle. The most important action this knowledge requires is to advocate for systemic change. A road map for change is presented later in the book.

Trauma-sensitive educational reform will not occur overnight. There are millions of children right now who need us to evolve our approaches to better meet their needs. They deserve hope for a healthy and fulfilling future. The good news for both school staff and students is that the science of neurobiology and trauma helps us improve our current approaches to behavioral management for students living with trauma.

Permission to Stop the Insanity!

Schools can no longer work off the assumption that young students' behaviors are results of well-thought-out choices made after weighing the possible outcomes and consequences. Unfortunately, too many in education continue to implement behavioral support systems that obviously fail to help struggling students. Nowhere is this failure more evident than in the fact that every year in the United States, we expel over one hundred thousand and suspend three million of our children from school (Greene, 2008).

The U.S. Department of Education (2014) found that students who receive suspensions and expulsions are

> 10 times more likely to drop out of high school, experience academic failure and grade retention, hold negative school attitudes, and face incarceration than those who are not…Not only do these practices have the potential to hinder social-emotional and behavioral development, they also remove children from early learning environments and the corresponding cognitively enriching experiences that contribute to healthy development and academic success later in life. Expulsion and suspension practices may also delay or interfere with the process of identifying and addressing underlying issues, which may include disabilities or mental health issues.

The only possible justification for expulsions and suspensions is that the school is incapable of keeping other students and staff safe if that student remains at school. If a school's strategy to keep students safe is getting rid of the students who need our help the most, we fail at a tragic level both as an educational system and as a society.

Understanding trauma, retraumatization, and rates of physical abuse, we cannot possibly justify the hundreds of thousands of paddlings that continue to occur in schools around the country. Striking a child or using a spanking paddle is another form of abuse. Doing so inflicts students living with trauma with additional harm.

This painful reality is even more devastating when we consider that black students receive over 36% of the paddlings, while making up only 17% of the student population. Students with disabilities are also over-represented in those being physically abused at school; 19% of those paddled have disabilities but only make up 14% of the student population [Human Rights Watch and American Civil Liberties Union (HRW/ACLU), 2010]. In part due to the trauma of this abuse, students then develop problems with peer relationships and school achievement. They drop out of school, display antisocial behavior, and suffer from depression, fear, and anger (Hickmon, 2008; Human Rights Watch, 2008).

Trauma devastates the mental, social, and emotional health of the child. Traditional behavioral-management systems often exacerbate the child's sense of unworthiness. They further establish a fixed mindset that was previously formed by the traumatic experience. Trauma-sensitive schools and classrooms are sanctuaries of hope, compassion, and success, rather than institutions that retraumatize their students, the very individuals they are there to serve.

Another problem with traditional systems is that they do not consider that many, if not most, of the extreme behaviors that get a student suspended or expelled are byproducts of retraumatization. Caleb experienced retraumatization when he saw Malik's mom give Malik affection. Caleb experienced an overwhelming flood of negative emotions due to his traumatic memories with his mother. It is highly unlikely that any classroom behavioral-management program would prevent this flood of powerful emotions from eliciting a highly inappropriate response.

Mental-health and social-work services take a pivotal role. First and foremost, if a child is living in a chaotic or dangerous situation, the resulting trauma will play out in the classroom. We must prioritize the safety of our students if we know or suspect that some of the students are experiencing abuse or neglect.

Second, when we identify a history of trauma, mental-health support is essential for any degree of behavioral success for most students. Trauma treatment provided by a competent mental-health professional will empower students to take power away from the memories that retraumatize them. Treatment helps to diminish many of the traumatic response behaviors we traditionally punish. In an ideal situation, the mental-health professional will help the child overcome their trauma and assist the teacher in helping the student thrive in the classroom.

A Skill-Based Approach

Science demonstrates that young students rarely make a conscious choice to misbehave. Those with trauma struggle to understand cause and effect. While it is nice to finally get an answer to why so many behavioral-management systems fail struggling students, schools need a new paradigm to view behaviors and help these children succeed. We find that a skills-based approach allows us to incorporate our understanding of trauma, neurobiology, and behavior into concrete strategies that help all students build skills for behavioral and academic success.

Before delving into action steps for addressing student behavior, schools should first explore two often overlooked questions. First, "Why did the behavior occur at this specific time?" School staff need to understand what is happening to the student that might have contributed to the behavior. Use the knowledge presented in the first several chapters to identify if social-work or mental-health support is needed

Second, "What skills does the student lack that contributed to their failing to follow the rules and expectations in this specific situation?" This simple question changes everything! Not only does it prevent school staff from getting into the mindset that this is just a "bad kid," it also helps proactively find solutions to prevent the problem behavior from reoccurring in the future. Bailey (2015) states, "Consequences do not teach new skills; they motivate us to repeat or stop using the skills we already possess. In order for a consequence to be effective, it must be applied to a connected child who already possesses the desired skill."

Below you will find a sequential approach to identifying and addressing trauma, and then helping to change student behavior through emotional regulation and skill building. Make sure you use the communication approaches in the previous chapter throughout this process:

1) Identify bigger issues, including trauma. As with Caleb in the last chapter, his behaviors were a result of trauma experienced earlier that morning. When trauma or high stress occurs in or outside of school, engage other professionals and services as appropriate.
2) Get as much information as possible from the student about what occurred before, during, and after the behavioral incident. Use OARS to explore the problem with empathy. Don't let one "I don't

know" or other flippant remark end the conversation. The student is likely expecting to get punished. It might take a while for them to understand that staff are here to support and collaboratively problem-solve with them. Try to end this conversation on a positive note if possible. If consequences are absolutely necessary, try to give them as gently as possible, as you are only halfway to solving the problem.

3) Identify which skills the student lacked to handle that specific situation in a way that meets expectations and follows the rules. For example, if the problem keeps occurring in music class, identify what skills the student would need to succeed in meeting expectations in that specific environment, with the students and adults present during those times. Don't overcomplicate this step! With younger students especially, staff are the ones thinking through this initially. A reasonable conclusion is one the student could easily understand.

Dr. Ross Greene is one of the leading experts on the relationship between skill deficits and behaviors in school settings, and we love how easy it is to adapt his work to a trauma-sensitive school environment. One tool he provides is the Assessment of Lagging Skills and Unsolved Problems. This short assessment gives a comprehensive list of lagging skills. It helps school staff, parents, and students collaboratively identify strategies for building the skills necessary for success in specific situations. The Assessment of Lagging Skills and Unsolved Problems is available free online. We highly encourage you to look at Dr. Greene's other tools and his book *Lost at School: Why Our Kids with Behavioral Challenges are Falling Through the Cracks and How We Can Help Them* (2008).

4) Come back together with the student and talk about how staff and the student will work together to build the skills necessary for success. Again, make it simple enough for the student to understand and implement with minimal support from staff (unless additional support or staff capacity is available). Check in with the student to make sure they know the task they are working on and to support them in any way possible to experience success. With younger students specifically, school staff need to check in frequently, as the student is more likely to get lost in the moment and forget previous conversations.

5) Support any positive effort and actions that demonstrate a growth mindset. Learning a new skill is a process with success and setbacks. Changing behavior requires the brain to change structure and functioning. Small positive relational reinforcement, such as a pat on the back, short check-in conversations, and a thumbs up, are more effective than a physical reward in supporting long term behavioral change. Also, see setbacks as natural. Try not to give consequences to the student for not yet having the ability to utilize the developing skill effectively. Process the attempt, search for any positive effort, and empathetically look for small adjustments the student might make.

6) Once a student experiences success in a particular situation, shift focus to generalizing the skill into other settings. "Look how great you did in music this week! Where else do you think you might use this new superpower you are developing?" Build the momentum slowly, as the young brain will take some time to generalize a skill in a specific situation into their overall strategy for interacting with the world.

Trauma-Sensitive Restorative Justice

Beyond identifying skill deficits, the problem remains of how schools should address incidents that are likely to occur involving a traumatized child. Restorative justice is one practice that is growing in popularity, due to its focus on empowering students and building healthy school communities. Restorative justice encourages the individuals involved in an incident to sit down together, discuss the situation, take ownership for inappropriate or harmful behavior, and find ways to move forward.

Usually, one party does something to make amends to those they harmed. A restorative-justice approach searches for solutions and ways to prevent future problems. It is counter to many traditional methods, which involve handing out consequences or punishments without providing opportunities for verbal processing and open discussion.

Restorative-justice approaches are well aligned with trauma-sensitive practices, in that they help students understand the impact of their behaviors on others. The building of empathy and emotional intelligence is crucial for children from traumatic backgrounds. However, without integrating trauma-sensitive principles, typical restorative-justice practices will fail to make a lasting positive change in behavior.

If the adults facilitating the restorative-justice practice fail to acknowledge the role of trauma, the process may reinforce that there is something wrong with the offending student. A trauma-sensitive restorative-justice approach starts with the adults asking themselves, "Might trauma or other stress in the school or home environment account for this behavior?" A "yes" to this question helps prompt the appropriate referrals and moves staff in the direction of addressing the underlying problems behind the behavior. Once those problems are understood, the restorative-justice process begins.

Let's apply this approach in the Malik/Caleb situation. Caleb's violent action triggers the staff to ask, "Might trauma play a role in his actions?" Based on what Dr. Griffin and Mrs. Vaughn already know about his family situation, the answer is very clearly "yes." Hopefully, that understanding will trigger the involvement of school and community social workers and prompt additional mental-health support.

Next, Caleb and Malik need to meet and work through the situation. Caleb needs to recognize that his actions hurt Malik without getting the message from adults that he is a bad kid. Instead, the focus is on the behavior and its impact on Malik. This restorative-justice approach reestablishes safety for Malik and helps the staff understand Caleb's level of insight and lacking skills.

Values: What Are the Rules by Which You Live?

Behaviors change when someone realizes that their values or the rules by which they live do not align with their actions. For those working with children with traumatic backgrounds, it is important to understand that to build the groundwork for behavioral change, a child must not only follow the external rules in their environment, but more importantly, they must also develop their own internal value system. While external rules and norms help them learn what behavior is appropriate in specific environments, internal values guide their actions across all aspects of life (Bennett, 2018; Miller & Rollnick, 2012).

It is never too early to get students thinking about their values. While values are complex, most children begin to learn about values very early in their education. Many of our most-treasured children's books focus on themes related to kindness, sharing, empathy, and honesty. Additionally, schools are becomingly increasingly aware that a focus on social and emotional learning (SEL) helps to reduce conduct problems and supports students in developing the skills necessary to better regulate their emotions.

External rules are everywhere in a young child's life. Mom has rules; dad has rules; teachers have rules; babysitters have rules; boardgames have rules. While exposure to these rules help young children learn social norms, they often become overwhelming for those who don't fully grasp the concept of cause and effect. Instead of setting them up for social success, the result is often struggle and failure.

Internalized rules and values are much more powerful motivators. Cognitive behavioral psychologists help their clients identify variances between their behavior and their values. This misalignment of values creates a specific type of stress termed cognitive dissonance. Cognitive dissonance, in this context, refers to holding two conflicting and unresolved beliefs concurrently. This conflict results in a sense of being uncomfortable, as well as an urgency to find a way to bring oneself back into alignment with one's rules. Often, it is this discomfort that provides the energy required for change in both children and adults (Miller & Rollnick, 2012).

Once you work with students to develop their own rules and values, it is essential that you keep these in front of them on a regular and, ideally, daily basis. Getting children at a young age to start thinking about their values and rules by which to live life helps establish a sense of self-worth. This moral compass will serve them well throughout their life. Early practice on this concept of rules and values helps build an understanding of ethical and moral action. Students will find that this is a key component in resiliency and positive, volitional decision making throughout their life (Siebert, 2005).

Finding a Starting Point

Mrs. Vaughn and Caleb walked back to the classroom in silence, neither quite sure what to make of this new type of conversation. Dr. Griffin was surprised at the calm way Caleb walked back into the room. She shot a quick glance at Mrs. Vaughn, who returned a satisfied smile and quick shrug.

"Class, let's give Dr. Griffin a big thank you for helping out this morning. We are going to get ready to go to gym class, so let's show Dr. Griffin how we take our ten belly breaths before transitions." The class put their hands on their bellies, "Dr. Griffin, why don't you join us!"

"Yay," whispered several members of the class. Mrs. Vaughn thought a few deep breaths might help get Dr. Griffin in a place where she might hear her argument for not suspending Caleb.

After the breathing, Mrs. Vaughn asked in a quiet voice, "Friends, please show me what zone you are in right now." Most indicated that they were in the Green Zone because they were feeling okay and ready for gym. However, Emilia said she was in the Blue Zone, and Malik said he was in the Yellow Zone. "All right, class, let's line up quietly. Emilia and Malik, can you please help Dr. Griffin and me with something quickly?"

The two came over to the two adults. Mrs. Vaughn said, "Hey, you two, would you like to share about your zones?"

Malik jumped right in, "I am in the Yellow Zone because I heard Caleb was hurting everyone this morning, and I'm worried that I'm next!"

Emilia, looking down like normal, whispered, "I'm sad and in the Blue Zone because Caleb will get kicked out of school again; I wish he could just stop hurting people."

"Dr. Griffin, see how insightful my students are becoming? They might be ready to be teachers themselves soon," commented Mrs. Vaughn.

Malik jumped a little with excitement and Emilia looked up with a smile, saying quietly, "Mrs. Vaughn, we are too young to be teachers."

"But Emilia, you teach me something every day. I want you two to know I talked to Caleb for a long time this morning and I think everything is okay. He had a rough morning but really wants us all to give him another chance today. Are you okay with that or would you like to stay back from gym?" Mrs. Vaughn said with a mischievous smile, knowing they both loved gym.

Both children nodded and said they were okay with giving Caleb another chance.

"Okay. Please get in line and let's go!" said Mrs. Vaughn, with a sigh of relief.

"Mrs. Vaughn, can you stop by my office after you drop the kids off at gym?" asked Dr. Griffin.

There was a collective "oooOOooo" from her class. "Oh my, Dr. Griffin, am I in trouble?" asked Mrs. Vaughn.

"We'll see!" declared Dr. Griffin. The class "oooOOooed" again before heading out the door.

A few moments later, Mrs. Vaughn was in Dr. Griffin's office with a cup of coffee in her hand. She was a little nervous that the kids were right, and she might have gotten herself into some trouble with Dr. Griffin.

Dr. Griffin began. "All right, here is where the rubber hits the road with this trauma stuff. We sent a kid that I'm going to need to suspend to gym class. Tell me about the conversation between you two."

"Let's follow the process Dr. Rodriguez gave us and see what conclusion we end up with," answered Mrs. Vaughn.

"Okay, go for it."

"First step, the bigger issues. A big yes on this one. Caleb disclosed disturbing information about an incident he had this morning at his house," said Mrs. Vaughn.

Dr. Griffin knew the reporting and paperwork required when allegations of abuse came to light, not to mention the emotional impact on her teachers when they know one of their students was suffering abuse. Luckily, Mrs. Vaughn was a veteran teacher, which, unfortunately, meant she was no stranger to the process.

"Please let me know what support I can give you when you call social services and begin the paper trail," she said, "Please go on."

"Caleb reported, and I believe him, that one of his mom's 'boyfriends' came over this morning and struck her so hard in the face that 'she fell asleep.'" At that moment, Dr. Griffin paused their conversation, picked up her phone, and called the police, asking for a wellness check at Caleb's address.

"Well, that's step one, and we are already calling the police and filing a report with Child Protective Services. That home is no place for a child." Dr. Griffin paused for a second, "So before this trauma stuff, I would have just suspended him. I would have solved the problem of his behavior by making him spend more hours in a dangerous home environment where his mom is getting punched in the face."

Mrs. Vaughn was somewhat relieved. She was worried that Dr. Griffin would not be open to hearing the 'why' behind Caleb's behavior. "You gave me that time to connect with him. The skills Dr. Rodriguez taught us worked wonderfully, even though it was one of the most difficult conversations of my entire career."

"I bet; hard enough hearing it second hand. I wonder how many other times Caleb got in trouble without us knowing why. How many other kids we expelled who behaved in a similar way?"

At that moment, the school administrative secretary, Donna, stuck her head in Dr. Griffin's door, "You have a call on Line 2." Dr. Griffin was on the phone briefly, and then said, "The police are on their way to Caleb's house."

"Carey, we still need to address the behavior. I understand why Caleb acted out. However; I am anticipating several parents contacting me about what he did to their kids this morning."

Mrs. Vaughn got up, "I know. Let me meet with Caleb at lunch and work up some possible strategies for the rest of Dr. Rodriguez's steps. Hopefully, we can create a good plan to move forward. It might be a long day for the kiddo. Maybe we should see if we can get our school social worker and counselor involved too."

"I think it is going to be a long day for all of us, but maybe one that actually makes a difference this time," Dr. Griffin replied.

The rest of the morning, Caleb was quiet and barely huffed at having to spend lunch with Mrs. Vaughn. Mrs. Vaughn had taken a quick moment to glance over her cheat sheet for serve-and-return and OARS.

She thought she would start with an affirmation, "Caleb, I just want to say that after a tough start to the day, your behavior and focus have been wonderful since our talk."

"Are you going to suspend me?" Caleb asked, seemingly ignoring Mrs. Vaughn's gallant try at starting the conversation out on a positive note.

"Dr. Griffin is giving you and me a chance to come up with a plan. We know that it was really hard for you to watch your mom get hit, and we need to figure out a plan to make sure some of your behaviors on the bus and in school this morning do not happen again."

"So, I'm not suspended?" asked Caleb.

"I can't promise anything right now, but the better the plan we come up with, the more we impress Dr. Griffin, the better chance you'll be in school tomorrow," answered Mrs. Vaughn.

"Okay, what do I need to do?" Caleb seemed ready to work on a plan.

Mrs. Vaughn thought to herself, step 2 is gathering information. "I think you know what you need to do or, maybe better, what not to do on the bus or before school."

"Yes, don't hurt kids," stated Caleb.

"Great, you know what to do, but days like today you do something else."

"Yeah."

"Well, now I'm confused," Mrs. Vaughn made a funny face that got a laugh out of Caleb. "We have a great mystery, Caleb. You know what to do, but sometimes, for reasons we do not fully understand, you do the opposite."

"I don't want to be bad."

"I believe you. Caleb; you are not bad. Today you made bad choices. So, let's focus on the bus, because that is one of the places where this mysterious behavior happens." Mrs. Vaughn was noticing that her short communications and Caleb's return of her serve were helping him match her emotional state of curiosity.

"Okay."

"So today, I bet the whole morning was tough because you were worried about your mom. I know I would have been really worried," said Mrs. Vaughn.

"Yeah," Caleb said in a sadder tone.

"Okay, so let's not think about today. I wonder why the bus is hard on other days," asked Mrs. Vaughn.

"I don't know," answered Caleb.

"Of course, because it is a mystery. Let's put on our detective hats and figure this out!"

"Okay."

"The bus, what is going on? Tell me what usually happens when you get on the bus," asked Mrs. Vaughn.

"I try to sit with Billy."

Mrs. Vaughn knew Caleb's neighbor Billy, who was a few grades older and gets in trouble himself quite often. "The mystery deepens. What happens next?"

"On some days, nothing."

"Great! On some days, your behavior is perfect. On other days…"

"Billy starts teasing me and other people."

"Go on, young detective."

"And sometimes kids get their feelings hurt or we start pushing."

"Let me see if I have things right so far. On some days, Billy behaves, and you have no problems at all," summarized Mrs. Vaughn.

"Yes."

"Then, on other days, Billy starts trouble, and you find yourself in trouble as well."

"Yes."

"I wonder, since today was a troubled day, what happened with Billy," stated Mrs. Vaughn.

"I was mad at my mom's boyfriend. Billy hit me in the arm and told me to pass it on."

Mrs. Vaughn knew this game all too well. One kid would hit another, say pass it on, and that kid would punch another. Boys! "And you did."

"Yeah, but pretty hard. The kid cried."

"I wonder what happened next."

"I called him a name."

Mrs. Vaughn thought she would try a summary, "Okay, let me see if I got this right. On any given day, Billy might do something that could get him in trouble. These are the days you also get in trouble. Today was especially hard because of your mom, and things got a little out of control."

"Yeah, I'm sorry. I should say sorry to the kid I hurt, even if I was sad and it was a game."

"Sounds like a plan is coming together, my friend. The first step is getting with the kids you hurt and apologizing."

"Yeah."

"But we are not done. What happens tomorrow when you get on the bus, and Billy starts trouble? I think we need a plan for that. What do you think?"

"Probably."

"I wonder if you have any ideas about solving this problem."

"Maybe I could sit somewhere else."

"Oh, I like your thinking! I wonder where you could sit and no trouble would find you?"

"In front probably." Caleb thought for a second, "Maybe with Emilia. She sits in the front row by herself. She never gets in trouble, and the bus driver will be right there too. No games happen in the front of the bus."

"I believe Dr. Griffin is going to like our plan. Maybe we could try to really impress her. What do you think?"

"Yeah."

"I know some kids really struggle when they get angry. Sometimes I see you get angry," said Mrs. Vaughn.

"Like this morning on the bus and before class."

"Right! And when you get angry, things happen."

"Yeah, I get in trouble."

"I know," Mrs. Vaughn worked on keeping her tone positive as visions of Caleb hitting Malik popped into her mind. "I think Dr. Griffin would like us to come up with a plan for what happens when you get angry."

"Okay."

"You do very well on the belly breathing."

"Yeah, I like that. It's fun, and I feel calm."

"Great, I love it too," affirmed Mrs. Vaughn. "I sometimes think that you get angry and you act before you can breathe or even think."

"Yeah."

"I have a proposal for you, Caleb. Would you like to hear it?"

"Yes!"

"I propose we start a team. The goal of this team is to help you breathe before your anger gets you in trouble," Mrs. Vaughn paused.

"Okay."

"When we talk to Dr. Griffin after school, I want to see if she will be part of our team and maybe get some other people involved as well."

"Ms. Smith, maybe?" asked Caleb.

"I think Ms. Smith would love to be a part of your team. You will need to ask her, though."

"Okay, who else?"

"Well, maybe some people you haven't met yet. We need the top experts on your team."

"Who?" Caleb said, excitedly.

"I don't even know right now, but would you be open to it?"

"Yeah, especially if Dr. Griffin doesn't kick me out of school."

"I have one last thought. Is it okay if I share?"

"Yeah."

"You mentioned you hurt a couple of kids this morning when you were angry. I wonder if there is anything we could do about that now," stated Mrs. Vaughn.

"Say I'm sorry."

"Should we do it now?"

"Okay."

Caleb was great for the rest of the day. He seemed to want to stay close to Mrs. Vaughn. He even helped Malik collect his things at the end of the day, and Mrs. Vaughn overheard him apologizing for the incident earlier in the year.

At the end of the day, Mrs. Vaughn and Caleb went down to Dr. Griffin's office. Donna at the front desk said that Dr. Griffin was down the hall, meeting with some folks about Caleb.

Caleb looked up at Mrs. Vaughn, "I must really be in trouble."

"Or maybe your team is meeting for the first time," Mrs. Vaughn said, unsure whether or not Caleb was right.

They walked into a small room with a round table. Mrs. Vaughn recognized the county social-service workers, the school social worker, the counselor, Dr. Griffin, and Caleb's cousins Jeremiah and Zion.

"Tough day, C?" asked Jeremiah frankly.

"Yeah, at least the first part." Caleb said, shyly.

"What did we tell you about fighting in school, C?" followed Zion with a stern fatherly voice.

"I know. Dr. G don't mess around," Caleb said without thinking about his words.

Everyone got a chuckle out of his answer. As Mrs. Vaughn and Caleb sat down, the social worker addressed Caleb directly. "Caleb, I'm sorry you saw your mom get hit this morning. We checked, and she is okay, but it isn't safe for you to go home tonight and maybe for a few more days. Your uncle agreed that you could stay with him, but since he is working right now, your cousins came to take you home tonight."

"Okay, am I in trouble?" asked Caleb.

Everyone turned to Dr. Griffin, who answered, "Caleb, I wonder why you think you would be in trouble."

Mrs. Vaughn was impressed that Dr. Griffin was practicing the skills Dr. Rodriguez taught them. Caleb looked at Mrs. Vaughn for the courage to continue; she returned the glance with a smile and nod.

"When I am angry, I hurt kids. I don't mean to do it, but I do it anyway," he said.

Dr. Griffin continued, "And you were angry this morning because you saw your mom get hit?"

"Yeah."

"You know what, Caleb?" Dr. Griffin was giving the whole serve-and-return thing a shot.

"What?"

"Sometimes, when I get mad, I am not always proud of what I do or say. If I saw someone hurt my mom and I couldn't protect her or hit him back, I might take it out on someone else too," Dr. Griffin admitted.

Caleb looked at Mrs. Vaughn for a moment, communicating his confusion about Dr. Griffin's comments. Zion and Jeremiah seemed equally surprised. Zion said, "You mean C's not suspended?"

Dr. Griffin continued, "Caleb, I understand why your morning was so tough. I also need to make sure you and all my students are safe on the bus and in school. I wonder if you have any thoughts about how we could make sure that the next time you get angry, kids don't get hurt."

"Um," Caleb was starting to feel nervous with all eyes on him.

As he turned to Mrs. Vaughn for help, Jeremiah spoke, "He knows that as long as he is under our roof, he better behave."

"Jeremiah, I'm not sure threats will change anything, at least over the long term. We need to support Caleb, because I am confident that he knows the answer," said Dr. Griffin.

Jeremiah and Zion exchanged looks. Who was this woman? The Dr. Griffin they knew spent most of their elementary years threatening to suspend them every day. Zion was going to say something about this when Dr. Griffin shot him a glance that brought him straight back to second grade in her office. Instead of pointing out the obvious, he played Dr. Griffin's game, "Okay, C, how we gonna fix this, and what can we do to help?"

Mrs. Vaughn nodded and smiled at Caleb, who managed to say through all the dynamics, "My team."

Everyone's expression except Mrs. Vaughn's was perplexed. Mrs. Vaughn jumped in, "Caleb, tell everyone the goal of your team."

"To help me not hurt kids when I'm angry," Caleb said quietly.

"Great, Caleb. Maybe I can tell them some of the details we discussed."

Caleb nodded appreciatively.

"Caleb and I had some great talks, and he turned one of his worst mornings into one of his best days. Caleb recognized that he has trouble controlling his emotions at times, especially anger, particularly when things are hard at home. Right now, he does things like hurt kids without even thinking about it first. Am I doing okay so far, Caleb?"

He nodded enthusiastically. "And I'm not going to sit by Billy on the bus. He gets me in trouble sometimes, and that makes my whole day bad. I'm going to sit in front with Emilia. She is nice, and the bus driver will help me make better choices."

Mrs. Vaughn continued, "Great job, Caleb! I know Dr. Griffin will like that we have a plan for the bus. Our goal is to help Caleb realize when he gets angry and give him tools to use to take power back from his anger and sadness. This process is a big undertaking, which is why we need everyone's help, if you all are willing."

The county workers, social worker, and counselor introduced themselves to Caleb and expressed how they really wanted to join his team. Caleb was a little nervous but open to meeting the new members of his team. The social worker said she would meet with Caleb on a weekly basis to make sure he was feeling safe outside of school and see if he needed anything like additional food or clothing. The counselor followed by asking if it was okay if she met with him one-on-one for an hour a week to talk more about controlling his anger. She also asked if he wanted to join a small group with other kids trying to conquer their anger too, and he agreed.

Caleb turned to Mrs. Vaughn, "Kids could join my team?"

"Of course; the bigger the team, the more powerful we are."

It was Dr. Griffin's turn, "Caleb, I would like to join your team as well. Maybe you can teach me a thing or two in the process."

"Like what, Dr. Griffin?"

"Maybe about how if we give kids a chance and not suspend them, that everyone wins. Being a part of your team might be good for me too!"

"Cool," Caleb said.

"What about us, C?" asked Zion.

"Yeah, C, I want to be part of your team," Jeremiah added.

"Heck yeah!" Caleb exploded. He idolized his cousins.

Dr. Griffin wrapped everything up, "Let me summarize everything so we can get Caleb's team off to a great start. Caleb, we have a plan in place for a safe bus ride tomorrow."

"Yes."

"You are going to start meeting with these two great new friends on a weekly basis," pointing to the social worker and counselor, "so they can help you."

"Yes."

"Jeremiah and Zion, you're the home side of his team for now." Although Caleb was technically living with his uncle, everyone knew that his cousins would be the ones watching him most of the time. "I think it would be great if you checked in with him every night about how school went and sent us back a report about his night."

"Whatever you say, Dr. G," Zion confirmed.

"I know Mrs. Vaughn is obviously on board. Caleb, this is quite a team you have here. I'm excited to see where you lead us all."

"I am in charge?" Caleb asked.

"It is your team, and we are all here to make sure you succeed," Dr. Griffin concluded.

As the meeting broke up, Mrs. Vaughn watched Caleb walk out with his two cousins. What a day for this kid. With domestic violence first thing this morning, then assaulting kids before school, maybe his conversation with her was the most positive interaction he ever had with another adult, and now he was ending the day excited to learn how to regulate his own emotions.

"Huh," was about the best her tired mind could come up with to describe this day.

CHAPTER 6
Positive Behavioral Supports for the Classroom

All the research we have covered so far definitely shows us one thing: it is difficult to emotionally regulate a large group of young students effectively enough to engage their cognitive brains. How can we expect children to grow academically when their bodies and emotions are out of control? The fact that, every day around the world, this small miracle occurs millions upon millions of times speaks to the brilliance of teachers and school staff. The previous chapter showed how much work and attention a student like Caleb needs in order to just make it through the day without a major outburst.

This chapter examines trauma-sensitive strategies for behavioral management in the classroom. As stated throughout this book, we need to rethink our conventional approaches when working with students with trauma. These systems unintentionally set them up for failure and embarrassment. At the same time, they reward students who would behave regardless of whether or not any behavioral management system existed at all.

While much of this book challenges traditional ways of thinking, for many teachers and administrators, this chapter will likely hit closest to home. Teachers are creative and adaptable. They get exposed to new behavior-management techniques by bloggers, colleagues, and social media. Inspired, they work tirelessly to bring these new ideas back into their classrooms. They spend hours laminating, cutting, and preparing the latest management trend. Classrooms fill up with pocket charts, stoplights, clip charts, "chill zones," and more to help motivate and reward good behavior.

Often, the latest trend in behavior management does, in fact, work well for many of our students. But what about the children like Caleb? If our current approaches fail certain children, students suffering from trauma, is it the students' fault or our ever-changing management systems?

We are not asking teachers and school staff to throw the baby out with the bathwater in this chapter. Most systems have far more positive aspects than negative ones for most of the students in the classrooms. The challenge, considering all the recent research on the brain and trauma, is to identify small steps toward a more trauma-sensitive behavioral-management support system in the classroom. For most teachers, this will simply entail tweaking their current approach, not throwing everything out and starting from scratch.

Shared Expectations & the Value of Repetition

The one essential aspect of any trauma-sensitive behavioral-management support approach is the establishment of shared expectations concerning rules and class norms. As mentioned in Chapter 1, students from chaotic home environments walk into the classroom without an understanding of cause and effect. They do not know what it means to "behave" in an educational setting. Additionally, the traumatized brain often struggles with issues related to memory.

These factors make learning behavioral expectations challenging for students from traumatic backgrounds. For most students, going over the rules early in the year and posting them somewhere in the classroom sets the expectation. Unfortunately, children struggling with trauma need more help comprehending the role and value of classroom rules. If these students lack a real comprehension of the rules, they will struggle to follow rules they don't fully understand.

The most important task, especially early in the school year, is to help students understand the rules and the "why" behind the rules. Teachers typically develop their classroom rules in collaboration with their students to promote buy-in and build community. After establishing rules, the students can commit those rules to long-term memory through daily review of the rules.

To avoid monotony, teachers can create accompanying hand gestures and movements to promote muscle memory recall of each rule. Teachers can review the rules in various voices—whispering, like a robot, and slow-motion, for example. It is also useful and fun to role-play classroom interactions with and without following the rules. The point is to not just develop the rules and expect students to follow them, but to review them day after day in ways that support all learning styles. This seemingly small step teaches the student critical life lessons not learned at home: that there are different expectations in different settings. Certain behaviors result in positive or negative consequences.

Remember, students coming into school in the morning or coming in from recess are in a different state or zone than the mental state that is required to engage academically. While switching physical environments automatically prompts many children to self-regulate their behavior, this may not automatically occur for the child with trauma. Young students need help in understanding these complex shifts in rules and expectations throughout the day.

We can realistically expect that by the end of the school year, most students will adapt to these changing environments. More frontloading will help all children, but it is crucial for those struggling with trauma. The key to establishing a trauma-sensitive behavioral-management system is repetition.

We encourage school staff to think about expectations in a universal and task-specific manner. Universal expectations are rules and norms that govern student and staff behavior school-wide. In contrast, task-specific expectations are those that guide behavior for specific tasks such as walking in the hallway, sitting on the rug, or turning and talking with a partner.

While universal expectations remain constant, task-specific expectations vary. For example, the task-specific expectations for behavior in the classroom during reading groups will change when it is time for indoor recess. Both tasks are within the classroom, but the behavioral expectations will differ.

Universal Expectations

Setting universal expectations is a collaborative process that might involve many different parties, including staff, administration, parents, and students. Universal expectations are expectations for anyone in the school building and apply equally to how adults treat students and how the adults interact with one another. In many schools, social-emotional programming provides the foundation for universal expectations.

These programs often offer lessons, guiding principles, and common language used throughout the school. Whether developed by the school or implemented as a part of a curriculum, the school should display universal expectations throughout the school building. Key areas include the school entrance, every classroom, each special room, and any other environment that staff and children occupy on a regular basis.

The first goal surrounding universal expectations is that every staff member receives training on these expectations, has agreed to lend support to the teaching of these expectations, and will do so with fidelity throughout the school year. Teachers, lunchroom staff, special teachers, volunteers, and custodial staff all need to know the expectations. For universal expectations to positively impact school culture, it is imperative that it is a team effort!

Next, a pacing guide needs to be created that instructs teachers on how to prioritize the teaching of each expectation. They also need to know the amount of time allocated to each. The school should be flooded with common language, visual displays, announcements, and modeling of each expectation as it is introduced and reinforced throughout the school year. Staff should try to incorporate the expectations into as many assignments and lessons as it makes sense to do. Short but frequent repetition will help students put the expectations in long-term memory.

Introductory lessons should focus on helping students understand "why" these expectations exist, how they guide behavior in different situations, and how the students might apply them to succeed in the school environment. In chaotic homes, expectations change depending on the psychological state, stress level, or level of sobriety of their family members. "Because I said so," is often the justification given under these less-than-ideal parenting situations. Teachers and school staff want to avoid sending the same message about our school-wide norms and expectations.

One major hurdle in teaching universal expectations is to make them accessible for younger students. As mentioned previously, there is great value in repeated exposure to expectations. It is not necessary to "drill and kill" students on expectations. Instead, school staff can reinforce learning in a variety of ways, tapping into multiple intelligences. The focus on making expectations visual, auditory, kinesthetic, and multisensory will be well worth the time.

For students who have experienced trauma, learning about and succeeding in a structured environment with social norms is the most important thing they will gain in their school life. Time spent on repetition will pay off in improved behavior and a lifelong understanding of the importance of norms for success in relationships, school, and work environments. Helping students understand the importance of rules and the principle of cause and effect will assist students in achieving positive outcomes that transcend their primary educational experience.

When students do break the norms, this deeper understanding provides the school staff with a foundation to explore the adverse effects of the behavior in a more profound way. This foundation is more likely to lead to change. When consequences or disciplinary actions are needed, discussing how the behavior was a violation of a universal expectation helps the student conceptualize "why" their behavior was an issue. It also opens the opportunity to explore how a different behavior or action could better align with the expectations (Miller & Rollnick, 2012).

Task-Specific Expectations

Task-specific expectations, as opposed to universal expectations, pose a much more significant challenge to students struggling with trauma. A task-specific expectation lets a child know what behavior is appropriate for specific tasks during a limited period of time. Some tasks are as simple as how to properly push in their chair, with more complex behaviors including developing good listening skills.

One essential task that students are asked to do repeatedly throughout their school day is transition. Children need to transition from home to school, classroom to playground, lunchroom to hallway, and the list goes on and on. Transitions are especially difficult for children dealing with trauma, with special-education needs, or attention-deficit or hyperactivity issues. A single transition requires a child to change environments, emotionally and physically regulate their body, and quickly adapt and focus in their new surroundings.

While setting task-specific expectations for transitions takes some time, the decrease in behavioral issues during transitions makes the time worth the investment. Let's say a class is preparing to line up and transition to music class. Time needs to be set aside to set the task-specific expectations for lining up: walking feet, safe hands, quiet voices, single-file line, and so forth.

Too often, school staff make the mistake of thinking, "They do these 100 times a day. They know the expectations." While this may be true, knowing the expectations and having the physical and cognitive ability to meet those expectations are not always congruent, particularly for those students with trauma.

It is also helpful to have cuing systems that give students a heads up that they are going to be changing environments and they will need to adjust their behavior expectations. The cuing system includes simple things such as turning off the lights each time the class is getting ready to transition. The teacher's voice may take a softer tone, and they may find it helpful to allot a short amount of time for mindful deep breathing to help students emotionally regulate before lining up. Regardless of the cues employed, they should be used consistently to maximize their effectiveness.

We recognize that expectations will vary at times due to the natural flow of the school year. There may be fire drills, schedule changes, and other events that require flexibility. When these changes occur, teachers and school staff must pay particular attention to students with trauma, as unpredictable things induce stress and cause additional heightened behavioral responses. Providing visual cues to these changes creates a sense of safety as well. School staff should write on the board that there is a schedule change and remind students a few times prior to that change. Using auditory and visual cues helps reduce the stress around the change.

Let's take an example every teacher loves: indoor recess! One of several reasons that teachers dread indoor recess is that students struggle with a coming together of different task-specific expectations. The expectations of indoor recess exist somewhere between expectations for classroom learning and outdoor recess. Students, especially those already experiencing the psychological effects of trauma, will find it hard to mix these competing sets of expectations without help from the teacher.

Another example is school-wide assemblies. These events are rare enough that most students will not learn a set of task-specific expectations that are unique to this specific environment. Plus, each assembly is different. Some want students to cheer and get excited; others require children to behave like they would in the classroom. The school administration should communicate ahead of time with the leaders of the assembly and help teachers understand the task-specific expectations concerning the event. Teachers should review these unique expectations with their students before attending.

Too many students leave primary education without an understanding of cause and effect. They do not know that different environments call for different states and behaviors. As these students advance in their school experience, they face more significant challenges, such as middle-school hallways during transitions, numerous teachers, peer pressure, romantic interests, and other forms of chaos. It is crucial to help students build the capacity to manage their emotions and states in the primary years, so they can succeed in these demanding environments later on in their education.

Rewards & Punishments

Currently, visual behavior-management systems, where students earn positive rewards for good behavior and consequences (or punishments) for negative behavior, are popular and widespread. While these systems give teachers and school staff a greater sense of control over managing student behavior, understanding trauma and its impact on the brain challenges educators to rethink the use of rewards and punishments, and the systems used to deliver them.

If one were to observe students in multiple classrooms under different behavioral-management systems, it would become clear that in nearly every circumstance, the same students thrive regardless of the system in place. Day after day, the same students earn the star stickers or make their way to "outstanding" on the clip chart. At the same time, it becomes apparent that if a student fails in one classroom system, they will likely struggle in a similar one, even if they are in a different environment. The child who doesn't earn star stickers is usually the same child who finds themselves on the bottom of the clip chart (Biffle, 2013; Greene, 2008).

The only instance where there is a deviation in this pattern is when the "failing" student develops a strong relationship with the teacher or when the "successful" student develops a negative relationship with the teacher or staff in the classroom. It becomes apparent that the relationship, not the threat of punishment or the promise of a reward, becomes a strong predictor of behavior (Hattie, 2009).

The Australian Society for Evidence Based Teaching (2019) found that, "In fact, the quality and nature of the relationships you have with your students have a larger effect on their results than socio-economic status, professional development or Reading Recovery programs." It is not that these other factors don't matter, but instead that the relationship is the most powerful indicator of behavioral and academic success for students with trauma.

In truth, most students who struggle in reward/punishment systems fail to make notable improvements in their behavior from year to year. They never seem to learn the lessons that the rewards and punishments were designed to teach. The children who struggled in the simple systems in elementary school often grow up to become the students suspended or expelled in later years. Even if one teacher could manage a student through rewards and punishments for a brief time, this learning never seems to transcend that specific environment in future years (Greene, 2008; Wisconsin Department of Public Instruction, 2019).

When viewing behaviors under the lens of trauma, one will be confronted with the idea that traditional approaches are punishing or withholding rewards from students who display the behavior and emotional symptoms of trauma. Ethically, this leave educators on shaky ground. Is it okay to hand out punishments to students for actions they use to survive in their home or community, actions that help them survive their trauma?

As mentioned, the inability to understand cause and effect is one symptom of a traumatic past. Not only are too many schools punishing children because their traumatized brains struggle with focus and emotional regulation, but students also fail to conceptualize the reasons behind the punishment or consequence in the first place. Few ever stop to think that the child who says, "I didn't do anything wrong!" might genuinely mean it (Cole et al., 2009; Van der Kolk, 2014).

Unfortunately, many behavioral-management reward-and-punishment systems reinforce fixed-mindset thinking. Trauma relays a message that the child is not a worthy person. Too many behavioral-management systems reinforce this internalized mindset with punishment or by withholding rewards. For many students with trauma, the emotional regulation and cognitive focus needed for appropriate behavior takes a tremendous amount of effort. School staff rarely reward or recognize these efforts, as the negative behaviors receive most of their attention (Dweck, 2006).

Sometimes teachers and school staff get so caught up in handing out rewards and punishments that they fail to address the underlying problems contributing to the behavior. In Chapter 4, Caleb's behavior would have led to him getting suspended from school. Someone who witnessed his actions on the bus and those behaviors he continued to exhibit in the school building would unquestionably believe that he deserved a suspension.

Jumping right to handing out punishments misses the opportunity to get the whole picture. The vast majority of negative behaviors result from much deeper issues. Punishment often makes these issues worse by reinforcing the message that the student is "bad" or "something is wrong with them." It does not affect future behavior, and most importantly, school staff lose an opportunity to find out the deeper cause behind the behavior. If school staff fail to identify these deeper causes in primary education, students will carry these issues with them into later grades and adult life.

Moving away from rewards and punishments does not mean we do not correct or reinforce behaviors. There are ample opportunities to point out desired behaviors after establishing universal and task-specific expectations. If the task-specific expectation is for students to come to the carpet for story time, then when students follow that direction, we would say they showed "expected behavior." They did precisely what we would anticipate, based on our previously set expectation.

On the other hand, if a student does not make their way to the rug and instead decides to go get a drink of water, that would be considered "unexpected behavior." When addressing the behavior, school staff would first ask the student whether they understood what the task-specific expectation was for that task. If they did not remember or were unclear about the expectation, the school staff would use that moment to reiterate the expectation. Then the child would be asked to try it again, this time showing "expected behavior."

The intent in labeling the behaviors as expected or unexpected is to prevent further negative messaging. Redirecting students with trauma keeps behavior management neutral and immediately provides the student with the opportunity for positive action. Compare this to the shame students often feel when they must "clip down" in front of all their peers (Kuypers, 2011).

Our conclusion, therefore, is that behavioral-management strategies that rely primarily on rewards and punishments to manage behavior do not have the intended effect. We now know and understand much more about the brain and trauma. Rewards do motivate some students and are useful when supporting growth mindsets and effort. Punishments that are given without first exploring the "why" behind the behavior should not exist in a trauma-sensitive school environment. They often do harm to the student whose brain does not possess the ability to focus, use volition to regulate their emotions, or understand cause and effect.

So, what do we do?

Trauma-Sensitive Positive Behavioral Support

Let's look at all the pieces laid out so far and think about how a trauma-sensitive positive behavioral support might work. We understand that it will look different, depending on the age of students. We will suggest powerful strategies that supplement the teacher's current system, rather than having them throw out everything that is currently working and start from scratch.

The brains of young students need short-term interventions. Even young children from healthy home environments struggle with long-term attention or memory, and the difficulties intensify for students with trauma. The goal is to help all students meet the task-specific expectations without violating any universal expectations. Let's examine a six-step process to help students bring the appropriate behavior to a specific task or situation.

Step 1: Regulate

As students begin or end their transition into a situation requiring a different set of expectations, give them a few moments for some deep breathing, a calming brain break, or a yoga pose. Not only will this help regulate their nervous system, over time, their brain will begin to see these regulatory activities as signals for changes in behaviors and external states. Follow this activity up with a quick check-in. What *Zone of Regulation*® are the students in? Are they in the Green Zone, demonstrating their readiness to learn? If not, it may take a more prolonged or targeted activity like a guided meditation to achieve the intended outcome.

Step 2: Relate

Take note of any children who express that they are in any zone besides the Green Zone. Try to find a quick moment to check in with these children as soon as possible. If several children signal that they are in the Yellow Zone, it is likely that something disruptive or over-stimulating happened in their last activity. Take a few minutes to discuss, "Class, I see that a bunch of friends feel they are in the Yellow Zone right now. That means they feel a little out of control and perhaps a bit silly or wiggly. I'm wondering if something happened in music class." This check-in allows the energy of the event to get processed and out in the open. While this discussion will take some time, it is more effective and efficient to spend a few minutes talking about what happened than to deal with the behaviors for the rest of the day.

Step 3: Establishing Task-Specific Expectations

As mentioned above, make sure these expectations are specific to the task at hand and easy for the students to recall. Remember, task-specific expectations only govern the next activity or period of time needed for student and class success. These task-specific expectations may include things as basic as how to walk safely with scissors to how students should listen to guest speakers who visit their classroom.

Write these down on a smartboard, whiteboard or flip-chart paper with picture cues. The action of writing them is a visual aid for those children who struggle with auditory processing. Once children get the hang of setting expectations, make it an efficient collaborative process. Many of the task-specific expectations will repeat over and over again. This repetition is a good thing, and if students recycle past expectation wording, that is a positive sign of learning group norms.

Regardless of whether the teacher is the one setting the expectations, or if they have progressed to a collaborative process, get student input and agreement on these expectations. Limit them to five expectations to avoid overwhelming students. Ask if everyone agrees to follow these expectations. The vast majority of the time, teachers get 100% agreement.

If a student gives a rebellious answer, don't engage immediately. "Well, class, it seems like we have almost full agreement. I'll chat with Matt once we get started and address his concerns." This approach helps to identify that something is up with Matt and lets everyone, including Matt, know that rebelling for rebellion's sake does not disrupt the process. It also sets a time to check in with Matt using the approaches listed in Chapter 4 and with the curiosity as to whether something bigger is going on.

Also rare is the student who does really have a problem with the expectations as worded. Negotiating group norms is a critical task of social development. Sometimes students make excellent points, prompting an adjustment to the expectations. The objective is to get "real" agreement and not just a robotic "yes." Don't see a student objection to the initial expectations as a challenge, but as a chance to help the class learn how to handle and resolve healthy conflict.

Step 4: Teach or Commence the Activity

Now the work of learning begins! We wish that taking the above steps would fix every problem and eliminate all negative or distracting behaviors, but we all know better. The next challenge is helping students maintain regulation during an activity. While the instructional strategies presented in Chapter 7 will answer a part of this challenge, next we will detail some behavioral-management strategies.

Step 5: Monitoring Task-Specific Expectations

This step monitors how well the class is meeting the task-specific and universal expectations. The primary goal is to help the entire class meet these specific expectations. Moving the goal to the whole class helps everyone focus on working together to meet the agreed-upon expectations. If it feels like rewards help the class stay focused, now is an excellent time to integrate more traditional behavioral-management systems.

Point out when student actions support the class in achieving the task-specific or universal expectations. When a student violates an expectation in a manner that disrupts the class, refocus everyone by reviewing all the shared expectations. The first attempt to re direct disruptive behavior is to address the progress of the group. Refocusing this way does not acknowledge the disruptive student. Instead, it brings everyone back to the expectations everyone agreed to follow.

If refocusing fails to change the disruptive behavior, check in with that specific student. Assume that the student is struggling with something, instead of falling prey to labeling the student a "bad kid." Check-in on the *Zones of Regulation*® using the communication strategies in the last chapter. If there is a specific plan or set of strategies developed for the student to help them regulate themselves and their behaviors, such as sensory activities, here is where those plans pay off.

Especially when there is only one adult in the room, it is hard to teach an entire class and conduct an effective behavioral intervention. Establishing a proactive strategy allows the teacher to implement an already agreed-upon intervention in an efficient manner that does not take too much time away from instruction. If the student continues to escalate, they are signaling that they are struggling to maintain regulation right now in this environment.

In an ideal world, another school staff member could help give the student the relational attention they need in the moment to process their emotions and regulate back to the required state. If no other adults are available, the next best approach is to isolate the student and encourage a task that will help them regulate. Ask them what calming strategy they would prefer. Do not give a choice as to whether or not to do one, but rather, provide them with a choice of which they would like to use. Any attempt to regulate physically and emotionally is a positive step, especially for students struggling with trauma.

What does not work for a dysregulated student in the moment? Punishment. Taking away points, going to red light, or other traditional punishments elicit emotions of shame, anger, or unworthiness. For students already struggling, systems that try to change behaviors through punishment and shaming are more likely to do harm and fail to teach them how to regulate better or handle their anxiety the next time they feel dysregulated.

Step 6: Collective Review

The final step is a collective review of how well the class did at meeting the task-specific expectations. The teacher might also want to review universal expectations or do that as a part of any shared time built into your daily schedule. Taking a little time to process the answer helps to show how vital these expectations are to you.

First, restate the agreed-upon expectations. Then ask the class, "Class, what are some positive things we did to meet these expectations?" Focus most of the time on the positive, reinforcing any student observations and adding the teacher's observations. Help students focus on specific behaviors of their classmates to support growth-mindset thinking. Also, encourage a few students to point out the positive actions of their peers. Peer recognition and any acknowledgment the teacher provides is much more motivating than a long-term reward. The teacher's recognition is the most powerful. Make sure to point out the positive behaviors of students who might not get recognized by their peers.

Second, ask "Class, as an entire group, what could we improve next time to better meet our expectations?" The second processing is a little more difficult, as you don't want students pointing out negative behaviors in other students.

A third step might entail a reward or a movement toward a greater class goal. In a trauma-sensitive environment, rewards are more about fun than motivation. We want students to develop internal motivation for success and not behave to achieve a specific reward. However, a fun class reward is a positive way to end the processing.

A Whole New Classroom

"Give up my light system? Are you nuts?" exploded Mr. Anderson, interrupting Dr. Rodriguez's presentation on why traditional behavior-management systems were not effective with students struggling with trauma.

Something about Mr. Anderson never returned to normal after he learned about the babysitter abusing one of his students. His smile and great sense of humor turned into a short fuse and harsh sarcasm that rubbed many of the staff the wrong way, including Ms. Smith. Mrs. Vaughn had not thought much about it, as Mr. Anderson always treated her with respect, and she had so much Caleb stuff going on that he took almost all her attention.

Dr. Rodriguez did not miss a beat, "Kevin, I'm not asking you to give anything up. I want to present you with what research is showing us and let you explore how it could help improve your current behavioral-management approaches. I understand that it might not make sense to make dramatic changes since we are already well into the school year."

"Rewards and consequences are the only way I prevent my classroom from turning into total chaos. You are asking me to give up one of my only effective behavioral-management tools. Without structure, these kids turn into animals!" Mrs. Vaughn was shocked by Mr. Anderson's words and the emotions behind them.

Dr. Griffin shared Mrs. Vaughn's concern about Mr. Anderson, but his behavior was not consistent with what she expected from her staff professionally, "Kevin, can I see you for a second in the hall?"

"Now I'm in trouble! At least there are no consequences in this school anymore." He said sarcastically, pushing his chair back so hard that it crashed to the floor.

With Dr. Griffin and Mr. Anderson in the hall, Dr. Rodriguez, Ms. Smith, and Mrs. Vaughn were left in the room sharing a moment of collective concerned silence.

Mrs. Vaughn broke the silence, "I'm sorry, Dr. Rodriguez. Kevin hasn't been himself lately."

"I'm not sure who this 'Kevin' is anymore," added Ms. Smith

"No worries," smiled Dr. Rodriguez. "Hearing someone challenge some of your long-standing teaching strategies is difficult. When we are trying to keep our heads above water, in addition to dealing with the larger community issues walking into our school each day, change naturally feels like criticism. I've heard much worse!"

Dr. Rodriguez seemed to have something else to say, but hesitated long enough for Dr. Griffin to re-enter the room. "I'm sorry. Mr. Anderson is under a lot of stress right now. I think we should start implementing these new behavior structures into your two classrooms and then bring him back in later." She shot Mrs. Vaughn a look that indicated something more was going on, but now wasn't the time to talk about it.

Getting the message, Mrs. Vaughn rolled forward, "When you say two classrooms, you really mean my room. Emma is already implementing this structure, and I've been learning a little more each week. I must admit, I'm impressed with how she manages her classroom with a mix of compassion, flexibility, and structure, but without the systems we traditionally implement. I initially worried that her lack of a more-traditional behavior system would leave her class a disaster. However, her class is thriving, and the students seem really invested in meeting her expectations."

Ms. Smith was nearly knocked out of her chair, hearing the words of her mentor. "Thank you" were the only words Ms. Smith managed to say. She knew her approach was seen as "outside the box" and "unstructured" by most of the school's teachers. Mrs. Vaughn was so busy with Caleb and implementing the new trauma-sensitive approaches that Ms. Smith was surprised she had even noticed.

Mrs. Vaughn shot Dr. Griffin one of those looks that didn't need words. Dr. Griffin rolled her eyes and said, "Yes, Mrs. Vaughn, you did hire the perfect person for a teammate. I'm a little tired of saying it, but you were right."

Ms. Smith and Dr. Rodriguez looked confused. Dr. Griffin continued, "I thought a first-year teacher would get eaten alive at this school. If I couldn't team her with one of the best teachers I've ever seen," she nodded towards Mrs. Vaughn in a sarcastic but respectful manner, "I would never have approved the hire. Emma, you are the best thing that has happened to this school in a long time."

At this point, Ms. Smith's face was beet red. Mrs. Vaughn smiled, "Okay, Emma, let's talk about implementing your system in my classroom."

The four of them came up with a strategy to introduce the new system after the Fall break coming up later that month. The break would make the changes seem less disruptive to Mrs. Vaughn's students, and she could prepare them for how things would change after the break. It also gave her more time to work with Caleb and some other students on their individual plans and get more comfortable with her new communication strategies.

The word that Mrs. Vaughn was implementing Ms. Smith's unique approach to behavioral management spread like wildfire through the school. Up to that point, any talk about "trauma-sensitive schools" seemed like every other "flavor-of-the-month" program that filtered in and out of schools without effecting any meaningful change. However, if a teacher like Mrs. Vaughn was taking it seriously, maybe there was something to this whole approach.

On Tuesday of the fall break, Mrs. Vaughn and Ms. Smith stood at the door of Mrs. Vaughn's classroom. "Let's do this thing!" Mrs. Vaughn said as she walked toward her clip chart and student star system. While versions of these systems changed over time, these laminated sheets of paper had played a central role in her classroom management for years.

She gently took each down as if they were old friends. She handed them to Ms. Smith.

"Where should I put these?" Ms. Smith asked.

"In the dumpster."

Next, Mrs. Vaughn and Ms. Smith created a "School Expectations" bulletin board that was similar to the display in the front of Ms. Smith's class. Each classroom had a laminated 11" x 17" sheet with these expectations on them, but Mrs. Vaughn, like most of the teachers in the school, posted this in the back of her room and hardly mentioned it. The school staff went on a retreat to create these a few years back. Unfortunately, once created, they got little attention.

Mrs. Vaughn stepped back from the bulletin board, "From the back of the class to the front."

Next, they rearranged Mrs. Vaughn's whiteboard to free up the right side for task-specific expectations. They both thought that writing these down next to the universal expectations made logical sense. Overall the physical changes were small when compared to how differently things would operate next Monday when the classroom filled with students.

"Okay, now it's time for you to teach me about these new approaches you use. I think I see you implementing some of those new communication approaches that I've used with Caleb with your entire class. I'm thinking, if I'm changing my behavioral-management system on Monday, maybe I need to look at my instructional style as well."

"Sounds like a great conversation to start over lunch," Mrs. Smith suggested.

"My treat!" Mrs. Vaughn said in a tone that left no room for argument.

As they left her classroom, Mrs. Vaughn felt surprisingly relieved that her old system was in the dumpster. There was something very freeing about getting out from under the old structure. However, she also knew that her work over this break was only half done.

CHAPTER 7
Trauma-Sensitive Academic Instruction

In the past, many believed that academic instruction and behavioral management were divergent topics. With our understanding that emotional regulation is crucial to both learning and behavioral management, it doesn't make sense to view them as unrelated topics. Instead of starting from scratch, trauma-sensitive academic instruction utilizes the neuroscience from Part 1 of the book to construct lessons and instructional routines that elicit states promoting emotional engagement and prefrontal cortex activation, as well as optimizing learning and retention.

The good news is that tools, approaches, and philosophies that support trauma-sensitive academic instruction already exist in our modern educational environment. These tools, routines, and philosophies are best practices because they create a brain-friendly learning environment. In this chapter, we don't attempt to reinvent the wheel. Instead, we want to help you make some adjustments to your existing approaches that help all students thrive academically, including those who are struggling with trauma.

One Size Fits One

Many students struggling with trauma are academically behind their peers. They are fighting to cope with difficulties in emotional regulation as well as in academic engagement. Differentiated instruction is crucial in helping these students catch up and experience academic success. Carol Ann Tomlinson describes differentiated instruction as the process of "ensuring that what a student learns, how he or she learns it, and how the student demonstrates what he or she has learned is a match for that student's readiness level, interests, and preferred mode of learning" (Ellis, Gable, Gregg, & Rock, 2008).

Differentiated instruction involves helping students find their island of competence. In the rough seas of trauma and the stress of their lives outside of school, their island of competence is where their strengths allow them to experience a certain level of success. The more time we allow a student to spend on their island, the more self-confidence and self-worth they develop. The goal of helping students find and experience success in one or more areas is to give them the experience of competency. This focus will provide them with the confidence to re-engage in other activities where they struggle (Brooks & Goldstein, 2012).

Ideally, school staff help students find an academic subject or topic where their current strengths and interests allow them to experience success. Once school staff and the student identify an academic island of competency, they can use it to help the student develop a growth mindset and experience a little success every day. Special projects, homework, or assignments establish a momentum of successful experiences.

For instance, let's say a student struggles with reading and writing activities, but enjoys anything math-related. The teacher can call on that child frequently during math time to explain their problem-solving in front of the class. The teacher might make a point of noticing when they complete a math task quickly and accurately, and let them know that they are clearly in need of an additional challenge. The student can help those who may struggle in math so that they experience the feeling of being a leader and learn that they too can help others.

The student, of course, continues to participate in other classroom activities and subjects. The challenge becomes helping them find ways to get small wins through differentiation. Continued failure reinforces fixed mindsets and does little to elicit motivation or engagement in learning. If not careful, teachers put students in situations where they lack the skills to succeed at the level of their peers. These struggles, failures, and setbacks add up over the years and put the student at risk of giving up altogether.

Unfortunately, due to the neurobiological and developmental impacts of trauma, many students lack competency across most academic subjects. A student without clear academic competency puts the teacher in a more challenging, but not impossible position. It is essential to try and broaden the view of what may be considered an academic strength. It may not be product-based, as in writing a detailed paragraph. Instead something as fundamental as a proper pencil grip or being able to retell a story using sequencing words like *first*, *then*, and *next* are academic skills that become a small island of competency to celebrate and build upon in future assignments.

Even non-academic activities, such as helping a classmate tie their shoes, leading the line down the hallway, or assisting a child with a physical limitation when getting their lunch, warrant praise and positive attention. Finding even the most straightforward task a student has the skills to complete provides a positive experience. If the school staff points out that their efforts lead to success, they are supporting a growth mindset.

Other students without an obvious academic island of competence can find success at art, music, or sports. Identifying ways for students to visit their island of competency for a few minutes a day lets the student feel good about themselves and experience being a valuable member of the class and school community. Keep in mind that even if the tasks the child can complete successfully are well below grade level, the repeated experiences of success can break patterns and feelings of failure often associated with school for students with trauma.

The island-of-competency approach to differentiated instruction challenges the teacher to adjust the learning environment, materials, and teaching strategies. The strategy is to maximize the skill strengths of the individual student, while preventing the devastating effects of repeated failures. The "one-size-fits-all" educational approach fails for students whose neurodevelopment is outside the "standard" range. Students with trauma often fall outside the "standard" range due to no fault of their own.

Once again, we find ourselves at a crossroads. Do we continue to force teachers into the standard "one-size-fits-all" paradigm of teaching? Or, do we understand that the inflexibility of modern educational expectations causes students with trauma to struggle? Trauma-sensitive classrooms take on the challenge of adjusting their environments, curriculum, and approaches to set their students up for success (Tomlinson, 2001; Tomlinson, 2003).

Trauma-Sensitive Lesson Planning

Trauma-sensitive lesson planning brings together everything learned so far. When designing lessons, teachers want to create an environment that promotes emotional regulation, prevents retraumatization, and maximizes cognitive engagement, in addition to effectively teaching a subject. The good news is that trauma-sensitive lesson planning builds on what most teachers are already doing.

Traditionally teachers are taught to utilize a few essential components in their lesson plans. These components include academic goals, delivery of content, practice opportunities, required materials, assessment, and follow-up. The assumption is that experienced teachers will have "good" behavior-management skills and therefore, will not need to allocate time to developing brain-friendly instructional routines to deliver their lessons.

The assertion is that a well-planned lesson will create an environment where all students will naturally maintain their focus and attention. For our students with trauma, even the most masterfully designed lessons will fail when teachers do not embed trauma-sensitive practices into their lessons. A trauma-sensitive teacher recognizes the value in establishing brain-friendly instructional routines. They understand the importance of allocating time for repeated exposure to the main ideas and goals of the lesson. Lastly, a trauma-sensitive teacher understands that avoiding retraumatization should be their priority in each and every lesson.

Emotional Regulation

One aspect of trauma-sensitive lesson planning that sets it apart from traditional lesson planning is the consideration and forethought put into emotional regulation. The emotional regulation step is especially crucial for students who suffer the effects of trauma. Traditional approaches to lesson planning leave us reacting to dysregulated students in real time without thinking how the lesson might minimize certain behaviors. A trauma-sensitive lesson is designed to teach academic objectives, while simultaneously building social-emotional competencies. Teaching students how to regulate their emotions, thoughts, and behaviors becomes part of every lesson, rather than being taught as isolated skills.

Before your lesson even begins, you must assess what emotional state your students are in. As we discussed in earlier chapters, optimal learning takes place when students are happy, focused, and ready to learn. With their amygdala calm and the prefrontal cortex ready and curious about upcoming learning activities, the student is ready to learn.

Many students need time to transition to a new lesson. These transitions are particularly important if they are being expected to change seating arrangements, alter their voice level, or demonstrate an ability to focus and attend to the instruction after participating in a less-structured activity such as recess or lunch. School staff should check in with students to assess their *Zone of Regulation*®. It is important for students to recognize that their emotional state is often the driving force behind their behavior. Teach your students how to use calming techniques, breathing exercises, sensory activities, and mindfulness activities to regulate their emotions and prepare for a learning activity.

Review universal expectations and the shared expectations for the lesson at hand. Help the students know what emotions may come up during the lesson and how to find strategies to manage those feelings. For instance, if the class is about to take a spelling test, discuss how they may be feeling anxious or nervous. It may be helpful to get a sip of water or do some belly breathing to prepare.

Far too often, teachers feel the pressure to maintain a rigid schedule and pacing. Rushing into a lesson in order to stay on a schedule before helping students regulate will only lead to frustration. Every teacher has tried to rush a lesson only to find themselves "putting out fires" and managing negative behaviors rather than teaching the intended lesson. The more front-loading the teacher does to help students achieve emotional regulation, the more effective the lesson. Be flexible with time and realistic with pacing. A commitment to help students regulate emotionally before a lesson is critical in delivering a successful lesson for students with trauma.

Once the time is taken to ensure students are in an emotional state that allows them to engage cognitively with academic content, the question then becomes, how do teachers keep them regulated throughout the entirety of the lesson? Teachers do their best to make lessons engaging, fun, and interactive. Despite their best efforts, students with trauma often need additional support and instructional routines designed to support their engagement for extended periods of time.

One of the best ways to help a student with trauma stay engaged in a learning activity is to keep their mind, mouth, and body active. The instructional routines established in a trauma-sensitive classroom are designed to maximize student engagement while providing instruction in a way that the brain is designed to learn.

One approach we have found that integrates brain-based neuroscience with effective teaching techniques is called Whole Brain Teaching. Established in 1999, Whole Brain Teaching asserted itself as a grassroots educational-reform movement. The approach was designed to maximize student engagement by the creation of brain-friendly instructional routines and pedagogical approaches. Let's explore some Whole Brain Teaching multi-sensory techniques easily modified for students with trauma (Biffle, 2013; Biffle, 2018).

Attention Grabbers

All teachers have some tactic for gaining the attention of their class. Ringing chimes, flashing lights, and using hand signals are just some of the numerous ways teachers attempt to secure the attention of their students. What is missing for our students with trauma is their participation in the routine.

As outlined previously, students with trauma benefit from the use of serve-and-return communication. In many forms of traditional attention grabbers, there is no role for the student. They are merely passive listeners. The teacher serves but does not allow space for the students to return. The goal in a trauma-sensitive classroom is to provide opportunities for collective or group serve-and-return communication.

We have found one method that is easily adaptable when promoting serve-and-return communication in the classroom. When the teacher wants to gain the attention of the class they say "Class!" and it is the students' job to respond "Yes!" The teacher uses variations on the word 'class' and the students are asked to mimic those variations when they return with 'yes'.

If the teacher whispers "Class," the students collectively whisper "Yes." The variations keep the routine engaging but provide predictability for students with trauma. If the teacher says "Classity," the students know to add -ity to their response, "Yesity." Even if a child struggles to figure out the correct response due to expressive language difficulties, the group's collective responses support their learning.

Using this serve-and-return method with your students activates their prefrontal cortex. They develop their receptive and expressive language skills while not being put on the spot. The repetition of the "class/yes" is also important because it activates the hippocampus, supporting the formation of new memories. This effective instructional routine strengthens memory and language areas often underdeveloped in students with trauma (Biffle, 2013; Biffle, 2018; Harvard National Scientific Council for the Developing Child, 2018).

Turn, Talk, Teach!

Oral language development is foundational for young learners. While all students need language to develop critical-thinking skills, knowledge, and understanding of the world around them, students with trauma face delays in their language development. These deficiencies often hinder the retention of instructional information, leading to slower academic growth and achievement (Cole et al., 2009).

One popular instructional routine that aims to support oral language development is called the Turn and Talk. It is an oral-language support strategy that encourages students to share their thinking with a partner. Turn and Talk allows all students to simultaneously share their thinking, rather than having a single student answering a question or responding to the content.

The Turn and Talk effectively maximizes student discussion throughout a lesson, because it provides students with an opportunity to share their thinking before, during, and after instruction. It typically involves the teacher presenting a topic or question and asking the students to turn and talk to their rug, seat, or table partner. Then when all students have had an opportunity to confer, the group comes back together to share out their thoughts.

While the Turn and Talk is effective in maintaining engagement and activating the speaking and listening parts of the brain, it does little to address the visual and motor parts of the brain. A more brain-friendly approach engages multiple sensory systems and provides students with additional ways to access, learn, and retain information.

One way to make the Turn and Talk multi-sensory and more trauma-sensitive is with the addition of Teach-OK-Switch. In using Teach-OK-Switch, the teacher introduces a concept or idea for a few short minutes. The teacher uses gestures to "act out" terms or ideas as they present the lesson (Biffle, 2013; Biffle, 2018).

When it is time to Turn and Talk, the teacher prompts the class to "Teach." The students collectively respond with "OK" and turn to their partners. Students discuss the content and are challenged to mimic the gestures of the teacher. Once one partner has had a chance to share, then the teacher says "Switch," and it is the other partner's turn.

The inclusion of motor movement in the Turn and Talk allows for the student to visually see the information and use their body to communicate. They are activating their prefrontal cortex and hippocampus with Turn and Talk. Also, during this practice, they engage multiple sensory systems with Teach-OK-Switch (Biffle, 2013; Biffle, 2018).

The information presented by the teacher has now been repeated three times: once during the lesson, once by the partner, and once again by the student. This repetition is critical in the learning process for students with trauma. Students with histories of physical or emotional trauma struggle with memory functioning. Providing students with multiple repetitions of the content using Teach-OK-Switch makes learning fun, engaging, and accessible to all students, not just those with histories of trauma.

Mirror

When searching for instructional routines that support students with trauma, we emphasize that our teaching practices need to reflect the way the brain is designed to learn. We try to embed routines into our everyday lessons that are multi-sensory, repetitive, and engaging.

Mirror is an instructional routine that teachers can include in the main part of the lesson, during the Turn and Talk or Teach-OK-Switch, or they can utilize it as a comprehension check. During this routine, students are asked to mirror the teacher's gestures with or without words. The teacher prompts this action by placing two hands in front of them, much like a mime would do when creating an invisible box and saying the prompt "Mirror."

The students would then repeat "Mirror" as a class, with their hands positioned just like the teacher. The teacher can then break the lesson into small, manageable pieces for the students to reflect on what they are learning. "Mirror" asks the students to mimic not only the motions and gestures, but also the precise speech of the teacher. This approach requires the teacher to have pre-planned the accompanying gestures and language goals for the lesson.

For students with trauma, having language modeled multiple times in simple sentences makes acquiring new vocabulary and formulating sentences more accessible. The teacher should speak slowly and in chunks for students who may process information at a slower rate than their peers. Mirror is also very effective for students who may not speak English as their first language. They are introduced to new words slowly and with visuals to help them attach meaning to new vocabulary.

Mirror allows the teacher to immediately assess who is on task and who may need additional support. It also activates both the motor and visual parts of the brain, rather than traditional lecturing, which only requires the student to use auditory processing.

Teachers must embed instructional routines that activate the auditory, motor, and visual parts of the brain. Lessons should include multiple opportunities for students to engage with the content using multiple sensory systems. Teachers need to provide enough repetition so that students with trauma have at least three opportunities to engage with the content of a lesson. This repetition allows for their hippocampus to make new, long-term memories (Biffle, 2013; Biffle, 2018).

Predicting and Preventing Retraumatization

One of the most challenging aspects of planning trauma-sensitive lessons is trying to prevent retraumatization in students who suffered the pain of traumatic experiences. Remember, retraumatization occurs when a student is emotionally activated by something in the environment that triggers a traumatic memory and forces them to relive their past trauma (Bloom & Farragher, 2011).

Understanding the trauma and stress facing your students is crucial, as it helps the teacher customize lessons to prevent triggering traumatic memories and the intense behaviors that follow. Let's use the Caleb example. Because Mrs. Vaughn knows about the domestic violence that Caleb witnessed and his suspected history of emotional and physical abuse, she will pay special attention to assignments that include the content of mothers, violence, or functional families, at least in the short term. She might still use the content, but customize it to avoid retraumatizing Caleb.

For some, this simple task might feel impossible, especially when your class contains many children potentially experiencing trauma at home or in the community. In this situation, let's look at some realistic approaches. First, pay attention to past triggers. If a student gets retraumatized every time they read a story about a family because her dad is in prison, avoid that subject as much as possible. Check in individually with the student to prepare them for the material or work with a mental-health professional to help develop a strategy specifically for that student.

Pay special attention to students who are going through a traumatic event that just occurred. If a student's parent just died of cancer, try not to expose them to something that reinjures the fresh wound. If it is impossible to adjust a lesson, find an activity for the student outside the classroom. Again, in an ideal situation, the student is receiving help. As the psychological wound heals, exposure to the material becomes tolerable over time.

Do consider that some favorite activities and holidays may be emotionally triggering for our students with trauma. A craft activity for Mother's Day or a birthday celebration is enjoyable for most students. For those suffering the loss of a parent or living in poverty, these celebratory activities can incite feelings of unworthiness or emotional pain. Do not avoid these topics altogether, but it is crucial to be cognizant of how activities emotionally impact your students with traumatic pasts and adjust accordingly.

Working with students with trauma means retraumatization will happen in the classroom. Often it is unpredictable. When it happens, it is an indicator that the student needs help, not that you failed in any way. Being proactive helps eliminate some of the obvious triggers, and that is your immediate goal when planning a lesson.

A Different Classroom

Mrs. Vaughn felt like a new teacher for the first time in decades. Not only had her classroom visibly changed to support universal and task-specific expectation setting, but her lesson plans were also dramatically different. With decades of teaching under her belt, lesson planning had become more of a formality than a strategic way to think about teaching. She spent a good portion of yesterday tweaking and studying her plans for the week.

In preparing her lessons, the thing that astonished her was how much of her material and the district's curriculum concerned issues that could trigger kids going through trauma like Caleb. While not all books featured the typical "nuclear" middle-class white family, none featured a character living with two cousins, or a mom regularly abused by her drug-dealing boyfriend. She found it difficult to strike a balance between avoiding triggers and presenting subject matter to which students in her community could relate.

She began to understand that transforming herself into a trauma-sensitive teacher meant much more than just taking a training or reading a book. It challenged her to rethink everything.

As her students began coming in, she made an extra effort to do a quick serve-and-return with each of them. It gave her a chance to practice replacing questions with statements and reconnecting with each of them personally after a long break. Most students did not notice the changes in room setup and new bulletin boards. Besides the universal-expectations bulletin board in the front of the class, she also made a chart over the break with the prompt/response structure she would teach her students today.

To her surprise, Caleb did notice. "Mrs. Vaughn, is that for me?" Caleb pointed to the universal-expectation bulletin board.

Mrs. Vaughn realized that Caleb's life required his brain to always be on watch. A little change for most kids goes unnoticed, while a small change for Caleb might signal danger. "Look who is wide awake this morning! Good observation, friend. Those are for me, you, and everyone. Since you were the very first student to notice them, I wonder if you might help me introduce them to the class once school starts?"

"Sure," Caleb shrugged but smiled a little.

"Caleb," Mrs. Vaughn whispered so no other students could hear.

"Yes," Caleb whispered back.

"I'm delighted you are here today."

"Me too."

As her class got settled, Mrs. Vaughn began, "Welcome back, friends. I hope you all had a wonderful break! I also want to welcome you back to your brand-new classroom!"

The students looked confused. Malik raised his hand, "But Mrs. Vaughn, this is the same classroom."

"Technically, it is the same room, but even though the room is the same, what goes on in the room is changing."

"How?" blurted several kids, too excited to raise their hands.

"Good question. I want to teach you a whole new way of learning. However, I want to start by going over something so important that I put it right in front of the classroom for you all to see."

The students all looked around. "Caleb was the first to notice, so I'm going to ask him to come up and help me introduce these important things to us."

More than one person shared a confused face. Caleb was usually in trouble when he was called out in class.

Mrs. Vaughn asked Caleb to read the first universal expectation, and then asked, "I wonder if anyone would like to share why this one is important." She let Caleb call on different students and took a few answers for each expectation as they worked through the list.

"Okay class, we are going to review these at the beginning of each day and after lunch. Your assignment is to catch your classmates following these expectations throughout the day. Let's see how many people we find being leaders today."

Malik raised his hand again, nervously this time. "Mrs. Vaughn, where is our behavior clip chart?"

Mrs. Vaughn looked around nervously. Other students followed her example; she even looked under her desk. "Does anyone see the clip chart?"

She chuckled as students looked around the room, in their desks, and even up at the ceiling. Maybe it was just as difficult for them to imagine life without the chart as it was for her.

"Anyone find it?" she asked.

"No," was the collective response.

"Then it must not exist anymore." At this, the students' eyes widened with uncertainty.

Malik, her little rule follower, raised his hand again. "But Mrs. Vaughn, does this mean we won't get to go to the treasure box anymore?" A majority of students nodded in shared concern.

"Before we went on fall break, we talked a lot about having a growth mindset. Does anyone remember what that means?" Mrs. Vaughn inquired.

Emilia slowing raised her hand and responded, "Our brain is like a muscle. The more challenges we try, and the harder we work, the stronger our brain gets."

"That's correct, Emilia!"

Mrs. Vaughn continued, "Our mistakes help us grow. I've been doing some thinking. It seems unfair to me that kids might receive punishments on our behavior chart for making mistakes if we are trying to have a growth-mindset approach to our learning."

"Everyone stand up for a second." The students all stood up. "Okay, sit down if you absolutely positively hate learning and don't want to become one ounce smarter than you are today."

Smiles broke out as everyone remained standing. "Interesting, okay, please sit down if you love getting in trouble and losing your privileges." A few students looked at Caleb's way, but all remained standing.

"Now, sit down if you want to be very smart when you grow up." All the students sat back down.

"Wait a minute, you mean I have a whole class that WANTS to learn?"

"Yes," was the collective response, as each student nodded in agreement.

"Therefore, I no longer think we need a clip chart." Mrs. Vaughn felt some of her own doubt creeping into her voice. "Instead, I want to try something new. Is that okay with you?"

"Yes," was the response from most, though her rule-followers seemed hesitant.

"Great, I was hoping we could start over. We will always try to follow the universal expectations. Next, I want you to share with me the rules you think we should set for ourselves. These will serve as the rules for our next lesson, which is math."

The students covered all the basics, such as raising your hand, listening when your teacher is talking, and being safe. After each response, Mrs. Vaughn asked the student why it was important. A few struggled, so she let others help them out. After she got a rationale for each explanation, she asked if everyone was okay with the new expectations and everyone seemed satisfied. It took about 5 minutes to get a nice set of five clear and concise expectations.

Mrs. Vaughn recognized that she needed to add some gestures for each expectation to make them more multi-sensory. She enlisted students to help her come up with actions that reflected their newly agreed-upon rules. The students enjoyed the task, as it resembled playing a game of charades.

"Class, I want to add one more if that is okay. I want to set the expectation that we have fun! I wonder if anyone knows why that might be important," added Mrs. Vaughn.

No hands went up, and confused looks met her. Mrs. Vaughn helped her students, "I learned something new recently. I learned that when we have fun learning, we learn more and remember it longer. To me, that is very important. I wonder who agrees with me." All hands shot up.

"All right, let's start." Mrs. Vaughn walked over to the bulletin board with the prompt/response list. "The first new thing is simple, but I think it is lots of fun. When I say 'Class' you all respond, 'Yes.' Let's practice." Mrs. Vaughn started, "Class."

"Yes," they all answered.

"Great, you all are such astute listeners! Now for the tricky part. I want you to match the volume of my voice. So, if I whisper 'Class,' you whisper back."

"Yes," the class whispered.

Next, she said it a little louder and louder and louder until her students yelled. Then she brought them back down, lowering her voice each time. Mrs. Vaughn found it fascinating to watch their emotions go up and down depending on the tone of her voice.

Mrs. Vaughn and the class had a great math lesson. Her students enjoyed the back and forth, and she noticed a sharp decline in the yawns that usually accompanied the morning lessons.

It was fast approaching time for library.

"It is time to transition for library." She walked over to the task-specific expectations and erased them. "I would like to set three expectations that we all agree to follow between now and when library time starts." She listed, 'no talking,' 'hands to self,' and 'eyes forward.'

Everyone agreed. "Class?" she said.

"Yes," about two-thirds of the class responded.

"Please stand up." Mrs. Vaughn had her class do three rounds of square breathing with prolonged and exaggerated breaths. Everyone followed right along. After 30 seconds of mindfulness, she whispered, "Class?"

All her student replied in a whisper, "Yes."

"Before we line up, please show me what zone you feel like you are in right now." Most students signed the letter 'G' for Green Zone. "Thank you for a great morning. Following our expectations, I will call one row at a time to line up for library."

After dropping the kids off, Mrs. Vaughn felt exhausted but happy. She was pleased with how engaged the students were with the serve-and-return communication. Mrs. Vaughn felt a little different and remembered Ms. Smith talking about how, when we engage in empathetic conversation with people we like and trust, we release oxytocin. She chuckled and enjoyed the small sense of accomplishment.

PART 3

Trauma-Sensitive Schools

No institutions are as central to a community as their local schools. Every day, millions of parents trust their child's well-being, academic instruction, and future success to teachers, principals, and school staff. Schools are unique in that they interact with children throughout critical developmental stages. Outside the family, few other factors influence a child's development and future success as much as their experiences in school.

For children whose home or communities are places of trauma and pain, schools take on an even greater significance. For them, their schools serve as sanctuaries and a second opportunity to find acceptance, self-confidence, and hope for the future. The concept of trauma-sensitive schools challenges many long-held notions of the nature of schools and their role in the community and students' lives.

At first glance, placing yet another responsibility on the shoulders of schools seems incredibly unfair. On the other hand, not getting children with trauma the help they need is both ethically and morally irresponsible. Through hard work and advocacy, we are encouraging schools to evolve and adapt to meet the needs of children afflicted by trauma.

An individual teacher can create a trauma-sensitive classroom in isolation. However, to fully maximize the effectiveness of trauma-sensitive practices, teachers need the support of an entire school community, with trauma-sensitive approaches prevalent throughout the school.

Envision a Russian Matryoshka nesting doll. The smallest doll represents a student struggling with trauma. The next largest doll represents the trauma-sensitive classroom, where they spend most of their time during the day. The trauma-sensitive classroom encircles the student and ensures that they get the social, emotional, and academic support they need for success.

The classroom doll exists within the broader context of a trauma-sensitive school that supports the classroom, its teachers, and other staff working with the student. Trauma-sensitive schools connect students and families to the resources they need to heal from their traumatic experiences and avoid future trauma. Like classrooms, schools do not operate in isolation.

The next doll represents the school district. A trauma-sensitive school thrives when supported by a trauma-sensitive school district. The school district aligns funding priorities, ensures resources are available, and advocates for the well-being and needs of all their students. Trauma-sensitive schools thrive when the district supports their efforts and are less successful if hindered by an inflexible district bureaucracy.

The community in which the district operates is our next doll. As any district administrator will tell you, the school district reflects the community in which it serves. The better the community understands the needs of students with trauma, the more likely they are to ensure their schools get funding to help every student succeed. Trauma-sensitive communities understand that helping their children who have experienced or are experiencing trauma is a worthy investment in the child's future success. It is also an investment in the safety, well-being, and economic vitality of the entire community.

Finally, our model needs to include dolls representing the state and nation. Hundreds of factors come together to determine the future life for a student struggling with trauma. State and federal policies and funding priorities are key variables that need to change to help children heal and achieve academic and personal success.

If we want every student to reach their potential, we need to spread this knowledge into our state and national legislative bodies. As we will explore, a trauma-sensitive school is a new model for education. Each doll must fit into place to fully realize the life-changing potential of the trauma-sensitive movement. We need to create educational environments where all students thrive.

An Uncomfortable Place

As the weeks passed, Mrs. Vaughn felt more and more comfortable integrating the emotional check-ins, mindfulness, expectations, and trauma-sensitive behavioral supports. There were still good days and tough ones; however, the "feel" of her class improved a little each week. Students were gaining the ability to identify and regulate their moods and demonstrate more attentiveness. She tracked a measurable decrease in negative behaviors.

Caleb was still Caleb. He moved back and forth between his mother's and uncle's houses. Mrs. Vaughn had hoped that once Child Protective Services got involved, he would get more stability in his home life. Unfortunately, as she had witnessed too many times in the past, just because the "system" gets involved, does not mean the trauma, disappointment, and chaos stop. Sitting next to Emilia on the bus helped him tremendously, and Emilia seemed to enjoy having a friend who did all the talking.

Most days, he got to the classroom in decent shape. Mrs. Vaughn huddled with him for a minute every morning, which they termed their "check-in time." "Check-in time," however brief, gave her a chance to do a quick emotional assessment of his state, practice some serve-and-return communication, and strategize with him about how to successfully manage his day. She could also alert him to any changes in the daily schedule.

Malik asked her one day, loud enough for everyone to hear, "Why does Caleb get to talk with you all by himself each morning? That's not fair."

Mrs. Vaughn could tell Malik's question, while genuinely curious, embarrassed Caleb. She was afraid his embarrassment could turn to anger. Luckily, she had an analogy she often used to explain how she differentiates in class and why sometimes students worked on different assignments or only completed a portion of what the rest of the class were expected to complete.

"Malik, I wonder if you like dogs."

Malik was confused by the statement, but answered, "Yes."

"Well, I think you would agree that all dogs need to eat." Mrs. Vaughn kept working to change questions into statements.

Malik was uncertain what dogs had to do with Caleb getting extra time with the teacher, but he answered anyway. "Right."

"Tell me the largest dog you can think of." Mrs. Vaughn asked.

"That one that carries a barrel around its neck and rescues people in the snow," Malik said.

"That is a St. Bernard, and you are right—those dogs are huge!" Mrs. Vaughn said with a smile. "Now tell me the smallest dog you can think of."

Malik proceeded, "My neighbor's Chihuahua named Nacho. He was so small he could fit in a purse."

Mrs. Vaughn then posed a more challenging statement, "Now this is a bit trickier. I wonder if you think it is fair to feed the St. Bernard the same amount of food as the Chihuahua."

At this point, Caleb was fully engaged with the conversation between Malik and Mrs. Vaughn and chimed in, "No way! The St. Bernard would starve!"

Malik added, "And if you fed Nacho what a St. Bernard would eat, he would probably get so fat! It would be way too much!"

"Exactly," said Mrs. Vaughn. "It is fair to give each dog what they need and what each dog needs to stay healthy is different. One dog is getting more food than the other. What is fair is not always equal or the same."

Mrs. Vaughn continued, "Caleb and I get extra time to talk each morning because that is what Caleb needs. Malik, you get extra help with getting your lunch because of your broken arm and that is what you need. Those two things are not the same, but you both are getting what you need. It is my job to make sure kids are getting what they need, even if those things are different."

Malik and Caleb both nodded "Oh," simultaneously, showing their understanding.

"All right, we have music this morning, so let's set our expectations for the hall and library and do some belly breathing. Before we do our breathing, please show me what zone you feel like you are in right now." She was not surprised to see that the majority of the class was in Green Zone after a great start to the morning.

As she looked up, Mrs. Vaughn realized Dr. Griffin was standing at the door. She seemed to enjoy the ad hoc fairness lesson as much as the students. As the students laid down on the floor for belly breathing, Dr. Griffin mouthed, "Can you see me once you drop the kids off?"

Mrs. Vaughn topped off her coffee and grabbed a cup for Dr. Griffin. "What's up, boss?"

"Oh, you are a saint." Dr. Griffin said, closing the door behind Mrs. Vaughn. "Carey, I need your opinion on something."

"Sure."

"So, we are a couple of months into this whole trauma-sensitive school thing. I love watching how you transformed your classroom and the positive results we see with Caleb," she paused. "Caleb is still Caleb, but he is doing better than I thought he ever would do."

"But," Mrs. Vaughn could tell there was a 'but.'

"Maybe more of an 'and.' I see trauma everywhere. I see it in every kid sent to my office for a behavior incident. I see it when I walk these halls. I see it when I talk to parents. I even see it in the eyes of many of our teachers," Dr. Griffin stated.

Mrs. Vaughn reflected, "Trauma is everywhere we look in our community."

Dr. Griffin continued: "Every grade level has one or two students facing situations similar to what Caleb is facing. I feel stuck in an outdated model of education as we continue to discipline and teach these students in ways that no longer make any sense. I'm a little jealous of you."

"Because of my huge paycheck?" Mrs. Vaughn tried to inject a little humor into the conversation.

Dr. Griffin smiled, sat back, and took a drink of her coffee. "While I know you see many areas for continued improvement, and Dr. Rodriguez continues to challenge us to think differently, you were able to transform your classroom and teaching to match our learning about trauma."

Mrs. Vaughn thought she knew where Dr. Griffin was going and tried a complex reflection, "Right. I'm trying to take concrete steps to evolve my teaching practices, and I'm getting some positive results. Unfortunately, you oversee a system still approaching student behavior and learning from an outdated paradigm."

Mrs. Vaughn paused long enough to get a nod from Dr. Griffin. "You know, I am so busy working on implementing these concepts that I didn't realize that we are all still working to support an antiquated system that doesn't work for many of our students and continues to inflict harm on our students with trauma."

"Every minute, every hour, every day, every week, I live in the knowledge that, as a school, we are not giving these kids what they really need." A sad look, bordering on despair, came over Dr. Griffin's face. She continued, "It's hard to work in a system that desperately needs change, and at the same time, I know better than to force a major change on my staff mid-year."

Mrs. Vaughn was about to offer another reflection, but Dr. Griffin continued. "Yes, I know I need to practice patience and approach the situation strategically. My problem is that I haven't figured out how to feel okay with the present or how to get to sleep at night. The faces of the kids we are failing haunt my thoughts." Dr. Griffin said taking another big gulp of coffee, hoping the caffeine might help with her constant fatigue from lack of sleep.

"If anyone can create a trauma-sensitive school, you can. This challenge isn't your first rodeo, and no one is respected as much as you are by our staff. Most of us would follow you over a cliff if you told us it was the right thing for the kids. We also trust you enough to know you wouldn't force us to change without including us in the process." Mrs. Vaughn wasn't sure how this affirmation would sit with Dr. Griffin.

"Thanks, Carey."

"Might I offer a suggestion?" Mrs. Vaughn asked.

"Of course."

"Winter break is coming up. I'll need a week to breathe; however, after that, I would love to spend some time planning out a strategy with you. While I know this is only happening in my class and Ms. Smith's, there is a buzz about Caleb's success, and people are curious. I feel comfortable enough now to talk about what I'm doing and why I'm doing it. Hopefully, that would get a few other people interested." Mrs. Vaughn paused.

Dr. Griffin smiled, "I really appreciate it. You are the perfect teacher to model what a trauma-sensitive classroom could look like in our school. Do you think Emma would join us?"

They both chuckled, and Mrs. Vaughn added, "Try to keep her away! I know she is in town over the break."

Mrs. Vaughn needed to pick her kids up from the library, so she summarized the conversation before she left the office. "Let me make sure I have our plan right. We'll find some time, maybe a day or two, the second week of winter break to meet and strategize over how to bring in more staff into our trauma-sensitive initiative. In the meantime, we will both be practicing mindful breathing and reminding ourselves that we are on the cutting edge of a new paradigm in education, and effective change takes a strong strategy and patience."

Dr. Griffin smiled, "Sounds about right." As Mrs. Vaughn got up, Dr. Griffin added one more thing, "And Carey, nice job using OARS on me!"

"Thanks," Mrs. Vaughn said with a sly smile.

On a snowy December day in that beautiful stretch between Christmas and New Year's, Mrs. Vaughn, Ms. Smith, Dr. Griffin, and Dr. Rodriguez turned the staff lounge into ground zero for planning a school transformation. Everyone seemed ready and excited to jump into the planning.

Dr. Griffin started the ball rolling, "You all impressed the heck out of me this semester. I want to take a moment to thank the two of you," looking at Mrs. Vaughn and Ms. Smith, "for taking a leadership role in this effort. Dr. Rodriguez, I also want to thank you for volunteering your time and energy. With that, I'll hand it over to you."

Dr. Rodriguez had dreamed of this day for several years. She worked with several schools who were interested in the research and information on trauma, but none to this point were as bought in as Dr. Griffin's team. "Thanks, Dr. Griffin. It is a true honor to work with you all. I'm so excited to move from research to action on the school level. I think a good place to start is to use the knowledge we learned about trauma to create a list of what concrete approaches and services we can provide. We really want to focus on those kids we have identified and help them heal from their trauma and succeed academically."

Dr. Griffin, Mrs. Vaughn, and Ms. Smith threw out a variety of ideas. Dr. Rodriguez challenged them not to let financial, structural, or staff-capacity issues block any possible solutions at this stage of the process. As they progressed, certain areas of focus began to emerge, with action steps supporting each area.

Eventually, there was a pause. Dr. Rodriguez, who was frantically writing ideas down on different pieces of flip-chart paper, used the silence to remove the sheets from the easel and tape each one to the wall. No one had realized the extent of the work they had done or the ambitious path they had set for themselves and the school until the whole picture manifested in front of them.

Dr. Rodriguez sensed that the end product was starting to overwhelm the group. "Wow, we did some work today! I think this is an excellent place to end today." Everyone nodded their heads in agreement, as their excitement started to yield to exhaustion.

Dr. Rodriguez continued, "It seems like the following focus areas provide us with a way to organize our efforts." Dr. Rodriguez wrote down *Family Partnerships, Access to Support & Resources, Trauma-Sensitive Classrooms, Staff Self-Care & Well-being, Trauma-Sensitive School Culture*, and T*rauma-Sensitive School Policies, Procedures, and Protocols* on a new piece of flip-chart paper.

Dr. Griffin was impressed with the list. "Action plan time. I feel like we have really dedicated a lot of time to implementing trauma-sensitive classroom approaches already with what Dr. Rodriguez taught us and the work Emma and Carey did to transform their classrooms. Dr. Rodriguez, maybe you and I could look at our professional-development schedule and find some time for you to train our entire staff? Maybe a short training this year and a more in-depth one at the beginning of next year?"

Dr. Rodriguez nodded in agreement.

"Great," Dr. Griffin continued. "I would also like to suggest we tackle a focus area each month, starting with family partnerships."

Mrs. Vaughn agreed, "I would love to start there. One of the nagging things about my understanding of trauma is our inability to give families what they need to help kids like Caleb. We are quick to demonize his mother, but we know her life is basically one long traumatic event."

Mrs. Smith added to Mrs. Vaughn's argument, "I agree. Sure, a trauma-sensitive classroom is a vast improvement over our traditional approaches to students with trauma. But so many go home to chaos, neglect, poverty, and even abuse. I'm worried that only using trauma-sensitive practices in the school setting will not be enough to offset years of trauma at home. We must figure out a way to help these families, or our students with trauma will probably become the next generation of struggling parents who might have a hard time being the parents their children need."

"Sounds like we have a starting point," Dr. Rodriguez said while circling *Family Partnerships* on the flip chart.

"Well done, team," said Dr. Griffin. "Let's leave this for now. Enjoy your evening, and let's come back together next month and start with family partnerships."

All agreed, and with the sense of exhaustion that comes after a good day's work, headed out to enjoy the rest of their day and winter break.

CHAPTER 8
Engaging Families as Partners

Challenges abound in transforming a traditional school environment into a trauma-sensitive one. Perhaps the greatest one involves changing the institutional focus from student-centered to family-centered; focusing on both families and the child is termed a "two-generation approach." Ever since we first entered the educational profession, we have heard people say, "Not a surprise that kid is a mess. You should meet his family," or "With parents like that, no wonder that kid is a train wreck," or "We do everything right, and she progresses each day; then she goes home, and all our success disappears overnight."

Students from traumatic, neglectful, or chaotic home environments do lose much of their progress once they go home at night. The survival traits needed to exist outside of school will prevent most children from developing the mental focus, emotional regulation, and academic curiosity required for success in the classroom. Considering what we now know about trauma, we face a crucial choice. We either continue to see our responsibility as limited to the time the student is in school, or we expand our focus.

It is time we realize that every child has a human right to a safe home environment. For too long, schools operated with the student as the sole recipient of the services. We must challenge ourselves to expand the focus of our resources to support families in need of help. Changing to a two-generation approach will not happen overnight. What might seem like a small adjustment in focus takes a different type of mindset, as well as additional resources and funding.

Now that we understand that an unhealthy home environment dramatically limits the ability of a student to develop, it is time for schools to rethink our traditional approach with families. We understand that this change will take a great deal of energy and advocacy from our school community. The lives and futures of millions of children depend on our making this crucial change.

Moving forward, we will use the word 'family' to represent parents, caregivers, foster parents, kinship providers, and others who fill the familial and parental roles for our students.

Partners, not Scapegoats

The actions and behaviors of individual families often become more frustrating than the behavioral challenges exhibited by our students. Not showing up to conferences or Individualized Education Plan (IEP) meetings, not helping their child with homework or projects, and getting frustrated with teachers when asked to participate in their child's education are just a few ways that family interactions cause frustration.

On the other extreme, some families seem overdemanding. They are frustrated that their child is not reading several levels above grade level and blame teachers every time something doesn't go perfectly. These families seem to forget that the teacher and school are responsible for more than just meeting the needs of their child.

While most families fall in the healthy middle between the detached and overbearing, those on the extremes frustrate teachers with their absence or insistence on dominating a teacher's already limited time. If school staff are not careful, a 'them' versus 'us' mentality starts to emerge. Families may become one of the biggest headaches vexing the modern educator. Unfortunately, some of the families who need the most help exist in these extremes.

It takes minimal effort to put the trauma-sensitive lens, developed in earlier chapters, on the family behavior that drives school staff nuts. So many of these families are carrying around pain and show traits from their own traumatic upbringing. Many of these parents or caregivers were raised by parents who were not able to establish healthy attachments, so they experienced abuse and neglect in their childhood. For most, they parent their children the way they were parented (Harris, 2018; Hughes, 2017).

What if the vast majority of neglectful, abusive, or extremely overdemanding families exhibit these behaviors because they never received the help they needed as children to deal with their trauma? Then as they became caregivers, they inherently used the attachment style and lessons their parents taught them to raise their own children in a similar way. In many families, these academic, social, and economic struggles go back generations. Many of the frustrating student behaviors that show up in our schools and classrooms are the product of traits and attachment styles that were passed down from previous generations.

The challenge in front of us is clear. We must invest time, resources, and energy into helping the students and their families heal. We must commit to establishing new ways of thinking and approaching parents and families, or realize that we are failing yet another generation. Someday the "bad kid" will grow up and become that "terrible parent." Schools are ideally positioned to identify families that need help and facilitate getting them the help that they need so that their child can succeed and break detrimental generational patterns.

A Continuum of Family Engagement

In their book *Beyond the Bake Sale: The Essential Guide to Family/School Partnerships*, Henderson, Mapp, Johnson, and Davies (2007) present a continuum of family involvement and engagement they saw in schools. They break schools down into *Fortress Schools, Come If We Call Schools, Open-Door Schools*, and *Partnership Schools*. With some small adjustments accounting for what we know about trauma's impact on students and families, we believe their concept of *Partnership Schools* provides a goal for trauma-sensitive schools to work toward in partnering with families. First, let's review the concepts of *Fortress, Come If We Call*, and *Open-Door Schools*.

Fortress Schools. These schools believe that families do not belong in schools. Poor parenting and dysfunctional families get the blame for students' academic and behavioral problems. The school focuses all its energy on what happens during school hours and within school walls. In

Fortress Schools, families are asked not to bother the school staff. Family involvement in school activities is discouraged.

Come If We Call Schools. In *Come If We Call Schools*, family involvement is highly dependent on what is convenient for the school. Families who are better off financially and who have flexible schedules attend more events; however, the schedules of working families are rarely taken into consideration when scheduling. Outside the limited opportunities for involvement, families are expected to find the resources to support their children's needs independently. The school staff provides little or no support, even when the student's behavioral issues are negatively impacting both the school environment and their academic achievement.

Open-Door Schools. These schools provide a variety of volunteer opportunities and activities for families. At this point on the continuum, the school works to involve families in a meaningful way in the education of their children. *Open-Door Schools* strive for inclusivity. These schools value the diverse cultural, socioeconomic, and linguistic backgrounds of their families. Staff communicates proactively with families, not just reactively when problems arise. The school creates partnerships in the community for students struggling with trauma, mental-health, or medical issues and refers students for help when issues occur (Henderson et al., 2007).

Each step we take down the continuum is a step in a positive direction. However, even *Open-Door Schools* only *involve* families. Our knowledge about trauma challenges us to go one step further to genuinely *engage* families and create *Partnership Schools* that are also trauma-sensitive. Larry Ferlazzo (2011) brilliantly sets forth the shift from involvement to engagement:

> To create the kinds of school–family partnerships that raise student achievement, improve local communities, and increase public support, we need to understand the difference between family involvement and family engagement. One of the dictionary definitions of involve is 'to enfold or envelope,' whereas one of the meanings of engage is 'to come together and interlock.' Thus, involvement implies doing to; in contrast, engagement implies doing with.

Trauma-sensitive schools spend a great deal of effort engaging families in their community. Establishing a true partnership requires concrete actions maintained over long periods of time. Henderson et al. (2007) provide five initiatives for schools who strive to become *Partnership Schools:* Building Relationships, A Team Approach, Sharing Power, Addressing Differences, and Supporting Advocacy.

Building Relationships

The importance of relationships and trust echo throughout this book and again play a central role when working effectively with families. Many family members view the schools their children attend as part of a more extensive system that does not value their input or respect their dignity as human beings. Many families perceive they were treated poorly or even traumatized in other systems, including criminal justice, social services, immigration, or health care. Unless the school takes an active approach to family engagement, these families naturally assume their family will experience similar disrespect and hardship when dealing with the school.

Building trust and relationships begins with a focus on creating a welcoming environment for families when they do choose to engage with the school. Many other systems treat people as problems or burdens, and customer service is something rarely considered. An excellent place to start building a partnership is asking, "How do we show our families that they are vital assets to the success of their children and the entire school?" Modern educational practices require schools to work harder to demonstrate this to families.

In many districts, family members must get a background check to enter the school when students are present. School buildings are evolving into highly secure locked-down facilities where doors are locked and families must show official identification to get "buzzed in." While these steps ensure the safety of students and school staff, it also actively communicates that families are potential threats to the security and lives of students and school staff. This reality is especially hard for family members with criminal records or fears about deportation due to their immigration status. Background checks are embarrassing or scary, and many will forgo involvement in their children's education to avoid humiliation.

While school security will likely continue to increase, the challenge for school staff is to make the family experience as welcoming as possible around these restrictions. Marked parking areas for families and visitors, friendly signs in the languages spoken by the families at the school, hallways decorated with student work, and well-thought-out color and paint choices are all ways of appreciating the family experience. Ensuring that security procedures are simple and clearly communicated to all families will help people feel more welcomed and less apprehensive. Take a moment to walk through the school with a mindset of a parent touring it for the first time. What messages does the physical space send to your families and community members? (Henderson et al., 2007)

While the physical space provides opportunities to communicate the value and importance of families, the most salient aspect of a school becomes evident when observing how the school staff treats family members. The administrative staff at the school play a crucial role in ensuring that families feel like valued assets and welcomed at the school. Whether over the phone or face-to-face, the power and influence of family-administrative contacts are some of the most critical interactions when helping families establish trust with the school.

Great administrative staff are gold and make everyone's experience better. A smile, a simple polite greeting, listening to concerns, and just being a friendly face in the office all help set the stage for a positive experience at the school. A trauma-sensitive school understands and supports its administrative staff, as they value their importance to the school's culture and the families' experience.

As mentioned in earlier chapters, people with trauma grapple with transitions. Critical transitions, such as starting a new school year or when new families enroll at the school for the first time, are opportunities to build trust and address concerns. As Will Rogers said, "You never get a second chance to make a first impression."

We recommend that schools establish a "Welcome Committee" comprised of teachers and families. This committee takes responsibility for reaching out and welcoming new families when they enroll throughout the school year. The members of this committee volunteer as a point person for new families to answer any questions and provide guidance on how to access school resources.

Meaningful events like back-to-school nights and open houses offer families opportunities to engage with the school and their children's education. Aside from general-classroom and grade-level presentations, it is essential that the school leadership, special teachers, mental-health and social workers, and specialists, such as special-education teachers, occupational therapists, and speech-language therapists, are all highly visible and available during these events. Meeting the people behind these resources and services will help families feel more comfortable accessing them if needed throughout the school year.

Transitioning new families provides an opportunity to set the student and family up for maximum success. Welcoming phone calls, individual tours, detailed descriptions of opportunities to partner with the school, and opportunities for new students to engage are all ways to set up for a great first day. They show that the school values the family and student as assets to their new community. Some families, especially those who experienced trauma in other systems, might hesitate to take advantage of the invitation to meet in the school environment. When this is the case, offer to meet them at a neutral location or even suggest a home visit. While this takes some additional effort on the part of the school staff, overcoming past negative experiences has lasting effects on their involvement in their child's education (Henderson et al., 2007).

Team Approach to Academic Achievement

A student's academic achievement is a team effort, especially for students struggling with trauma. The stronger the communication between teachers, school staff, therapists, social workers, parents, older siblings, and other caregivers, the greater the opportunity for cognitive growth. Outreach to families pays off for the student and the school. Studies demonstrate dramatic jumps in attendance and standardized test results when families feel they are an essential part of their child's education (Henderson & Mapp, 2002; U.S. Department of Education, 2001).

What works? The U.S. Department of Education (2001) showed Title I elementary schools that scheduled in-person meetings at the beginning of the school year, sent families strategies to help their children on assignments at home, and telephoned routinely to provide updates on academics and behaviors (both positive and negative) saw up to a 50%

improvement in student performance in math and reading.

The primary-school experience provides an opportunity to help families learn how to effectively engage with teachers and school staff throughout their child's school years. Many families, due to immigration status, past negative experiences, shame associated with homelessness, poverty, past involvement with child welfare, or absence of their own personal success at school will often lack confidence in their ability to engage productively or advocate in their child's education. Helping these families find their voice and confidence will serve their child well for years to come.

Back-to-school nights and other events provide school staff with an opportunity to coach families on how to effectively ask questions and advocate for their child's needs. A critical and too-often-overlooked first step is establishing a shared language. "Proficient," "standards," "standardized test scores," and other academic lingo are mysteries to many families. Going through key terms helps build confidence and allows families to not feel lost when these terms repeat throughout the school year.

Once a common language is established, help families know what key academic questions to ask throughout the school year. Henderson et al. (2007) provide important questions that families might want to ask. When providing these questions to families, make sure they know when and why they should ask these questions, and what different answers might mean.

- Is my child performing at a proficient level (up to standard) in basic skills? If not, is my child above or below? What is your plan for helping my child catch up? How can I help?
- What do my child's test scores show? What are their strengths and weaknesses?
- Can we go over some examples of my child's work? Will you explain the grading standards?
- Does my child need extra help in any area? What do you recommend? How can we work together to help my child?
- Does my child do all the assigned work, including homework?
- Does my child seem to like school and get along with classmates?
- Have you noticed any changes in my child over the year?

Before problems do arise, proactively establish clear and transparent processes for conflict resolution with families. One proactive strategy for addressing potential conflict is for the school or district to work with their Parent Teacher Association/Organization (PTA/PTO) to create a student and family Bill of Rights. The Bill of Rights should clearly outline what the family should expect from the school regarding the treatment of their child, teacher/family communication, and disciplinary action. It also includes specifics on how to handle conflict with teachers and other school staff. Many of the same components that schools use in implementing restorative justice for student conflict should guide their family conflict-resolution approaches.

Another critical step in establishing family engagement is to involve families in making critical decisions. While PTA/PTOs are a good start, many schools find that the same small group of families with flexible work schedules or those who are already highly involved tend to dominate these groups. Outreach specifically directed toward immigrant families and those from diverse cultures will help ensure that materials and curricula honor all cultures that walk into the school. Schools, students, and communities thrive when families and school staff see each other as partners in the academic achievement of the children in their community.

Schools that take family engagement seriously create a natural opportunity to train families on critical parenting approaches that support social, emotional, and cognitive development. Parenting workshops could include topics like trauma, child development and attachment, serve-and-return communication, stress management, effective discipline at home, supporting academic achievement, and other issues specific to the community. Work with family members to identify issues and find internal or community expertise to provide training. Setting the expectation that the school is a learning place for families as well as students increases engagement in the school's success. Schools, families, and students thrive when everyone works together in the best interests of children and the community (Bennett, 2018; Henderson et al., 2007).

Addressing Trauma at Home

Few people would argue against the concept of family engagement. There is another challenge inherent in the shift to trauma-sensitive schools. The more schools assess for trauma and connect with the home life of their students, the more likely the chance that school staff will discover the the traumas of their students and needs of families.

Over both our careers, we have both been legally mandated to make dozens of calls and reports to Child Protective Services concerning the abuse and neglect that our students experienced at the hands of their family members. We spent months building trust and safety with students and these families. At times it was gut-wrenching to take the required steps that we knew would damage, if not permanently destroy, the relationships we worked so hard to create. Even harder at times, after we reported, we got little or no feedback on the actions taken to keep the students we cared so deeply about safe and to prevent future trauma.

From our positions as school staff, the current system seems to painfully separate us from children, families, and their trauma, as if school staff existed in a silo. The system fails to recognize teachers and school staff as partners in ensuring student well-being and safety while helping them recover from their traumatic experiences. So, we report the incident and hope that someone we might never meet or talk to takes proper action. It feels like we throw something of incredible importance out into the universe and pray that something positive happens.

Obviously, we do not encourage anyone to act against state laws and district policies around confidentiality. However, schools must rethink this approach to helping families and students. As the trauma research forces schools to shift thinking about student behavior, they need to approach families with the same empathy and understanding. Part of this shift in thinking challenges school staff to stop viewing abuse and neglect by families as a signal that they lack the necessary skills or the emotional stability to parent their children effectively.

Many abusive or neglectful family-members' parenting styles evolved out of their own traumatic experiences and their families' inability to adequately care for them. Families inflict trauma when they lack the skills to manage their stress and frustration effectively. The question for those seeking to create trauma-sensitive schools becomes: how do we help families manage stress and build skills to parent our students effectively?

While schools will continue to report abuse, the critical change for trauma-sensitive schools is what happens next. Trauma-sensitive schools ensure they follow up with families after a report. They work to rebuild trust and rally all available resources within the school to support the student and family as much as possible. Too often, when students need schools at their best, policies and procedures force professionals to stay in their silos.

Ideally, the school staff, community agencies, the family, and the child would come together to form a treatment team. This team would meet and communicate on an ongoing basis through daily reports and calls to family, regular meetings, and open communication (with some limited restrictions, such as confidentiality in mental-health therapy). When the barriers to effective communication disappear, the team maximizes its efforts to ensure the child's safety, well-being, and academic achievement. Although the regulations of many states and school districts make open communication difficult, we are not encouraging anyone to act contrary to them; however, we need to advocate for change, while maximizing opportunities for communication and partnership where they do exist.

A Call

Mrs. Vaughn sat like a statue staring at the black phone in her classroom. She promised herself that she would make this call. Every excuse she tried to come up with played itself out, and she couldn't procrastinate any longer.

Two days earlier, the team met to discuss how trauma-sensitive schools approached family engagement. Dr. Rodriguez reviewed *Fortress Schools, Come If We Call Schools, Open-Door Schools,* and *Partnership Schools*. To their collective embarrassment, they were at best a *Come If We Call School*.

Mrs. Vaughn's classroom was no exception. Sure, she was okay if people like Malik's parents reached out about volunteering in her class. As she thought back over the last several years, the only family volunteers for the classroom, PTA, or help with holiday parties were from the families of her best-behaved students. They were all intrinsically motivated, felt confident in approaching her to offer their time, and were fluent English speakers.

She realized that she was working under the assumption that other families were not as invested in their children's education, due to their own struggles or general lack of interest. Why bother to reach out to families who do not even show up for parent conferences? Mrs. Vaughn struggled with the truth that she had created a *Come If I Call* classroom in a school with a similar philosophy.

On her computer screen, she had contact information for Caleb's mom, Hannah. While Caleb's school behavior continued to improve, he was still back and forth between his uncle and mom. His cousins, Jeremiah and Zion, enjoyed their roles on his team. It was amazing how these two less-than-traditional role models brought a mix of love and structure into Caleb's life!

His mental-health therapist "loved working with that child," which was the first time anyone in the school had ever uttered those words about Caleb. While Caleb had good days and bad days, overall, his behavior improved a little each week. His improvement included better emotional regulation and an increased ability to focus on tasks. Mrs. Vaughn would love to see inside his young brain, as she knew things were changing rapidly in that little head of his.

Even though the nature of the call was to provide positive news on Caleb's steady progress, her dread came from her anger at his mom. It was easy for Mrs. Vaughn to demonize the woman whose actions traumatized a student she grew fonder of each day.

Okay Carey, dial the stupid phone. She picked up the receiver and dialed the number. As it rang, she took a deep breath.

"Yeah," a weak voice came across the line.

"Hi, it's Mrs. Vaughn, Caleb's teacher." She wasn't sure if his mom even knew her name, which in hindsight was demeaning.

"What did he do now?" Hannah said with a hint of anger in her voice.

"A lot actually," but before she could continue with the great news, Hannah interrupted.

"I guess you all are suspending him again. How many days this time?"

"Oh, no. Actually, Caleb is doing amazingly well." Amazing was a little bit of a stretch, but true for his progress throughout the year. "I know the only times you've heard from the school this year was when Dr. Griffin called you with bad news." Mrs. Vaughn took another breath.

"Doesn't seem like anyone over there has a problem calling social services on me," Hannah said with resigned anger.

"That is true. When we heard about the abuse from his…" Mrs. Vaughn could not think of the right word.

"His mom's abusive boyfriend," Hannah filled in the blank.

"We had to act. Please know, I hate how sometimes the regulations set us up as enemies instead of partners for the kids we both love," Mrs. Vaughn commented.

"I just hope you never have the state come to take your children away," Hannah's anger seemed to fade to sadness.

"I can't imagine how hard that was." Mrs. Vaughn thought if OARS worked with the students, she would give it a try here.

"You have no idea. Just surviving most days is hard enough; then there's all the trouble with Caleb."

"You are juggling a lot. I'm sure getting calls from Dr. Griffin adds even more stress." Mrs. Vaughn tried a complex reflection.

"Yeah, pretty sure no one at this point thinks I'm a decent mom or person," stated Hannah.

"Well, I think you raised a pretty amazing young man," Mrs. Vaughn said with pride, as she felt herself choke up a little. "Hannah…"

"Yeah."

Mrs. Vaughn took another breath, "I'm sorry that it took me over half the school year to reach out to you. I'm sorry because I assumed you were not invested in Caleb's academics. I'm sorry for never inviting you to school events. I'm sorry that this call is the first time you are hearing my voice." Mrs. Vaughn's apologies were not exclusively for Hannah. It was for all the moms and dads she assumed did not care about their child's education or even for their child at all.

There was just silence. Both women used the silence to hide their hurt from one another.

"Hannah," Mrs. Vaughn said, after 45 seconds that seemed like 45 minutes.

"Yeah."

"I have a little over five months left with Caleb, and I want you to feel like this classroom and school are open to you. I would love to work with you as a team for Caleb."

"Does that mean I could join Caleb's team?" Hannah asked with a mix of curiosity, hurt, and anticipation.

"You know about his team?" She was horrified that a team had been working with Caleb for over a month. Apparently, since the state was involved, no one felt like it was important to keep Hannah in the loop.

"Caleb never shuts up about it, but I'm not sure I'm getting the full picture," commented Hannah.

"Well, after the…" Mrs. Vaughn searched for the word.

"Abuse," Hannah filled in the blank.

"Yes. We put together a team consisting of his cousins, a social worker, a school mental-health professional, and a few teachers, with Dr. Griffin in the mix as well. I again apologize for not communicating sooner about our efforts to help Caleb," explained Mrs. Vaughn.

"Thanks for the apology. Caleb can't stop talking about it. I felt really left out."

"I'm sure that was tough. I wonder if I could make a suggestion," Mrs. Vaughn asked.

"Sure."

"I think it would be great if we got Caleb's permission for you to join the team. Bringing you on at some point is crucial; however, I want to make sure the team remains a safe place for him to talk about stuff outside of school as well." Mrs. Vaughn wondered if she had gone too far.

"That makes sense. Caleb asked me several times already if I would come to a team meeting, so I'm assuming it will be cool with him."

"I'm sure he'll be thrilled. Hannah, I know our school might not seem like a safe place for you with everything that's happened this year. We probably both feel like we've been working more against each other than together. I would love to meet with you and Caleb at the school to go over all his progress. However, if the school doesn't seem like the best place, I'm happy to meet at the diner down the street from your house."

"Thanks for that offer. If I'm accepted onto Caleb's team, though, I need to start being okay going back to that school building," Hannah stated.

"I would love that. I wonder if it would be okay if Caleb joined us. I think he would love to show off in front of his mom. How about a week from this Thursday after school?" Mrs. Vaughn asked with hope in her voice.

"Of course! Listen, I have to run, but thanks for the call. I guess it probably wasn't easy."

"Thanks, Hannah. I am really looking forward to Thursday," Mrs. Vaughn finished with words filled with truth and hope.

CHAPTER 9
Accessing Support & Resources

A student cannot overcome childhood trauma without a great deal of help and support. Most families often need a similar level of support to deal effectively with their child's pain and suffering, while maintaining their own well-being in the process. If a trauma happens outside the family system, the entire family needs to heal along with their child. In homes where trauma occurs in the family system, the family needs an additional level of support to learn new ways of parenting, handling stress, and how to create a safe environment and secure attachment.

As argued in the last chapter, schools play a crucial role in identifying trauma and rallying around the student and family to support the healing and growth process. The sooner the child receives mental-health services and support after the traumatic event, the faster the transition from pain to healing. In this chapter, we explore how trauma-sensitive schools connect students and families to the support and resources they need.

Assessing for Trauma

In an ideal world, we would hand out trauma assessments at regular intervals during the school year. Schools could then continue monitoring students who experienced trauma and identify new cases or instances of traumatic experiences. While this approach is feasible for older students, the verbal limitations as well as cognitive and emotional development of children in the primary years makes implementing standardized trauma assessments difficult. Without an efficient or effective way to assess the entire student body, those working with students in primary grades must take a more creative approach.

One way to identify many children who could benefit from mental-health trauma treatment is to ask parents. Not all parents will truthfully answer the questions, especially if the trauma is happening at home. However, the answers the school does get back will provide them with a starting point and a group of families to help immediately. Here is a sample letter that a school could send home with students. Please ensure that it meets all district and state regulations and policies before distributing.

Recent research has shown a powerful link between childhood trauma, behavior, mental health, medical health, and academic success. The good news is that trauma is treatable. The right mix of support and resources helps children become more resilient and develop the strength and confidence that will serve them well throughout their lives. As part of our efforts to help our students grow emotionally and socially, as well as academically, we want to ensure that our students who experience trauma and their families get the help and resources they need.

According to The National Child Traumatic Stress Network, the following situations might traumatize a young child and cause some resulting behaviors.

Possible traumas:

- Physical, emotional, or sexual abuse
- Abandonment or neglect
- Death or loss of a loved one
- Life-threatening illness in a caregiver
- Witnessing domestic violence
- Automobile accidents or other serious accidents
- Bullying
- Life-threatening health situations and/or painful medical procedures
- Witnessing or experiencing community violence (e.g., shootings, stabbings, robbery, or fighting at home, in the neighborhood, or at school)
- Witnessing police activity or having a close relative incarcerated
- Potentially life-threatening natural disasters

- Acts or threats of terrorism
- Homelessness, housing instability, and hunger

Resulting behaviors to look out for:

- Separation anxiety or clinginess toward caregivers or regression in previously mastered stages of development (e.g., baby talk or bedwetting/toileting accidents)
- Lack of developmental progress (e.g., not progressing at the same level as peers)
- Re-creating the traumatic event (e.g., repeatedly talking about, "playing" out, or drawing the event)
- Difficulty at naptime or bedtime (e.g., avoiding sleep, waking up, or nightmares)
- Increased somatic complaints (e.g., headaches, stomachaches, or overreacting to minor bumps and bruises)
- Changes in behavior (e.g., changes in appetite, unexplained absences, angry outbursts, decreased attention, or withdrawal)
- Over- or underreacting to physical contact, bright lighting, sudden movements, or loud sounds (e.g., bells, slamming doors, or sirens)
- Changes in school performance
- Increased moodiness
- Anxiety, fear, or worry about the safety of self and others, worry about a recurrence of the traumatic event, or new fears (e.g., fear of the dark, animals, or monsters)
- Statements and questions about death and dying

Not all the above situations will traumatize every child. Similarly, not all children exhibiting one of the resulting behaviors do so because they experienced a traumatic event. Our goal is to get every child who has gone through a difficult time the help that they need to ensure they do not carry the pain into the future.

If you are concerned about your child or if one of the above things happens to your child during the school year, we are here to help. As part of our efforts, *Insert School Staff name and position here* is the dedicated contact person to help ensure all our students and families get the resources and support they need. Please feel free to contact them at the phone number, email, or address below with any questions or concerns.

You may remain anonymous if you decide not to state your name. If you email or mail in your concerns, *Insert name here* will reach out and set up a time to meet or talk over the phone. All communications are confidential unless there is a reason to believe that your child or another's safety or life is in danger (*include any state or district confidentiality procedures here as well*).

When sending out a letter like the one above, be ready. Make sure the contact person has the right training and capacity to handle the influx of communications and can respond appropriately to each. A school might consider sending the letter out to one grade or even one classroom at a time until they get a handle on the response rate. Next, we'll discuss how to ensure adequate resources and support are available for the families that respond.

Unfortunately, due to their shame or fear, many parents will not disclose trauma. Alternately, assess children who are struggling behaviorally, socially, or academically by asking questions mentioned in earlier chapters. School staff might check to see if they feel safe. Ask if there is anything they want to share with you. Vigilant eyes and the letter home will help you identify many of the children who need help.

Resources and Support

While hope exists for everyone, the sooner trauma is recognized and treated, the less pain the student experiences. In most cases, they will suffer fewer and less-severe symptoms. A trauma-sensitive school develops the capacity and expertise to assess and identify when trauma occurs. The next challenge for a trauma-sensitive school is to create a resource-rich menu to match services to the needs of their students and families.

Trauma-sensitive schools maximize their position within the community and neighborhood in a way that helps students and families get the resources and support they need. One of the essential aspects of a *Partnership School* mentioned in the last chapter is the creation of a family center. The concept of a family center is central to ensuring children and families struggling with trauma get the help and resources they need to survive and eventually thrive (Henderson et al., 2007).

Unfortunately, due to past negative experiences, stigmas exist about accessing many services. This list may include mental-health and healthcare services due to immigration status, cultural perspectives, or poverty. Many families are just trying to survive their economic, psychological, and social struggles. They are afraid and unwilling to access resources in the community and may lack time to explore their options. Since their children spend so much time in school, school staff often develop a level of trust that families do not hold for other service providers. Trauma-sensitive schools utilize this trust to provide or connect families to the services, resources, and support they need.

A family center is a tangible way for the school to support families and promote aspects of their student's wellness. Depending on the needs, struggles, and demographics of a community, a family center will look different, depending on the specific needs of that school's families. The shift in thinking about the school building being only a physical space for academic learning to its including a resource hub for families poses the most significant challenge for school and district administration to consider in their journey toward trauma-sensitive schools. Assisting families in accessing services to improve their health is the right thing to do for our students. It also improves their overall academic performance (Bruns, Walrath, Glass-Siegel, & Weist, 2004; Roche & Strobach, 2016).

A school-based family center utilizes a mix of community-based and district-funded services to provide a one-stop shop for families. It is designed to help them meet their basic needs, as well as access the mental-health and medical services necessary to heal trauma. Consider that 1.3 million students in the United States' public-school system are homeless and 13 million children lack food security, often going to bed and coming to school hungry (Bridgeland & Raikes, 2018; Seaton, 2017).

Schools have an ethical obligation to ensure all children in our country access their fundamental human rights of food and housing. In many communities, resources such as food banks and family shelters exist to address these needs. School-based family centers provide a bridge connecting identified families to life-saving resources.

In an ideal situation, the school would provide space and administrative oversight to fill the family center with community agencies. Potential services could include support, resources, medical care, therapy, adult education, tutoring, mentor programs, language translation, education services, and after-school programming for students whose families work outside the typical 9 am to 5 pm work hours. These partnerships are ideal, as many of these agencies already receive funding to provide these services. Collaborations create effective ways to engage communities, families, and students who could benefit from them. However, if a community lacks a resource that students and their families desperately need, the school must then problem-solve with the district and community partners to find funding to address the need.

Few would argue that a school-based family center sounds good in theory. Most schools face a significant challenge in creating a physical space to house these vital resources, let alone the staff and equipment necessary to provide mental-health and social-work services, and medical care. When it comes to space, schools are a fascinating concept to explore in terms of new ways to use that space.

The community builds school buildings funded through tax dollars. However, the vast majority of the time, these immense structures sit empty or underutilized outside of school hours. Our current thinking about schools and school schedules makes it difficult to imagine how a typical school could support a small medical clinic or a team of mental-health professionals. A little creativity, such as a mobile medical van or allowing classrooms to become therapy offices after hours, provides dramatic steps toward giving students what they need to succeed.

Building family centers within schools takes innovative thinking, but school and district staff could succeed if they followed a simple process.

1) List the resources and support needed for students with trauma to succeed socially and academically.
2) List resources that exist in the district already and brainstorm how to maximize existing capacity.
3) With those needs not met by existing capacity, work with the school, district, community social workers, and other experts to identify community organizations that are already funded and operating to address these needs.

4) Create a school or district initiative to formalize partnerships with community agencies.
5) Creatively address crucial issues in the creation of community partnerships. These issues often include funding for additional programming, space utilization, confidentiality agreements, and scheduling. Many social-service and medical providers operate in funding and regulatory environments entirely different from those in education. Working through these issues in advance avoids frustration during implementation.
6) Figure out how to create time and space for the family center to operate on school grounds.
7) If the lack of infrastructure, community resources, and space become an issue, search for grant opportunities and other funding options to build additional capacity.

Let's look at a couple of additional notes for creating community partnerships. Don't expect every community agency to understand the effects of trauma. The trauma research is still relatively new to many in the professions of medicine, social work, psychology, and other related occupations. The school might find themselves in a position to educate community partners, policymakers, and community members on this paradigm-shattering research.

Some community partners are amazing and highly motivated to partner with schools. Others might lack the financial means or creativity to consider such partnerships. For schools and districts in larger and resource-rich communities, several options may exist for the same service. Time spent finding the best partner is time well spent and has the potential to pay off for years, if not decades.

In smaller communities where options are limited, creativity is needed. A partner who is not a good fit for the school's students, family, or school will create headache after headache if they are not willing to adapt and innovate. A district might find it easier to build their own infrastructure and customize it specifically for the school environment and the unique needs of their students and families.

When creating a family center, remember to balance safety with access. A family center invites families to the school in a very different way. The safety of school staff and students remains the top priority. However, whenever possible, family centers should remain open for as many hours as feasible. If possible, a separate entrance and parking area helps family-center staff welcome families into the center without background checks, showing identification, and other school security measures that might turn many families off.

Trauma Treatment

Family centers play a crucial role in connecting families to resources to help meet urgent and basic needs. Whether provided by the district or through community partnerships, families need access to mental-health trauma treatment. Here we provide a brief overview of some of the common goals and approaches that are effective in healing trauma. The realm of trauma treatment is progressing at a rapid and exciting rate. We want to cover the basics to help schools evaluate whether mental-health services are appropriate for your students suffering from trauma.

Traditionally, most people viewed mental-health support in schools as something separate from what happens in the classrooms, at recess, in the lunchroom, or during other activities during the school day. Trauma treatment in trauma-sensitive schools might involve pulling children out of the classroom. However, this approach must include helping the student succeed emotionally, socially, behaviorally, and academically throughout the school day. Trauma-sensitive schools push mental-health support into the classroom, partnering with teachers and school staff as often as they pull students out.

Creating collaboration between mental-health professionals and other school staff allows for a collective focus on helping the student succeed in a variety of school settings as part of their healing experience. This collaboration might focus on a range of issues, but usually includes assisting the student in regulating emotional distress, learning to engage with and trust others, inhibiting risky or ineffective behaviors, and utilizing problem-solving and life-management tactics. Mental-health support helps maximize concepts such as mindfulness, growth mindset, and behavioral management, as presented in Part 2 (Courtois & Ford, 2009).

Helping a struggling student succeed socially and academically is an essential step in many students' growth and healing processes. Healing trauma is a complex and individualized process. Most treatment methods include versions of the following goals:

- Help the student rethink the false notion that one is defective, failing, incompetent, dependent, or damaged
- Create a sense of self as whole, integrated, worthy, and efficacious
- Prevent reenactments of the trauma and revictimization
- Restore an existential sense that life is worth living

There are several critical tasks associated with the healing process. Many younger students struggle to label their emotions. They find it difficult, if not impossible, to put their traumatic experiences into words.

When thinking about trauma treatment for primary-aged students, do not get stuck in the traditional model of talk therapy. The trauma healing might occur through play therapy, yoga, mindfulness, or music or art therapy. Modern mental-health and trauma treatment looks vastly different than the traditional model of two people sitting across from each other and talking.

The first task of most trauma-treatment approaches is emotional regulation. We covered emotional regulation in detail in Part 2. Just as physical and psychological safety is a focus of trauma-sensitive classrooms, the relationship with the therapist plays a central role in healing. Therapy often focuses on working through past attachment and relational problems to create a secure base with the therapist (Courtois & Ford, 2009).

The therapist/student relationship is the model of a secure attachment that many students failed to develop with their parents. The student often brings a negative relationship template into the therapeutic relationship. The therapist works through trust and abandonment issues as a foundational part of treatment, often dedicating many sessions to the relational dynamics before beginning to address the trauma. The therapeutic relationship in trauma treatment provides the student with a new relational model that they can eventually apply in other aspects of their life.

Other essential focuses of the emotional regulation task include awareness and management of fight/flight/freeze responses and retraumatization. The therapist works with the student to identify their traumatic triggers underlying these arousal states and behaviors. Working through trauma triggers is intense and powerful work. Often through this process, the student begins to realize for the first time that they are not a bad or defective person.

In therapy, the student starts to gain some control over their feelings and behaviors. Here the healing begins when the student begins to control their traumatic triggers instead of the triggers controlling them. By integrating mindfulness into the classroom, the teacher supports emotional regulation in therapy (Ogden, Minton, & Pain, 2006).

Specific trauma-treatment approaches handle traumatic memories in different ways. Some treatments enact memories through play, others discuss the memories directly, and still others work through the memories through art or music. All have the goal of taking power away from these memories and returning a sense of control to the student (Foa, Keane, Friedman, & Cohen, 2009).

A powerful, but sometimes necessary, side effect of this step is the emergence of new traumatic memories. As the student starts to gain control over one set of memories, they might open repressed memories. The brain will often suppress memories that are too overwhelming for it to handle, and these memories can remain implicit for many years. These hidden memories still impact the student's thinking, behaviors, and health, even if the student cannot readily access the memory of the actual event.

As the student gains strength in treatment, the brain can release these memories with all the intense emotions, bodily sensations, and images associated with them. While there has been quite a bit of controversy around recovered memories, this misses the point of treatment. Trauma treatment is not about recovering every traumatic memory. Instead, it focuses on building a student's strength to deal with the memories and their emotional power over the student (Van der Kolk, 2014).

The second task in the journey to post-traumatic growth is integration. The mastery of arousal states gives the student a sense of control over themselves and their behaviors. They are no longer victims of their emotions and thoughts. Instead, the student develops mindfulness and other coping skills to regulate emotions more appropriate to their age.

Trauma is a thief. It steals a favorable view of self and the world. In this task, the student works with the therapist to reclaim a positive sense of self by integrating their traumatic experiences into a positive personal narrative or story of their life. To regain control of their narrative, the student must answer the question, "Why did this happen to me?"

As long as the "Why did this happen to me" question goes unanswered, it is difficult to stop the pain and suffering resulting from the experience. Without a positive and coherent personal narrative, the student has no place to put the traumatic experience, which allows the trauma to control the narrative. When the student finds their answer to "Why did this happen to me," they start to regain control of their narrative and their lives (Herman, 1997).

There are often no easy answers to this question, especially for a young child. The key here is to find a meaning for the trauma in the present situation, not in the context of the past. Finding meaning helps make a significant shift. Before integration, the trauma is still in the present, due to the pain and suffering it continues to cause in the student's life. Integration helps put the trauma in its appropriate context, which is to place it as something that happened in the past that is now over.

Once there is a "why," then the therapist works with the student to integrate the "why" into a coherent and integrative narrative of self and the world — finding the "why" puts the trauma in a box. Integration finds where that box fits in the story of the student and their world. It does not take away the impact and devastation that the trauma caused in the past, but dramatically reduces the power it has in the present and future (Foa, Keane, Friedman, & Cohen, 2009).

This shift helps address the fixed mindset and the feeling that the student has no control over their situation or problems. Instead, a growth mindset emerges, along with coping strategies that help the student take responsibility for their behaviors and achievement. Meaning does not come easily or quickly, but when the therapist and student come through this struggle, the growth mindset starts to emerge. The emergence of power where there was once a weakness, purpose where there was previously a sense of being lost, and meaning where there was once only pain is a powerful experience for both student and therapist (Courtois & Ford, 2009; Dweck, 2006; Herman, 1997).

As a growth mindset emerges, the student can now also start to redefine their world. For many students up to this point, trauma created the narrative of the world as a dangerous and harmful place, with people out to hurt the student. The student learns to balance the pain in the world with the joy and hope that it also holds. The student also redefines the role others take in their world. The student identifies the abuser, parents, teachers, and other students as characters with flaws and their own pain. For some students, forgiveness is a part of this step in the journey. The critical task here is retaking the ability to define one's world (Bennett, 2017).

Integration, like emotional regulation, is a difficult task. The journey to post-traumatic growth has no easy steps. In emotional regulation, the student faces their trauma. In integration, they work hard to find meaning and to deal with the loss caused by the trauma.

The final task in the healing journey is post-traumatic growth. Here the therapist works to strategically bring the strength discovered in the first two tasks to the demands and stress of the school environment and the dynamics of one's family and community. The therapist helps the student translate their work in therapy to the greater world.

The combination of knowledge, insight, and judgment creates wisdom, which is not a word usually associated with young people. Trauma treatment focuses on building these attributes in the student and helps them to bring this newfound strength into the world. This process is transformative and, as with any journey worth taking, has inherent challenges. Detours and pitfalls occur along the way, but in the end, the reward is unparalleled.

When It Rains

Dr. Griffin, Dr. Rodriguez, Mrs. Vaughn, and Ms. Smith quickly realized that, when considering integrating trauma sensitive and the *Partnership School* concepts into their school, it would take more than four people. The Trauma-Sensitive Transformation Team, as they started to call themselves, picked up momentum with every day.

Dr. Griffin invited several parents to join, many of whom had little previous involvement in the school. Each grade level chose a representative to join the committee, and Mrs. Vaughn could feel the idea of trauma-sensitive schools turning into a full-blown movement.

The school district sent an assistant superintendent who oversaw social work and mental health in the district to the Trauma-Sensitive Transformation Team. Thanks in significant part to the relentless advocacy of Dr. Griffin, the district agreed to test out the idea of piloting a trauma-sensitive school. If it worked at their school, the district was open to potentially expanding to other schools.

Dr. Rodriguez set up the school as an intern site for several social-work and psychology students from the university. They enthusiastically went to work setting up a family center at the school and providing services to families, under the supervision of the assistant superintendent and Dr. Rodriguez. It felt like everyone's eyes were on the school and, more specifically, Ms. Smith's and Mrs. Vaughn's classrooms.

Mrs. Vaughn was in a rush after school and feeling a little nervous, as Caleb's next meeting with his mom in attendance was fast approaching. However, she could never pass by the emerging family center without checking in with the interns and seeing how the physical space was rapidly developing. Dr. Griffin and the assistant superintendent pulled off a real miracle. They convinced the district to give them a portable classroom unit that another school no longer needed.

The interns and district worked hard to identify and connect with community agencies, filling the structure with brochures and fliers, and more importantly, workspaces where families could connect with professionals in the community. Currently, interns staffed the family center before and after school for about an hour, but were also flexible in making appointments with families who couldn't make those hours. Staff extended evening hours on Thursdays, when many community partners showed up to answer questions that families had about resources. The hope was to add an additional evening each month, until it was open five days a week until 8 pm.

Dr. Griffin acted like a child on Christmas morning. She finally had a place on the school grounds to help improve the home life of her families and students. As Mrs. Vaughn was walking into the family center, Dr. Griffin was coming out. "You can't stay away, either, can you?" Dr. Griffin asked Mrs. Vaughn.

Mrs. Vaughn just smiled and nodded with pride.

"I lost count a decade or so ago of how many times I gave families numbers to reach out to in order to find resources and prayed they would call. Now I walk them over here and introduce them to people who help them right away, with no phone messages, no language barriers, and no excuses. I feel like I've done more good in the last couple of weeks than I usually do in an entire year." A small moment of sadness interjected into her excitement with the last sentence.

Mrs. Vaughn was ready to console her, until she caught sight of a large white RV in the corner of her eye. "Is that it?"

Dr. Griffin turned, and a huge smile came across her face, as a mobile medical unit from the local public hospital pulled into the parking lot. Dr. Griffin never dreamed that a school would ever provide medical services to her students, much less the parents. However, she found the local public hospital was excited to partner with the school one day a week. So many families did not feel like they had access to medical care due to past negative experiences, believing that they couldn't afford it, or because of fear due to their immigration status. Sending the mobile medical unit to the school helped the hospital outreach to their target population and helped get eligible people signed up for the state's insurance program.

A tear fell down Dr. Griffin's cheek. Mrs. Vaughn felt herself start to choke up as well, as the RV parked and a nurse in scrubs walked out. Mrs. Vaughn hugged Dr. Griffin without needing to speak a word.

Finally, Mrs. Vaughn uttered softly, "Well if all this isn't enough, I have a meeting with Caleb's mom right now."

They both felt like bawling their eyes out, but Dr. Griffin needed to welcome the mobile medical providers, and Mrs. Vaughn had a meeting that sounded like a breakthrough on paper, but left her apprehensive at the thought of what the next hour held.

As Mrs. Vaughn hurried to her classroom, she heard Caleb's voice coming from Ms. Smith's room. She peeked her head in to see Caleb excitedly showing off his math work to his mom.

"And this was my last math assignment!" Caleb's excitement touched

Mrs. Vaughn, as she remembered the kid everyone feared just a few months earlier.

"Caleb is one of my star math students. I'm so proud Caleb could make so much progress in such a short time." Ms. Smith's excitement matched Caleb's. "I'm a little jealous. I only get him for math," she said, seeing Mrs. Vaughn in her doorway.

Mrs. Vaughn took a second to let Caleb brag a little more. The appearance of his mother, Hannah, struck her. While they had seen each other frequently when they were in school together, it had been many years since the last time they had seen each other. Hannah looked twenty years older than her age, and her body carried her trauma and addiction. She seemed weighed down and burdened by life. Mrs. Vaughn could see her visibly trying to hold it together in a foreign and probably triggering environment.

"Ms. Smith, you are not trying to steal one of my favorite students, are you?" Mrs. Vaughn said, with the biggest smile she could muster.

"Mrs. Vaughn!" Caleb ran at her full speed and embraced her lower body in a huge hug. She could feel his mix of excitement and fear. Here was a kid who, for a brief moment, had a normal situation with his mom, and was afraid that it would slide away and back into the chaos that was so common at home. Caleb released Mrs. Vaughn and ran over and hugged Ms. Smith with the same energy. Mrs. Vaughn was pleased to see him get all the support and love he could before the meeting.

As the three of them left Ms. Smith's room, Mrs. Vaughn smiled and whispered to Ms. Smith, "You need to go outside to the family center. There is a miracle on four wheels out there that you have to see." Mrs. Vaughn couldn't look at Ms. Smith long, as she started to choke up again. As a veteran teacher, she couldn't remember ever feeling the rush of emotions that the last couple of weeks had brought.

The meeting with Caleb's mom was surprisingly ordinary. While it was apparent that Hannah was doing her best to hold it together, the reports about Caleb's behavior and academic improvement brought smile after smile to her face. Mrs. Vaughn felt like Hannah couldn't outwardly express too much joy, or the floodgates would open, unleashing an unpredictable rush of emotions.

After bringing Hannah up to speed on his progress, Mrs. Vaughn asked, "Caleb, would you mind doing a little homework at your desk so your mom and I can chat for a second? I promise I only have more good stuff to say about you!"

"Sure," Caleb seemed a little hesitant to leave the two of them alone. It seemed he was more worried about his mom's behavior than anything Mrs. Vaughn might say.

"Thanks," Hannah said, trying to fight back the intense emotions rising inside her.

"Your little man has taught me so much this year. I wanted to offer you one thing before you leave. We just opened a family center that offers a wide variety of resources. No pressure, but if you want to take a look before heading home, I know the staff there would love to meet Caleb's mom and help out in any way they can."

Hannah hesitated.

Mrs. Vaughn realized that she was adding more stress to an already intense day for Hannah. She remembered something Dr. Rodriguez mentioned about a warm hand off, and how when one school staff member builds trust and introduces a parent to someone else, a little of that trust gets transferred. "I'm happy to accompany you. Honestly, I love the place, and we'll look at it as an information-gathering process; no pressure, I promise."

Hannah nodded.

"Hey Caleb, want to join us in the family center for a little bit?"

"Yeah!"

As they walked into the family center, the social worker who was on Caleb's team met them, calling out, "Caleb!"

Caleb gave him the same power hug that he had given his teachers, which the social worker was thrilled to accept. In the last hour, Caleb seemed like Tarzan. Instead of swinging from vine to vine, he moved from one safe and trusted adult to the next. The social worker said, "Caleb, we have some snacks and toys in the last workspace, if you want to join some other kids."

Caleb looked at his mom. Mrs. Vaughn realized that he was checking in, not for permission, but to see if she was going to be okay if he left her. Hannah nodded, and Caleb joined the other kids in the play area.

Mrs. Vaughn loved seeing the portable classroom alive with multiple families. Some were meeting with social workers and representatives from community agencies, while others browsed for resources on their own. The social worker offered them both some water and asked if they would like to sit down and chat in one of the open workspaces.

Mrs. Vaughn was very impressed by the social worker's approach. Knowing that he was aware of Caleb's situation, she was worried that he might aggressively push Hannah to get help. Instead, he asked her permission to share some of the available resources without ever implying that she needed any of them.

For each resource, he provided a brochure or flier. After providing one on mental-health and substance-abuse counseling, he brilliantly added, "I know you probably don't need all of what I'm offering; however, I love providing more than is necessary, in case you know others who might need assistance."

He offered to answer any questions, but Hannah just nodded in appreciation. "Hannah, it was great to meet you today. I really enjoy the interactions I get to have with Caleb. Since I bombarded you with a bunch of resources, would you mind if I called you in a few days to check up and answer any questions?"

"That would be great. Thank you." Hannah said softly.

Mrs. Vaughn could tell Hannah had hit her limit. She thanked the social worker and walked Caleb and Hannah out of the family center. Just then, Dr. Griffin approached. Mrs. Vaughn was initially worried that another interaction would push Hannah over the edge.

"Hannah and Caleb!" Dr. Griffin said with excitement. "So glad you got to see our family center. Hannah, I won't keep you. I do want to take a moment to apologize to you and Caleb. I know our interactions over of the last couple of years were overwhelmingly negative. I realize that a big part of Caleb's struggles was our inability as a school to help him find success. I hope you can give us another chance and accept our apology."

Mrs. Vaughn wondered who was more stunned by Dr. Griffin's words, her, Hannah, or Caleb. All Hannah could muster was a soft, "Thank you." As they walked away, Mrs. Vaughn appreciated what a different experience this was for Hannah. Not once did anyone make her feel like a terrible mother or a problem. Instead, they surrounded her and Caleb with support and options.

As Mrs. Vaughn exhaled, Emilia and her mother, Maria, approached. She could tell from the looks on their faces that something was wrong. Then Mrs. Vaughn saw the letter in Emilia's mom's left hand.

A week ago, the Trauma-Sensitive Transformation Team sent out letters to parents of students in Ms. Smith's and her class, as a test run. The group wanted to start small to measure both the responses they received and to ensure their current mental-health support capacity could handle the number of responses. Ms. Smith had had a couple of parents respond, but until now, Mrs. Vaughn hadn't heard anything.

Ever since learning about the freeze response that is common for victims of physical and sexual abuse, Mrs. Vaughn was worried about Emilia. With the focus on Caleb and all the changes, she was never able to act on her worry. It seemed like the letter might have set things in motion.

In her usual barely audible whisper, Emilia said, "Mrs. Vaughn, my mom would like to talk with you."

"Sure, Emilia. Why don't I get an interpreter, as you know my Spanish is far from perfect," Mrs. Vaughn said, trying to use her normal voice to hide her nervousness about the impending conversation.

A loud "No!" came from Maria.

"Mrs. Vaughn, my mom won't talk to anyone but you. We are scared that talking might mean we have to go back to Nicaragua."

Mrs. Vaughn's students often served as interpreters for their parents. She was amazed by how quickly young students like Emilia took on adult roles in conversations. "Emilia, what if I ask Dr. Griffin to join us? You know Dr. Griffin and that she is a safe adult. Plus, her Spanish is much better than mine."

Emilia turned to her mother and seemed to convince her that Dr. Griffin could also be trusted. The four of them walked to Dr. Griffin's office. Just as she sat down, Maria started crying uncontrollably.

"Emilia, why don't you ask Mrs. Simon at the front desk to walk you down to the family center; there is a room there where some kiddos are playing. Does that sound okay?" Mrs. Vaughn asked gently, assuming Emilia's afternoon had already been extremely stressful.

"Okay." Emilia got up, letting her mom know what was happening and giving her a big hug, which seemed to allow her mom to catch her breath.

Dr. Griffin started in Spanish, speaking slowly enough for Mrs. Vaughn to understand most of what she was saying, "Maria, I want you to know that we will do everything in our power to protect you and Emilia and get you help. However, I want to be up front and let you know that if someone is hurting Emilia, we would need to report it to the local Child Protective Services. We've done this dozens of times with migrant families, and they have never called ICE or gotten any of our families deported."

Maria hesitated, looking down at the letter in her hand. Mrs. Vaughn was struck by how the current system facing immigrants forces a mother to choose between the well-being of their child and entering a system she believes might force them to return to a horrible situation in a country Emilia hardly remembered.

"Dr. Griffin," Mrs. Vaughn looked at Maria, "Please tell Maria that Emilia is such a wonderful child and that our school is working hard to help kids like her get the help they need."

Tears fell down Maria's cheeks. "When we got the letter, I asked her about how her dad's detention with ICE was impacting her. We talked for a while about how we were both afraid that he and maybe our entire family could get deported back to Maturin. I noticed that she has been more withdrawn and quieter over the last year, and I assumed it was because of the stress and worry about her father."

Here Maria paused, knowing that her next words would set forth events that were mostly out of her control. Mrs. Vaughn gently squeezed her hand. "I asked her if anything else was happening. That is when she told me about her cousin and how he abused her almost every day in such terrible ways. When I asked her why she didn't tell me, she said that her cousin would threaten to call ICE and deport me."

At this, Maria collapsed into Mrs. Vaughn's arms and cried uncontrollably.

CHAPTER 10
Transforming Schools One Practice at a Time

Few people enjoy the idea of reviewing and revising policies and procedures. Visions of additional committees, bureaucracy, reviewing district policies, and understanding state and local regulations stop many from moving forward to this crucial stage of the trauma-sensitive journey. The easy part of the change journey is dedicating a staff meeting or staff development to trauma-sensitive practices, or by reading a book. The work of transforming a school or district seems a daunting task to many. We get it!

There are volumes of books written on why the current educational system is failing. Every elected official, parent, and person on the street thinks they know how to fix the system. Schools and districts try hard to maintain focus or find consistency, due to the shifting winds of politics, changes in leadership, or "flavor of the month" educational initiatives.

In this chapter, we put our heads down and provide a structure for creating a trauma-sensitive school. It's hard work! Making the challenge even more daunting, a school's culture, resources, student population, staff, and history all present unique challenges to that specific school. The goal of this chapter is to provide a detailed road map to guide a school on the trauma-sensitive change process.

Fueling the Transformative Journey

The crucial first step on the trauma-sensitive school journey requires creating a shared understanding of the impact of trauma on students' academic success, emotional health, and behavior. Each school and district must find the right way to deliver this knowledge to all their staff. We hope our book helps many, but we also recognize the importance of professional learning communities and in-person professional-development trainings. Powerful change occurs when an entire school's staff goes through a shared learning experience, with time to assess current practices and brainstorm initial solutions in a safe and nonjudgmental training environment.

Choose the learning method carefully. Trauma is a tricky subject because so many of the staff will have a history of trauma themselves. Many might currently struggle with problems in their marriages, with their children, or with unresolved trauma from their own childhood. Any good trauma trainer will recognize this reality and create strategies for safe learning opportunities. If you are considering bringing in a trainer, we suggest asking them the following questions:

- How do you create a safe learning environment for an audience with their own traumatic histories?
- How do you present the information about trauma so that staff do not come away overwhelmed and devastated that they failed many of their past students?
- What should we do after the training to begin integrating the know edge you taught into our policies, procedures, and practices?

If you like their answers to these questions, request references from past trainings conducted by the trainer. You want to hear that people enjoyed the training experience, learned new material, and felt excited and motivated afterward. Also, ask references how the training changed any practices and approaches at their school or district.

Finding the Sweet Spot

The trauma-sensitive change process succeeds when it focuses on the areas of most importance to the school's staff. We suggest an easy two-step assessment to create a shared focus and help structure a successful process. The first step is the Trauma-Sensitive School Checklist developed by Lesley University, Massachusetts Advocates for Children, and Legal Services Center of Harvard Law School. You can find the online version of the assessment and great additional information about trauma at the

Lesley Institute for Trauma Sensitivity website, under Tools for Assessing Your Own School (2019).

We suggest giving this assessment to every staff member. If community members, district staff, or parents were involved in the initial training, have them take the assessment as well.

We thank the folks at Lesley University for permitting us to reprint aspects of the assessment here (Lesley Institute for Trauma Sensitivity, 2019). We broke elements into five categories. Rank the elements on a four-point scale:

1) Element is not at all in place
2) Element is partially in place
3) Element is mostly in place
4) Element is fully in place

School-wide Policies and Practices

- The school contains predictable and safe environments (including classrooms, hallways, playgrounds, and school buses) that are attentive to transitions and sensory needs.
- Leadership (including principal and/or superintendent) develops and implements a trauma-sensitive action plan, identifies barriers to progress, and evaluates success.
- General and special educators consider the role that trauma may be playing in learning difficulties at school.
- Discipline policies balance accountability with an understanding of trauma.
- Support for staff is available on a regular basis, including supervision and/or consultation with a trauma expert, classroom observations, and opportunities for group work.
- Opportunities exist for confidential discussions about students.
- The school participates in safety planning, including enforcement of court orders, transferring records safely, restricting access to student record information, and sensitive handling of reports of suspected incidents of abuse or neglect.
- Ongoing professional-development opportunities occur as dete mined by staff needs assessments.

Classroom Strategies and Techniques

- Expectations are communicated in clear, concise, and positive ways, and goals for achievement of students affected by traumatic experiences are consistent with the rest of the class.
- Students' strengths and interests are encouraged and incorporated.
- Activities are structured in predictable and emotionally safe ways.
- Opportunities exist for students to learn and practice regulation of emotions and modulation of behaviors.
- Classrooms employ positive supports for behavior.
- Information is presented and learning is assessed using multiple modes.
- Opportunities exist for learning how to interact effectively with others.
- Opportunities exist for learning how to plan and follow through on assignments.

Collaborations and Linkages with Mental-Health Support

- Policies describe how, when, and where to refer families for mental health supports, and staff actively facilitate and follow through in supporting families' access to trauma-competent mental-health services.
- Access exists to trauma-competent services for prevention, early intervention, treatment, and crisis intervention.
- Protocols exist for helping students transition back to school from other placements.
- Mental-health services are linguistically appropriate and culturally competent.
- Staff has regular opportunities for assistance from mental-health providers in responding appropriately and confidentially to families.

Family Partnerships

- Staff uses a repertoire of skills to actively engage and build positive relationships with families.
- Strategies to involve parents are tailored to meet individual family

needs, and include flexibility in selecting times and places for meetings, availability of interpreters, and translated materials.
- All communications with and regarding families respect the bounds of confidentiality.

Community Linkage
- School develops and maintains ongoing partnerships with state human-service agencies and with community-based agencies to facilitate access to resources.
- When possible, school and community agencies leverage funding to increase the array of supports available.

The results of the Trauma-Sensitive School Checklist provide schools with a starting point in identifying both strengths and areas for improvement. We encourage schools to view their initial findings as neither positive nor negative. Instead, the first measure provides you with a baseline in which to direct improvement efforts. Readminister the checklist after each semester to gauge improvement and identify any emerging issues to address.

To further focus change efforts, schools should conduct a process termed "Stop, Start, Continue, Change." This exercise is a common process-management activity customized here for trauma-sensitive schools. We suggest asking the school staff the following questions after learning about trauma-sensitive schools (The Wisconsin Department of Public Instruction, 2017).

- Stop: What current practices or approaches do not work well for students with trauma?
- Start: What could we start doing to help all students succeed academically and behaviorally?
- Continue: Which of our practices and approaches work well for students with trauma?
- Change: What should we continue to do, but tweak to better meet the needs of students with trauma?

Using the Trauma-Sensitive School Checklist with the "Stop, Start, Continue, Change" activity will provide trauma-sensitive implementation efforts with focus. Since everyone is involved in the assessment stage, starting with the areas they identified will help more people buy into the process, thus increasing overall motivation for decisive action. Any significant change process is complicated. Beginning with the right focus is essential.

Development of a Trauma-Sensitive Transformation Team

After the assessment, the next critical step is establishing a Trauma-Sensitive Transformation Team. These teams will look different in each school. The initial tasks of forming a Trauma-Sensitive Transformation Team involve getting the right people at the table and informing those people about the process. Here are some key questions to consider in developing a Trauma-Sensitive Transformation Team:

- Who will lead the process?
- Does the leader or leaders possess the skills, training, and capacity to facilitate the process? Or, do you need external expertise or capacity to facilitate a successful change process?
- What sort of representation does the team need from school/district staff, including teachers, grade levels, administration (school and district), specialty teachers, social workers, therapists (speech, mental-health, occupational, and others), and coaches?
- Is participation mandatory or voluntary?
- What is the best way to structure family involvement? Make sure to diversify parent representation as much as possible to get all points of view.
- Does it make sense to bring in a partner or potential partner organization such as a mental-health organization, county/state social services or Child Protective Services, a child-and-family service organization, policymakers, or others? Even if it does not make sense to bring some of these people to the table initially, keep this question in mind as the process moves forward.
- What are the responsibilities and expectations of team members? Create a clear understanding about time and work expectations,

including time and place of meetings, length of meetings, the estimated time frame of the overall work (if not ongoing), and any expectations about work done outside meetings.
- What information or trainings do group members need in order to understand trauma-sensitive schools?

These questions help get the Trauma-Sensitive Transformation Team off to a great start. However, in our experience, staff meetings and committees are an almost universal source of frustration for teachers and school staff. If the Trauma-Sensitive Transformation Team functions like most meetings or committees, it too will become ineffective and a source of frustration, rather than bringing excitement and transformation.

The section below will help structure the team. However, if staff are already frustrated with how meetings and committee structures function at the school, leaders should consider bringing in an outside facilitator. An outside, objective perspective helps schools avoid the pitfalls that lead many change initiatives to fail. The small investment in an outside expert will pay off in increased motivation and buy-in, and help schools achieve the outcomes associated with trauma-sensitive schools.

Trauma-Sensitive Transformation Work Plan

A robust work plan serves as an overall map with directions for the trauma-sensitive school journey. A successful journey requires a clear goal. For teams charged with transforming a traditional school into a trauma-sensitive school, the goal is to align policies, practices, and approaches with the research on effective strategies for students with trauma, as presented in previous chapters.

What are some standard components of a strong Trauma-Sensitive Transformation Work Plan? Right away, state the goal of aligning policies, practices, and approaches with research on trauma. Since the work plan is a living document, make sure that the larger goal is prevalent, to remind everyone why they are doing the work.

The next components of the work plan are the objectives. These state how the school will reach the goal of aligning policies, practices, and approaches with the research on trauma. Common objectives for a

Trauma-Sensitive Transformation Work Plan include:

- Educate all staff on trauma.
- All classrooms and specialty teachers will create plans to ensure every learning environment approaches academic instruction and behavioral management in a trauma-sensitive way.
- Align school-wide behavioral-management approaches with trauma sensitive approaches.
- Establish a procedure for assessing and identifying students suffering from trauma.
- Ensure trauma treatment is available to the children and families who are struggling with trauma.
- Create a robust social-work and resource infrastructure (potentially with community partners) to help families meet basic financial, housing, medical, food, employment, and other needs, and get the support necessary to create safe, stable, and healthy environments for their children.
- Assess school staff regularly on the overall health and well-being of staff and school culture (more information in chapters 11 and 13).
- Train all staff on self-care strategies (more information in Chapter 12).
- Provide supportive supervision and coaching to all staff and ensure access to mental-health services when needed (more information in Chapter 13).
- Ensure staff provide feedback to leadership on how they are doing in providing supervision and support for staff.
- At the district level, ensure all Human Resource policies align with trauma-informed practices (grievance policies, availability of access to an Employee Assistance Program or affordable mental-health services, and effective employee evaluation processes).

These examples should serve as a starting point for the Trauma-Sensitive Transformation Team's task of identifying objectives. Each school's journey is unique, so please add objectives or reword the ones listed above.

The next task involves creating action steps for each objective. Action steps outline how the school will achieve each objective and accomplish a larger goal. While action steps can change over time, working on them at the beginning of the process gives everyone a detailed understanding of the scope of the work and what needs to be accomplished to reach the goal. Action steps are specific and precise, making it easy for everyone to know when the team completes them.

The next task is assigning responsibilities. This section designates a specific party who will be responsible for the completion of a particular action step. This person or team will own the associated action step and will report back to the team on their progress. When reading the list objectives above, this might seem overwhelming! Some schools create teams to work on specific objectives, which speeds up the process. Those without this capacity may decide to keep all the work within the Trauma-Sensitive Transformation Team. Regardless of the approach, the responsibilities section clearly states who is responsible for each objective.

The next task involves creating a timeline. The timeline states the completion date for each action step and the broader objective. While timelines change for a variety of reasons, setting an actual date helps the team establish accountability and expectations. It also helps the team conceptualize the scope of the entire project.

The next task answers the question, "What resources are available to accomplish this action step?" Even if the school or district does not currently have all their resources lined up, identifying what additional resources are needed starts the brainstorming process. If current resources or capacity does not exist to meet an objective, the Trauma-Sensitive Transformation Team should create an action step to secure that resource or ask appropriate district personnel how they could help secure the resource.

The next task is identifying potential barriers. Many teams skip this step, which unfortunately ends up with them hitting roadblocks later that slow down or stop the process altogether. Having people think of possible obstacles for success at the beginning of the process helps to adjust action steps or establish new ones that address these barriers proactively, leading to a better probability of success.

The final task is the communication plan. The communication plan helps the Trauma-Sensitive Transformation Team think about who to communicate with and the methods of communication. Most schools include parents, district leadership, community partners and stakeholders, and other school staff in their communication plan. While the Trauma-Sensitive Transformation Team will do most of the work, how they communicate with key partners will determine the effectiveness of implementation.

The team creates the work plan as a road map to help the school understand where it wants to go and what it will take to reach their destination. Like any trip, expect changes in the plan, as maps can't predict all the roadblocks and other obstacles that they might encounter. Make sure that the work plan is a living document and changes to reflect what the Trauma-Sensitive Transformation Team learns along their journey. The success of a team doesn't depend on making the work plan perfect; instead, success relies on a flexible strategy that changes when new information becomes available.

Effective Review Process

Each objective written above will take weeks, if not months, to accomplish. Larger schools might create smaller workgroups to address specific objectives and report back to the Trauma-Sensitive Transformation Team. In smaller schools, the team will need to take on one objective at a time.

Starting with the most critical areas identified in the Trauma-Sensitive School Checklist and the "Stop, Start, Continue, Change" assessment will help the Trauma-Sensitive Transformation Team feel like they are accomplishing meaningful results for the broader school community. Such a transformational process takes time and patience. A slow and steady approach avoids overwhelming people with too much change all at once. The team grows as a group and learns lessons that improve their effectiveness and efficiency.

Make sure to celebrate each success and accomplishment. Remain open to feedback from the broader school community. Early in the process, take implementation slowly. Do not jump right into the next objective. When given negative feedback, see it as an opportunity to learn and innovate. No transformational change process goes smoothly at each step. Keep flexible and adapt the work plan as needed.

And maybe more importantly, celebrate every success!

Biting Off a Big Chunk!

Mrs. Vaughn sat in a large meeting room at the City-County Building, amazed, and a little overwhelmed to see where the trauma work had taken her in such a short time. Flanked by Dr. Griffin, Ms. Smith, a couple of involved parents, an assistant superintendent, and a lawyer from the district, she sat across a long table from representatives and lawyers for the child welfare/protection system, foster care, the police department, and several other folks from different family/children departments. Dr. Rodriguez and the Director of Human Services for the County sat at the head of the table as co-facilitators.

Over the last couple of months, their Trauma-Sensitive Transformation Team had started addressing the school's approach to positive behavioral supports. The school already implemented limiting suspensions to very extreme situations and sending out trauma information letters in all grades. The team was establishing a positive momentum and building excitement in the school.

However, an issue kept coming up over and over in their assessments, team meetings, and the conversations between the team and staff. School staff tried hard to understand how to help the students most in need when there was so little communication between county staff and the school after reports of abuse. The Trauma-Sensitive Transformation Team kept hearing some version of, "We make these calls and don't ever hear anything back from the county or law enforcement. How do we help these kids when we don't know if they are continuing to get abused every night at home?"

The team initially thought that taking on this issue, which crossed bureaucracies of several systems, was well beyond its ability or scope. However, with such a huge and agreed-upon barrier standing between them and their goal of becoming a trauma-sensitive school, they decided to take it head-on.

Mrs. Vaughn started to champion the idea after trying to help Emilia and her mother, Maria. Due to what Emilia disclosed about her cousin, they called Child Protective Services. Despite Dr. Griffin's pleas for some updates over the next few weeks, none came. Per district policy, school staff were not allowed to discuss the matter with Emilia or Maria while the case was under investigation.

Mrs. Vaughn would check in with Emilia, but kept it general. Already a quiet girl, the most Mrs. Vaughn got back when she asked Emilia how she was doing was, "I'm fine." The school worked so hard to create a family center, connect with community resources, and address its practices, yet confidentiality policies at the district and county prevented the school from reaching out to help the family or even from asking if Emilia was safe each night when she went home.

Years of anger with this "report-and-pray" system, sadness with the inability of the school to reach out to identified struggling families, and not wanting to tell one more of her staff that, "This is just the way it has always been," prompted Dr. Griffin to advocate at the district level for a change. Even with district involvement in the Trauma-Sensitive Transformation Team, Dr. Griffin had to work her way up the district ladder. Her persistence led to the district sending a member of their legal team to the school to meet with the team.

The legal personnel quickly saw how current practices hindered the school's ability to help students and families. Even though the team's arguments were logical, passionate, and convincing, legally, it was a little trickier. The district's flexibility could improve, but what about the county and state regulations?

This response was all Dr. Griffin and Dr. Rodriguez needed to go to the head of Human Services at the county. During an initial meeting, they agreed to start a partnership to create a collaborative trauma-sensitive approach for the well-being of the children. All the people sitting around the table demonstrated the intense nature of the bureaucracy that many families and children find themselves facing after a report of abuse or even just asking for help.

Ms. Smith and Mrs. Vaughn were representing their Trauma-Sensitive Transformation Team at the meeting to provide the teacher perspective. While most at the table seemed comfortable at these sort of high-level meetings, Mrs. Vaughn and her young teammate felt like they had just entered an entirely different world. Mrs. Vaughn never missed her classroom and children more.

"Welcome everyone," Dr. Rodriguez began. "I want to thank everyone here for coming together around this important issue. I'm excited about this meeting, because I feel there is a great deal of room for us to collaborate in ways that could help children in our community."

Dr. Rodriguez turned it over to Dr. Griffin to detail the efforts her school had made to become trauma-sensitive. To Mrs. Vaughn's surprise, some of the county officials and even the police representatives had heard about some of the new research on trauma and shared some of their own efforts. Dr. Rodriguez then asked Mrs. Vaughn to talk about her experience and how some current practices hinder her ability to help her students and families.

Mrs. Vaughn took a deep breath, "Good morning, everyone. As we embark on our trauma-sensitive school journey, we are identifying more and more students who are experiencing trauma. We are working incredibly hard to create an environment with all the resources and support our students and families need."

"Due to our success in assessing and identifying students experiencing trauma, we are making many more reports of abuse and neglect to the county and law enforcement. The problem, from a teacher's perspective, is that once I report, I am in the dark. I don't know if the student is still living with the abusive family member, what action you took to stop the abuse, and whether the family is getting the help they need to create a healthy and safe home environment." Mrs. Vaughn felt her emotions taking control, and her sadness and frustration became apparent to everyone.

"A few weeks ago, a mom of one of my students reached out to us after we sent home some general information about trauma. After receiving the material from the school, the mom talked to her daughter and learned about the horrific sexual abuse her older cousin inflicted on her almost daily." Mrs. Vaughn felt the tears rolling down her cheek. She did not want to cry in front of all these people she didn't know.

Ms. Smith put her hand on Mrs. Vaughn's back, and the tears made it impossible to get out the words she so wanted to say. Everyone stayed silent. Through her tears, she saw Dr. Rodriguez smile, a smile that communicated reassurance and support. "I'm sorry. My tears are not just for this student. They are for the hundreds of students that we failed to help over the years."

She gathered herself. "The mom did not want to disclose the abuse for fear of deportation, but took the risk in hopes of stopping the abuse and getting her daughter help. We fulfilled our obligation by calling it in and filing a report. However, we heard nothing back, and due to our policies, I can't reach out to the mom or the student to offer additional support or resources."

Mrs. Vaughn felt something come from deep inside of her. It wasn't anger or frustration. Instead, she sensed herself speaking, not for herself or even her school, but for her past, present, and future students. "I want to become a trauma-sensitive teacher. I feel like the current structure says to me and my fellow teachers, 'Stay in your lane; your job is education and nothing more.'"

She realized Ms. Smith had grabbed her hand under the table. This small gesture of support added even more conviction to her voice.

"I spend more time with these children than anyone else outside their family. I can do more; I want to do more. If I don't do more, these kids might end up in jail, shot dead in the street, or overdosing in a back alley with a needle in their arm. They need everyone at this table to give them every opportunity to heal and change the direction of their lives. I'm done staying in my lane. If you want me to educate them, you must bring us into the healing process." Another tear rolled down her cheek as the room fell into silence.

Ms. Smith wiped the tears from her own eyes, as her mentor's words touched her deeply. Ms. Smith added, "As teachers, we don't come to the table without solutions. We propose the following: First, offer families that we report the option to sign a release of information form that allows the school to communicate with county personnel around how the school might help the family. We don't need information on the specifics of your investigation. However, we want to keep communication open to provide the family with the support and resources they need during a difficult time."

Now Mrs. Vaughn was squeezing Ms. Smith's hand, "Second, for families with continued involvement in your systems, we propose forming a treatment team that includes teachers, therapists, county workers, and others involved in the case. We want to do our part by rallying all our resources around these students and their families, and it is impossible to succeed if we are not all at the table."

"Finally, we created a Trauma-Sensitive Transformation Team at our school. If we are successful, it will spread throughout the district. I want to extend an invitation to each department here to send a representative to our team. If we radically change the way we work together, we need to set this process up for success and adjust it as we learn how to efficiently and effectively work in partnership." Ms. Smith's assertiveness and conviction carried just as much weight as Mrs. Vaughn's experience and passion.

As the room sat in silence, Mrs. Vaughn realized something. Too often, school staff feel disrespected and unimportant in their work. Here, in this room of influential community leaders, their voice carried power and force. They were educating these leaders' children, and their ability to succeed directly impacted the future of the entire community. For too long, Mrs. Vaughn saw herself as powerless in the modern education system. At this moment, she felt like an advocate for all the community's children.

The assistant superintendent broke the silence, "The district supports our teachers' desire to change how we work together. For too long, we assumed the current structure worked because we received few complaints. When they came to us wanting to do more to help change the lives of the children we serve, we took them seriously."

The head of Human Services was affirmatively nodding his head, "Thank you, Mrs. Vaughn and Ms. Smith. We are so lucky to have such powerful teachers and advocates in our community. I know my workers also feel overwhelmed by the trauma inflicted on our children, and creating a partnership with schools could help the effectiveness of our interventions."

The assistant superintendent went next, "Obviously, we all must work inside the current regulatory structure. However, I believe we could each become more flexible and find ways to partner. The release of information opens a great many possibilities. Let's get our legal folks and department leaders together to work out the legal details. My directive is to find areas to improve flexibility and open up our communication."

As the meeting broke up, a supervisor from Child Protective Services came up to Mrs. Vaughn and said, "Thank you. I never viewed schools as potential partners in the way you described, and I apologize for my ignorance."

Mrs. Vaughn chuckled, "No apology needed. Before learning about the impact of trauma, I never thought of anything like we proposed today. Without this knowledge, we find it easier to stay in our lanes and pray that others are doing a halfway decent job."

"I'm pretty sure I know the family you brought up as an example. I can't say much, but we are at the point in the process where I can propose a written release to her mother. Let me see if she is open to it."

Two days later, Mrs. Vaughn got a call from the CPS supervisor with one of his caseworkers on the line, "Hi, Mrs. Vaughn. Emilia's mother signed the release. She was open to our sharing certain information about the case, and was very interested in the treatment-team approach your fellow teacher proposed."

"That is great! Could you give me any information on how they are doing?"

"We probably could; however, I would prefer if the mother updated everyone in person at Emilia's first meeting. How's next Thursday work after school?"

"I can make that work." Mrs. Vaughn was taken aback by how quickly this all was moving.

"Mrs. Vaughn," the supervisor said compassionately.

"Yes."

"I can share that Emilia is safe."

Mrs. Vaughn paused, as a sense of relief washed over her. "Thank you! That little piece of news means so very much to me."

"I now have a deeper appreciation for how important these sort of updates are for teachers," he said. "Now, I need to contact some other teachers from your school to set up meetings for their students. Since we are just starting this process, I'll attend the meeting on Thursday, if that is okay?"

"Absolutely," Mrs. Vaughn said, humbled by the leadership investment.

"Also, if it is okay with you, Ms. Smith, and Dr. Griffin, I would like to join your Trauma-Sensitive Transformation Team with one of my case workers. I'm interested in the possibility of assigning one of my workers to handle all the cases at your school. Hopefully, we both would add some value to the team."

"Thank you," was all Mrs. Vaughn could say.

PART 4

The Role of a Healthy School Environment and Self-Care in a Trauma-Sensitive School

A trauma-sensitive school seeks to align its behavior-management practices and academic instruction with the most current research on trauma. The success or failure of these efforts depends heavily on three variables. The health of the staff, the culture and climate of the school, and strong leadership all play critical roles in determining the success of any trauma transformation effort. Without any one of these three, the school will struggle to achieve the true life-changing power of trauma-sensitive educational reform. Unfortunately, due to the stress of modern education, many schools lack these three critical elements.

Let's address the troublesome and concerning facts about educational careers right up front. Primary teachers and principals rank among the top five professions with the highest rates for burnout. Social workers and nurses, who also work in schools, also make the top five (White, 2019). The stress isn't just wearing teachers out. More than two in five new teachers leave education within five years (McLaughlin, 2018). Working in the modern educational system is strongly correlated with emotional, physical, and mental exhaustion. Stated simply, working in schools may be harmful to your health!

The Nature of Stress in Education

To understand why working in modern education is so stressful, it is essential to explore the nature of stress. Stress is a person's internal reaction to changes in the environment. Three factors determine the degree to which an event creates stress and whether someone experiences negative consequences. These intensifying factors are duration, importance, and uncertainty (The American Institute of Stress, 2012).

The first intensifier of stress is duration. The longer a stressor is present, the greater its impact on wellness. While most educational settings include breaks throughout the year, the breaks are not enough to offset the long stretches of intense stress.

For many, the school year feels like a series of long sprints, with school staff reaching the school breaks on the verge of burnout or worse. Some schools add the expectation that teachers spend their breaks in professional-development classes, checking emails, learning new curriculum, or working to implement further reforms. This extra work prevents school staff from getting the downtime they genuinely need.

The expectation that primary teachers spend some of their evenings grading papers or lesson planning has always existed. Now with modern technology, most school staff also communicate with parents and co-workers via email and text. Too many school staff fall into the trap of working well into the evening and even over their vacations. These practices make it difficult to escape or recover from the stress prevalent in their day-to-day duties.

The second of these factors is importance. The more important something is to the person, the more stress it causes. All school staff care deeply about the students in their classes and schools. It is painful to watch students that everyone cares about struggling academically or socially. Witnessing them go through traumatic events is devastating, especially when school staff feel powerless to ensure their safety and stop the trauma.

The final intensifier is uncertainty. People feel less stress when a situation is predictable. Unfortunately, the nature of traumatic events carries a high degree of uncertainty. When students experience trauma, school staff often possess little ability or power to affect the situation. They end up hoping that someone else will take the necessary steps to keep their students safe from dangerous situations.

In Part 4, we'll use a simple analogy to summarize a great deal of intricate research on stress, trauma, and burnout. We use a cup analogy to demonstrate the impact of stress and trauma on the physical, cognitive, and mental health of school staff members.

The first part of the cup analogy involves robustness. According to Merriam-Webster's Dictionary (2014), robustness entails "having or exhibiting strength or vigorous health and being capable of performing with success or without failure under a wide range of conditions."

The cup analogy provides a visual to demonstrate the impact of stress and trauma on the school staff's ability to perform at their best. The cup analogy starts with the size or capacity of the cup, which represents the amount of robustness one brings to their work and lives. The larger the cup, the more stress a person can hold without it negatively impacting our cognitive, emotional, and social functioning.

The ability to manage stress, or the size of our cup, increases when a person lives a healthy and happy life, both personally and professionally. Chapter 12 focuses on specific strategies to build capacity and effectively manage the stress of modern education. The size of the cup decreases slightly in the short term with small things like the weather, illness, hunger, and frustrating interactions with other people. Things like trauma, constant stress, chronic diseases, and unhealthy social or professional relationships decrease capacity dramatically and leave the person with a small cup or limited ability to manage stress.

Connecting the cup analogy to the science learned in Part 1, the stronger the prefrontal cortex and the less dominant the amygdala, the larger the cup. For students, age is also a key determinant of robustness. As a child ages, the prefrontal cortex normally gains greater and greater power to manage stress and keep the amygdala calm. In healthy development, the older the student, the more stress they can handle. Unfortunately, trauma disrupts normal prefrontal cortex development (Nakazawa, 2016).

The next component of this analogy concerns the level of water in our cup. The water in the cup is the amount of stress and trauma held in the body at any given time. As a cup fills with stress, the person starts to lose their capacity for cognitive engagement and emotional regulation. The higher the water, the more the brain shifts activation from the thinking parts of the brain to the emotional and reactive parts.

Some people react to stress by trying to organize and control their world, which indicates a rigid response. In an educational setting, rigid staff members are highly rule-based, providing little flexibility to consider possible traumatic reasons behind the behavior or academic struggles of their students. These staff members are more likely to rely on one-size-fits-all approaches and find it difficult to differentiate academic lessons or behavioral interventions.

While chaotic reactions are more common with students, some school staff also react chaotically when the water in their cups starts to reach capacity. Chaos is an effective way for people to protect themselves or to avoid dealing with their stress, burnout, and other issues. Yelling at a teammate, storming out of a meeting, or other disruptive behaviors gets the staff a short-term reprieve from what is causing them stress, thus allowing them to avoid having to face their inability to handle their stress effectively. Over time, school staff in the chaos response will fail to provide the structure needed to effectively manage their classrooms. Their workspace will often look cluttered and disorganized, and they will fail to meet deadlines for tasks like report cards.

Rigidity and chaos are rarely well-thought-out choices or strategies. Instead, rigidity and chaos are reactive behaviors to stress in the environment. If rigidity or chaos does not alleviate the stress, people will react in one of three survival modes: fight, flight, or freeze. When professionals display these behaviors, we know that they are under a great deal of stress, and their cup is overflowing, spilling the stress everywhere (Bennett, 2018).

As we will explore in the next chapter, school staff often experience different forms of trauma in their work. Trauma occurs when a stressor in the environment overwhelms their cup's capacity or their ability to cope with the intensity of the stress. The intensified stress submerges the cup in the trauma, taking away the person's ability to access their cognitive ability. Everything becomes focused on surviving the event and preventing it from recurring.

An Opportunity for Reflection

An amazing buzz built around the trauma transformation work at Dr. Griffin's school. The team leading the transition was on fire, tackling one big issue after another. The family center was so successful that it was now open five days a week, with some thought of opening on the weekend. Community partners were excited, and the team approach to handling abuse and neglect reports was transforming interagency communication and cooperation in ways Dr. Griffin never imagined possible.

She was wired and tired. Dr. Griffin's mind kept her up at night as new ideas never stopped. Yet, managing the excitement with all the other stress of running a school was exhausting.

Her excitement, the evident successes, and strong coffee got her through the days. However, she always felt on edge and caught herself recently with less and less patience for those staff members who had a tough time getting on board with the rapid progress. In her wired-and-tired state, the piece of paper sitting in front of her felt like a punch in the gut, as much for its truth as for the hard reality it named. It was a feedback form from one of her staff after their short trauma training with Dr. Rodriguez.

Dr. Rodriguez's training was terrific. However, why aren't we talking about the fact that most of our staff are acting like they are traumatized?

Mrs. Vaughn popped her head in Dr. Griffin's office door with a fresh cup of coffee. "Need a pick-me-up?"

Dr. Griffin just slid the piece of paper across the desk. Mrs. Vaughn sat the cup down next to Dr. Griffin and picked up the paper while taking a seat.

Mrs. Vaughn read the paper and pushed it back. In a joking but gentle voice, she said, "Yeah boss, what about us?"

"If I'm honest, the same thought occurred to me several times during our training and conversations. There is a huge amount of work just to give our students what they need for their trauma. Thinking about how all our students' traumas impact us is something that seemed easier to ignore than to address directly," Dr. Griffin said to one of the few staff she trusted with such vulnerability.

"We are far from models of health and well-being." Mrs. Vaughn was enjoying these complex reflections.

"I know; I see it in the faces of staff as I walk these halls. While most of us are surviving, too many of us are walking around like zombies. Those who are doing okay are carrying our trauma transformation efforts. Others are falling even further behind. That's not to mention that, as our practices evolve, other areas of our instruction are falling to the wayside."

"Sounds like you think we need to put the trauma-sensitive lens on ourselves," Mrs. Vaughn stated.

"How? Modern education is a burnout machine. Besides Ms. Smith's unending energy and enthusiasm, most of us barely keep our hearts beating until the next vacation or break." Dr. Griffin showed a level of resignation Mrs. Vaughn rarely saw in her leader.

"I wonder if I could throw something out," Mrs. Vaughn inquired.

"Of course! Go right ahead."

"Sure, modern education chews people up and spits them out. I also feel like many of my co-workers walk these halls with their students' and their own trauma weighing heavy on their hearts. However, when was the last time we talked about staff health? I can't remember us ever talking about self-care. I think part of our problem is that we view teachers and other staff as cogs in the modern education machine and not as human beings. I think just acknowledging the stress and trauma inherent to our work, and also supporting self-care would go a long way." Mrs. Vaughn waited to see the response to her words.

"You're right. The trauma stuff does provide us with a language and understanding we could use to think about ourselves and our own struggles."

"Another hill to climb in our journey," Mrs. Vaughn said, while getting up to go get her class from gym.

CHAPTER 11
Stress, Burnout, and Trauma of School Staff

As the field of trauma research evolved, researchers came to a startling realization. They discovered that many in the educational, mental-health, medical, and social-work fields who worked with people struggling with trauma displayed many of the same trauma symptoms as their students, patients, and clients. When researchers assessed these professionals, they found that many met the diagnostic criteria for Post-Traumatic Stress Disorder or PTSD. In these professionals, the PTSD diagnosis was not a result of divorce, death, abuse, or another horrific event. The only identifiable trauma was their work with others' pain and suffering (Bloom & Farragher, 2011; Lipsky & Burk, 2009).

In Chapter 4, we learned the importance of students feeling that the school staff understands their pain, and how OARS helps school staff effectively communicate empathy. Unfortunately, while empathy is essential to effective trauma-sensitive communication, connecting deeply with a student's pain puts the person in a vulnerable position. Human beings are naturally emotionally impacted by the pain and suffering of others. This impact intensifies when we care about the person suffering, even more so if they are a small child.

Empathetic Intensity

Empathetic intensity is the emotional impact of sitting with someone else's trauma, pain, and suffering. In the course of a typical school year, teachers witness multiple students suffering from traumatic experiences. Also, staff are continuously faced with issues such as poverty, racism, food scarcity, violence in their communities, immigration, fear, and other issues impacting their students and their families (Stamm, 2010; Wilson & Lindy, 1994).

Early in my career, I worked at an elementary school in Harlem, New York. There were many instances where I carried the weight of my students' trauma with me. Many of the students I worked with lived in dangerous neighborhoods, dealt with food and housing insecurity, and faced various forms of abuse and neglect. I lost sleep because I worried about their safety. I found it impossible to find the energy to exercise. My eating habits derailed, and I battled persistent headaches from unconsciously clenching my teeth throughout the day. I knew all these things were related to my worry and anxiety for my students and my inability to remedy their pain. Yet every day, I would put on a brave face and pretend everything was just fine. What I did not realize at the time was that I was experiencing empathetic intensity and my struggles got progressively worse with time.

The risk is real. When our empathetic intensity overwhelms our capacity to cope, we find ourselves disoriented, furious, depressed, hopeless, and confused. Over time, our student's hurt, suffering, and pain becomes our trauma, especially when we feel powerless to stop the trauma and get the student the help they need (Bloom, 2006; Bloom & Farragher, 2011).

We are also at risk of experiencing retraumatization from our work. This trauma occurs when the student's traumatic story connects with our past experiences. When we experience retraumatization, the emotions we felt during our trauma come flooding back, overwhelming us with fear, sadness, and pain (Lipsky & Burk, 2009).

Most people experienced some form of trauma in their past. I am no exception. Understanding empathetic intensity forces me to pay special attention to my reactions to traumatic stories that hit a little close to home. In fact, sometimes things do trigger my traumatic memories. When I find myself overreacting to a situation or when I feel physical changes like a lump in my throat or my face getting flushed, often my body is reacting to something traumatic from my past. Now that I recognize how trauma impacts my ability to support my students, this knowledge has given me the motivation to seek out mental-health help to support my own recovery processes.

These traumatic reactions are authentic traumatic experiences. Without treatment and healing, they threaten long-term psychological, social, and medical health. Any reactions might result in emotional numbing and an inability to experience pleasure. People may feel detached from work or lose interest in work or other activities altogether. They may find that they avoid emotionally intense subjects with students, co-workers, and in their personal life. School staff are also at risk of experiencing anxiety, which can include symptoms like difficulty concentrating. They may feel hypervigilant and have trouble sleeping. They may experience feelings of constant anxiety or irritability, or suffer from angry outbursts (Bloom & Farragher, 2011; Geller and Madsen, 2004; Harris & Fallot, 2001).

Researchers also found other residual implications of trauma on the school staff. An important piece is the development of a negative world view. School staff experience the dark side of society and human nature, as trauma usually results from someone doing something terrible to a child. Without careful attention, school staff begin to miss the positive aspects of their communities. They may view work and perhaps the entire world in a negative light (Bloom, 2011).

This negative perspective can also lead to a sense of hopelessness, in that school staff believe they lack the ability to help their students find a healthy and prosperous future. With all their struggles and the reality of their situation, hope is sometimes hard to find. School staff may struggle to see how to help students or how they could positively impact the situation.

If school staff are lucky, they will have caring and observant friends, principals, and co-workers. Other staff will see their difficulties and assist them in finding the resources, coping skills, and help they need to overcome the trauma. If this support does not come, school staff may end up developing negative attitudes towards their work, their co-workers, and even their students. When school staff lose their positive mindset, they lose the greatest gift they have to offer students–hope (Bloom & Farragher, 2011; Geisinger Health System, 2008; Geller & Madsen, 2004; Harris & Fallot, 2001; Lipsky & Burk, 2009).

Another danger that is always present for school staff is burnout. As we mentioned in the introduction to Part 4, primary teachers, principals, social workers, and nurses occupy the top five occupations for burnout. If empathetic intensity fills their cups with the emotional aspects of their work, burnout results from all the other stress inherent in working in modern education. One reason teachers and principals rank so high on the burnout list is that most assessments are measuring both empathetic intensity and everyday work stress.

While burnout happens over time, if school staff are not careful, it progresses without their ability to identify what is occurring. Too many papers to grade, conflicts with parents, managing student behavior, testing, and even their co-workers add small amounts of stress to their cups each day. If school staff do not proactively implement strategies to manage and eliminate this stress, they find themselves just trying to survive to the next vacation or the end of the semester.

There is a great deal of research surrounding burnout and the long-term consequences of work stress. Here are just some of the findings on the severe nature of occupational stress and burnout (Achor, 2010; Fernandez, 2006; Hoopes & Kelly, 2004; Maslach & Leiter, 1997; Siebert, 2005).

Impact on physical/medical health:

- Heart disease
- Stroke
- Type II diabetes
- Musculoskeletal disorder
- Cancer
- Chronic fatigue
- Sexual issues
- Gastrointestinal problems
- Headaches
- Colds and flu
- Back problems

Impact on psychological health:

- Feelings of incompetence and doubt
- Negative attitude
- Memory loss
- Cognitive decline

- Early-onset Alzheimer's disease
- Sleep problems
- Shame
- Mental fatigue
- Anxiety and irritability
- Depression
- Guilt
- Aggression

Impact on social/occupational health:
- Social isolation or relationship issues
- Poor job performance
- Absenteeism
- Tardiness
- Theft at work
- Dehumanization of students
- Turnover or leaving education
- Parent- and employee-filed grievances and complaints
- Litigation
- Low job satisfaction
- Blurred boundaries

Are You at Risk?

Everyone working in modern education is at risk of experiencing burnout and trauma. How do you know if the stress and emotional intensity of your work is negatively impacting you? We provide a simple self-assessment below. The more statements you respond to with "yes," the higher the risk that you may experience the negative repercussions we covered above.

- I am preoccupied with more than one student.
- I jump or am startled by unexpected sounds.
- I find it difficult to separate my personal life from my job.

- I am not as productive at work because I am losing sleep over the traumatic experiences of a student.
- I think that I might have been affected by the traumatic stress of my students.
- I feel trapped by my job in education.
- Because of my job, I have felt "on edge" about various things.
- I feel depressed because of the traumatic experiences of the students.
- I feel worn out because of my work.
- I feel overwhelmed because my workload seems endless.
- I avoid certain activities or situations because they remind me of the frightening experiences of my students.
- As a result of my work with students, I have intrusive, frightening thoughts.
- I feel "bogged down" by the system.
- I can't recall important parts of my work with trauma victims.

You are at greater risk if you answer "no" to the following questions.
- I am happy.
- I get satisfaction from being able to work with students.
- I feel connected to others.
- I feel invigorated after working with students.
- I like my work in education.
- I have beliefs that sustain me.
- I am the person I always wanted to be.
- My work makes me feel satisfied.
- I have happy thoughts and feelings about my students and how I help them.
- I believe I can make a difference through my work.
- I am proud of what I can do to help my students.
- I have thoughts that I am a "success" as an educator.
- I am a very caring person.
- I am happy that I chose to do this work.

- I am pleased with how I am able to keep up with new educational techniques and protocols.

Note: The assessment above draws extensively on the Professional Quality of Life Measure (PRoQOL), administered by the Centre for Victims of Torture (CVT). The original ProQOL measure, with administration instructions, can be downloaded free of charge for personal use from **www.proqol.org**.

Stages of Education Fatigue

Burnout, empathetic intensity, and trauma all easily fill up school staff's cups throughout the school year. Each day they wake up with more water in their cup from the days and weeks before. If people carry high levels of stress and trauma in their cups and bodies for long periods of time, their psychological, social/occupational, and physical/medical health start to decline. Their ability to do their jobs effectively diminishes. A four-stage model of education fatigue helps demonstrate the escalating effects of stress and trauma on people's well-being. The four stages are 1) Exhaustion, 2) Guilt, Doubt, and Shame, 3) Cynicism and Callousness, and 4) Crisis.

While each stage is unique, many people embody the characteristics of the stage they are in, as well as the previous stages they went through. The higher the stage, the more anxiety and the lower the quality of their work. The utility of this model is that it helps people identify how stress is affecting them. With this knowledge, people can self-correct before the stress moves on to the next phase. Since each succeeding stage is more detrimental than the past one, people can recognize where they are on the scale and act to regain wellness (Maslach & Leiter, 1997).

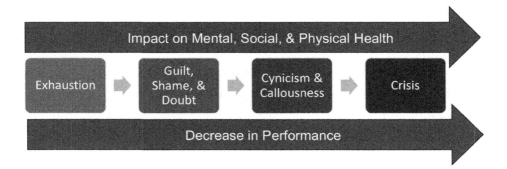

Exhaustion

The first stage, exhaustion, is something every school staff member struggles with at some time during the school year. It seems like every little task is its own mountain, taking a tremendous amount of effort to accomplish. Identifying exhaustion is critical, because if people don't act to address it, they are at risk of quickly moving into more harmful stages. By recognizing that they are in a state of exhaustion, small actions can help get them out of the stage and back into wellness, thus avoiding the negative consequences of later stages.

Signs that you are in the exhaustion stage.

One key aspect of addressing exhaustion is knowing your physical, psychological, and social triggers. These are signs that your work and overall stress levels are starting to negatively impact your functioning. Think of these triggers as your mind and body telling you that something is going wrong and it is time to do things differently.

Notice your physical state. Physical triggers are often the easiest to identify. Common physical triggers include stiff necks, sore backs, strained muscles, headaches, colds that will not go away, and other little aches and pains that are more annoying than debilitating. An excellent way to distinguish the physical triggers associated with education fatigue from typical illnesses or pain is what happens when you address the pain. When you get a massage, take a pain killer, or treat a cold, if the pain returns quickly after the treatment or if another physical sign of stress replaces the one you treated, you may be in a state of exhaustion.

While physical triggers are the most obvious, a little insight helps you identify your psychological triggers. Take a moment to think about the characteristics of your mood when you are tired or irritable, or did not get enough sleep. Now compare those characteristics to your mood when you are your best self, or maybe to how you feel in mid-July if you get summers off.

Notice your state of mind. Psychological triggers include dreaming about work, trouble sleeping, obsessive worry or thinking about work, and minor depression or anxiety. These triggers are not at the level of a mental-health diagnosis. They do put you at risk of more significant threats to your mental health if you do not take action to get out of the exhaustion stage.

While physical and psychological triggers exist within your body, social triggers show up in your relationships. In your personal life, social triggers include a lack of desire to connect with friends and family in meaningful ways and less patience with your children and loved ones. The good thing about social triggers is that these people might give you some feedback that you are being less social or patient with those you love.

Unlike many jobs, education is a highly social occupation. When you are in the exhaustion stage, you may find that it becomes harder to empathize and be present with students. Empathetic listening is an intense activity that takes lots of focus, energy, and attention. As exhaustion creeps in, you will find it harder to engage fully in conversation and connect emotionally to students.

As with the other triggers in this stage, social triggers will not result in marriages breaking up, friendships ending, or getting fired from jobs. However, if unaddressed, these small changes in relationships often become more significant issues with greater consequences. The important thing with all triggers is to recognize when your mind and body are telling you something is wrong and then act to correct the problem.

In addition to triggers, the exhaustion stage also diminishes the capacity for creativity and cognitive flexibility, and the ability to handle the complexity of work. School staff do not get nearly enough credit for how complex and intense the work is, both emotionally and intellectually. Helping students with trauma requires lots of creativity and innovative thinking. Unfortunately, these are some of the first things to weaken when you enter the exhaustion stage.

In exhaustion, healthier coping skills shift to unhealthy ones. Instead of jogging or going to the gym, you may opt for another glass of wine, binge-watching a new favorite television show, or spending hours lost on social media. While none of these activities is inherently bad, they should not be the primary coping skills to stress and exhaustion. The more time spent in the exhaustion stage, the harder it becomes to get out of bed in the morning, find excitement in work, and locate the energy for social interactions in your personal and professional life.

The good news is that if you identify that you are in this stage, a long weekend, a few great workouts, and some time with good friends can take some of the stress out of your cup. You can find your way back into wellness.

If people don't notice and work to fix education fatigue at the exhaustion stage, they are at risk of moving to the next stage: guilt, doubt, and shame.

Guilt, Doubt, and Shame

School staff know that students need them at their best every day. Hopefully, when school staff realize they are in the exhaustion stage, they react to restore their wellness. However, if they fail to act, they begin to recognize the decreasing quality of their work. This realization leads to feelings of doubt about their ability to ever regain their former quality and level of work. A sense of guilt and shame usually accompanies this doubt, as they do not live up to their own expectations, realize they are failing their students, and cannot be the co-worker or teammate that their fellow school staff members can depend on.

School staff also experience doubt and shame when they are overwhelmed by the intensity of the problems their students face and their limited power to change the realities that are harming their students. They start to believe that they can never do enough to counterbalance the pain and suffering their students are experiencing. This reality creates feelings of helplessness and hopelessness in the face of their students' pain.

Signs that you are in the guilt, doubt, and shame stage.

In this stage, you may have increased awareness and internal unrest about the privilege in your life. You may find that it becomes harder to go home and enjoy your family, friends, and life when you know that so many students you care about are homeless, hungry, experiencing violence, or alone after they leave school. You become hyperaware of the divide between the "haves" and "have-nots," and the social and economic injustice behind this divide.

As you work with, support, and try to help those impacted by this injustice, you have a difficult time leaving work and then enjoying the social and economic stability you have established in your life. The sense of guilt resulting from this awareness starts to deteriorate your ability to get pleasure out of your work. If you do not feel like you are significantly impacting the situations facing our students, you feel like you are part of a system designed to simply manage these issues instead of solving them.

One of the results of guilt, doubt, and shame is a sense of hypervigilance. You start to work longer hours and on weekends. Over vacations, you try to counteract the feeling that you are never doing enough. Just because you are working longer hours does not mean the quality or impact of your work increases. In fact, the opposite is true. The more extended hours are often unproductive, and the resulting exhaustion decreases the energy you use to engage students and maintain a high quality of work (Rock, 2009).

You may also have trouble disconnecting. You may start checking work emails at home in the evening and even on vacation. You cannot disconnect when someone always needs you. There is never enough time in the school day to do all your work. Unfortunately, continually working never gives your brain a chance to refresh, disconnect, and relax. Working harder and longer to alleviate the doubt and shame just makes the problem worse, as your exhaustion increases, and you get less and less done (Schwartz, 2010).

In the second stage, you may find that you need to talk to someone else to release and process these feelings. Often an empathetic co-worker, supervisor, or friend serves as an adequate source of support. If you exist in this stage for long periods of time, you might need to access your own mental-health therapy to resolve your guilt, doubt, and shame fully. Time off is a good idea, because the exhaustion still exists, and you need to get some of that stress out of your cup in order to be yourself again.

Cynicism and Callousness

People can only hold guilt, doubt, and shame for so long before it triggers a defensive reaction, leading to the third stage of education fatigue: cynicism and callousness. Cynicism and callousness are a natural reaction to continuous experiences of exhaustion, shame, guilt, and doubt. If school staff do not address the causes behind their progression from stage 1 to stage 2, they must do something to cope and be able to continue to show up to work every day. The human response to exhaustion, guilt, doubt, and shame is to withdraw empathy and compassion. This response leads to the inability to connect emotionally with students and their struggles.

Signs that you are in the cynicism and callousness stage.

As you withdraw empathetically, your sympathy and caring dissolves into a cynical view of the work, students, and co-workers. You may find yourself disrespecting students by talking about them harshly and acting passive-aggressively toward them and their families. You will struggle to find empathy and understanding for your students' trauma. Instead, those students start to seem like an inconvenience and annoyance.

In this stage, your passive-aggressive response also impacts your relationships with co-workers. You spend more time gossiping about your co-workers and complaining about administration and other professionals. Instead of realizing how traumatized and burned out you are, you start to put down others. You act passive-aggressively in meetings, instead of honestly and respectfully confronting issues. Lashing out at others or withdrawing empathy are forms of the fight-or-flight responses. Here your intense stress responses often hurt other people.

A sense of self-importance also develops in this stage. "No one here works longer and harder than I do." "These parents are so entitled. They think their child is the only one I teach!" "You think it is bad now; I've been putting up with this for 25 years!" Cynical people need to ensure that everyone sees their burdens and notices how strong they are for carrying these burdens every day.

We describe callousness as someone's heart becoming a concrete monument to who they once were. Every new school staff member, principal, or teacher we meet is full of excitement and energy. Most everyone enters education for altruistic reasons. Years of trauma exposure and stress can destroy this initial passion and compassion.

Those who realize that they are a shadow of their former selves often view their lack of achievement as persecution. They see themselves as victims of everything that is wrong with education and are happy to tell everyone they feel this way. Their focus is on their own pain, leaving little energy to focus on the needs of their students or supporting their co-workers.

While most of the people we meet in the education field are caring individuals, we must acknowledge that cynicism and callousness are way too prevalent in education. Education does not attract mean or cruel people. The stress of modern education leads many once-empathetic and -passionate people to end up unable to find the kindness and patience needed to work with students successfully. Unfortunately, because they did not get help in earlier stages, they are left in a dark place and create an unhealthy environment for students and co-workers.

The devastation of stage 3 demonstrates why school staff must address education fatigue in stages 1 and 2, before they progress to cynicism and callousness. Everyone finds it challenging to work with people at this stage. Negative experiences between people in stage 3 and co-workers, families, and others make it hard to recover without drastic action. Individuals in this stage cause real hurt to others. Resentment and frustration grow beyond the point where a simple apology gets everyone back on the same page.

Usually, mental-health services are needed to recover from stage 3. Exhaustion, guilt, doubt, and shame are states that change back with some limited effort. Cynicism and callousness become personality traits that impact relationships at work and in a person's personal life. If you find yourself in this stage, know that the path back to wellness will take time and considerable effort. However, the final stage, crisis, is where no person wants to end up professionally or personally.

Crisis

People in the crisis stage are actively experiencing trauma from work. Due to high levels of stress and trauma over long periods of time, they are no longer able to function, either personally or professionally, from a healthy place. People must do so much personal and professional work to recover from crisis that rarely does anyone in this stage stay in the field of education. If the person in crisis somehow manages to keep their job, they most likely isolate from their caring co-workers. Rarely can co-workers maintain a healthy working relationship with someone in so much pain.

The trauma of crisis transcends the work environment and prevents the person from being a decent spouse, partner, friend, or parent. Divorce and other extreme relational issues often happen when someone is in crisis due to work stress. Addiction is common and makes all the person's difficulties much more intense.

A trauma-sensitive school requires a healthy and engaged staff. Burnout, empathetic intensity, and trauma will occur in any school. Despite this inevitability, a trauma-sensitive school and staff can proactively implement strategies to prevent and minimize these dangers. When they do occur, everyone rallies around their teammates to help them recover from the experience.

Heart disease, cancer, mental illness, Alzheimer's, relationship issues, and the other scary impacts of work stress should not be the price school staff pay for dedicating their professional lives to the service of the children in our communities. Unfortunately, the stress and trauma associated with working with students with trauma threaten to take years, if not decades, off our lives. In the next chapter, we will examine best practices to prevent and recover from trauma.

What Happened to Us?

The Trauma-Sensitive Transformation Team continued to identify and change policies and approaches in the school. The family center kept growing in people and resources, to the point where the space of the modular classroom could not host all the people and resources that filled it. The team approach for students identified for trauma was transforming the role of the school and teachers, and how the community worked for its children.

With all this excitement, Mrs. Vaughn loved her time with the Trauma-Sensitive Transformation Team, while dreading her own team meetings with Ms. Smith and Mr. Anderson. On the one hand, Ms. Smith's excitement pushed everything forward at a dizzying pace. On the other hand, Mr. Anderson had never seemed to recover his usual wit and good sense of humor after he had discovered the abuse of one of his students.

At this point in the school year, Mrs. Vaughn would typically shrug off such exhaustion and frustration as the normal emotional state of teachers after eight months of difficult teaching. However, her growing understanding of trauma made it impossible to ignore the fact that Mr.

Anderson was displaying many of the symptoms of trauma that she was taught to identify in her students.

He seemed to have a short temper and lack of cognitive focus on tasks. He failed to follow through and pull his weight on the team. He withdrew from any school activity outside his regular duties and contract hours. His attitude frustrated Mrs. Vaughn. The hardest part was that she felt her longtime friend and partner was fading into someone very different, and she hated feeling like she was losing a friend.

After a recent Trauma-Sensitive Transformation Team meeting, Mrs. Vaughn asked Dr. Rodriguez if she had a moment.

"I'm worried about someone. I'm not really sure how to state it, but is it possible to experience trauma because of your exposure to someone else's trauma?" Mrs. Vaughn felt herself struggle to get the words out coherently. "Does that even make sense?"

Dr. Rodriguez smiled. The absence of Mr. Anderson was suspicious. Of the three-member teaching team, two teachers were highly motivated and were helping to transform not only the school, but how the entire community worked with its children. One teacher on their team was visibly absent from all the excitement and success. She wanted to respect that Mrs. Vaughn might not wish to disclose that her concern was for her absentee teammate.

"Yes. In fact, some studies show that exposure to another's trauma puts us at risk of PTSD." She paused, wanting Mrs. Vaughn to direct where the conversation went next.

In an almost inaudible voice, Mrs. Vaughn mumbled, "What happened to…us?"

"Exactly. School staff are especially vulnerable to experiencing trauma from their work when exposed to the pain and suffering of their students. You care deeply about the safety and success of your young students. When someone hurts them, we feel their pain and trauma. Their pain too often becomes our pain."

Mrs. Vaughn nodded.

"Until this year, I'm sure you often felt there was little you could do to help your students once you learned about and reported their trauma.

School staff feel like they are powerless to stop the trauma." Dr. Rodriguez knew her words would resonate close to the heart of any teacher, especially one with the compassion of Mrs. Vaughn.

After a moment of contemplation, Mrs. Vaughn shared her thoughts. "Okay, so we know that many of the disruptive behaviors and academic struggles of students relate to unresolved past trauma." She paused to find the right words. "It is also possible that much of the frustrating and even passive-aggressive behavior of our staff is rooted in their own traumatic reactions to the trauma of their students."

"Absolutely." Dr. Rodriguez always had trouble with the next part, as it often hit too close to home. "Also, the majority of those in education come from their own histories of trauma. If untreated, they might struggle with their own social and emotional health."

"Or be retraumatized by the trauma of their students," Mrs. Vaughn added.

"Yes. If something about their students' traumas triggers memories of their own past trauma, they risk retraumatization," Dr. Rodriguez continued. "Staff can also become traumatized as a result of consistent exposure to their students' pain and suffering over time. They are especially vulnerable when they learn about their suffering but feel they are powerless to stop it or help in a meaningful way."

"If that were true, every teacher in the country would be traumatized!" Mrs. Vaughn felt somewhat defensive without really knowing why.

Dr. Rodriguez said nothing, as she allowed time for Mrs. Vaughn's statement to sink in.

"Sorry, I wanted to talk to you about my co-workers. Now I am wondering, do you think I'm traumatized?" Mrs. Vaughn said, with a chuckle that communicated her uncomfortableness with the question.

"I'm careful when I use the word 'trauma,' and without a much longer conversation, I couldn't give you a concrete answer. In general, without a great deal of focus on their own wellness and self-care, I cannot see how any teacher, administrator, or school staff who cares about their students and the quality of their work does not at some point in their career experience psychological distress that impacts their mental health. While we know primary-school teachers and administrators burn out more than almost any other profession, whether it reaches the point of trauma would necessitate a closer look," Dr. Rodriguez said in a quiet voice.

Mrs. Vaughn spoke much more excitedly, "How do we create trauma-sensitive schools for our students and families when we are traumatized ourselves?"

Mrs. Vaughn's question hung like a black cloud over the two of them. Ms. Smith walked up just in time to hear Mrs. Vaughn's question. "You are talking about Mr. Anderson, aren't you?"

Two heads turned, shooting her looks that communicated both the truth in her statement and how uncomfortable it was to narrow the focus from every teacher in the country to their teammate.

Mrs. Vaughn wasn't ready to discuss Mr. Anderson. She knew Ms. Smith was aware of his problems, but she felt protective of her friend and, until recently, esteemed teaching partner. "I think we are talking about all of us; well, maybe not you." Mrs. Vaughn caught herself for the first time feeling envious of Ms. Smith's energy, which she somehow had maintained throughout this particularly challenging school year.

"Finally, we are talking about education fatigue." Dr. Rodriguez glanced at Mrs. Vaughn, not wanting to disclose their private conversation.

Mrs. Vaughn smiled, "Just include her." With that, Dr. Rodriguez nodded. Education fatigue and self-care was an entire semester-long class in the teacher-education program that Ms. Smith had completed.

"When we identified our own self-care as one of the topics over winter break, I thought we might start there." Ms. Smith looked at Mrs. Vaughn. "The health of the staff at our school is miserable. It seems like everyone just holds on long enough for the next break or long weekend."

"We aren't all young teachers." Mrs. Vaughn felt herself getting defensive and a little angry.

"I know. Sorry, I meant no offense." Ms. Smith said lowering her head slightly as she realized her overstep.

"I know you didn't. I also know you are right. Many of us carry the great burden of our students' trauma, behaviors, and struggles from one year to the next, wondering if we are making any meaningful difference. It's exhausting and, now I know, maybe traumatizing." Mrs. Vaughn said with sadness in her voice.

Dr. Rodriguez said, "I decided not to start with the self-care piece because I find it better if people come to this realization on their own. Having an outsider or a new energetic teacher," she smiled at Ms. Smith, "come in and tell everyone they are traumatized or burned out, and that their mental health is preventing them from being effective, threatens to stop a process before it gets off the ground."

"Really, Dr. Rodriguez, you think a teacher would react defensively to someone telling them that they are traumatized?" Mrs. Vaughn lightly kicked Ms. Smith's leg in a joking manner. "Let's try to meet with Dr. Griffin before our next Trauma-Sensitive Transformation Team meeting. I believe the end of the year is a great time to start planning for some concrete steps to address our own wellness for the next school year."

CHAPTER 12
Self-Care for Educational Excellence

In all the debates about education, rarely does school-staff wellness come into the conversation. News stories feature former educators so frustrated that they felt compelled to leave the field of education entirely. However, few debates or stories address the core issue. Unhealthy, burnt-out, and traumatized educators will often fail to create vibrant educational and emotionally healthy environments for our children.

We will address the role that schools and districts play in educator health in the next chapter. While the school environment and the treatment of educators significantly impacts staff wellness and effectiveness, the individual must take personal action to ensure their health. A trauma-sensitive school requires a healthy and motivated staff to implement trauma-sensitive practices effectively.

In this chapter, we present best practices for work effectiveness and ways to stay mentally healthy in an occupation fraught with burnout and trauma. This section allows for a comparison of current strategies and lifestyles to some research-based self-care approaches. The challenge is to identify small changes in routines, mindsets, and habits that could improve health, work, and overall well-being.

Physical Health

Physical health is the basis of our emotional, cognitive, and social functioning. Most people know the importance of sleep, nutrition, and exercise on well-being. Fewer think about the relationships between physical health and the ability to provide students with the education and services they need.

Please note: This section comes from years of research on physical health. However, we are not medical professionals. Please check with your medical provider to see if the strategies presented here are appropriate for you.

Sleep

Let's start the examination of physical health by exploring the importance of sleep. If someone were to do one single thing to ensure they could bring their best self to work tomorrow, it would entail getting eight hours of sleep tonight. Unfortunately, getting a good night's sleep is increasingly difficult as people become busier, more stressed, and more connected to technology.

Sleep helps to reset all the body's systems to ensure the mind and body work effectively the next day. A good analogy to demonstrate the power of sleep is thinking about a cell phone. Eventually, due to the number of apps running, battery drain, and just everyday use, phones slow down. In most cases, the solution to the problem is a quick restart. During the reboot, the phone closes apps, installs updates, and ensures everything is operating correctly.

Sleep is like restarting a phone for the mind and body. Everyone knows how great a good night's sleep feels. While research shows that most people need a full eight hours of sleep a night, the average person gets only 6.7 hours.

There is a lucky minority of people who need slightly less sleep than eight hours. Someone waking up feeling refreshed after six or seven hours of sleep might find themselves in that group. Most people do need eight hours. Unfortunately, many fall short with grave consequences (Rath & Harter, 2010).

Well beyond just being tired, insufficient sleep has a devastating impact on well-being and work performance. Lack of sleep has much the same effect as drinking. Very few people would drink a six-pack of beer before work, but lack of sleep and intoxication have some very similar characteristics.

Like drinking too much, lack of sleep increases the number of mistakes people make and decreases productivity and effectiveness. When sleep-deprived, people do and say things they usually would never say or do and might regret later. While those around them might easily notice the change in behavior, they remain unaware of how impaired the lack of sleep has made them (Stulberg & Magness, 2017).

Besides limiting social and cognitive abilities, lack of sleep hinders the ability to learn. During sleep, the brain files information learned that day with similar knowledge gained in the past. As mentioned in an earlier chapter, this brain process is called sequential memory. Sleep is where many long-term memories form. Without sleep, the person fails to retain knowledge. If you ever crammed all night for a test in college, you probably did okay on the test itself, because you had the information in your short-term memory. But what did you remember a few weeks later? Probably not much (Schwartz, 2010).

Now it gets alarming as the research shows that lack of sleep over long stretches leads to weight gain, type 2 diabetes, and even early death. Sleep deprivation leaves the person more likely to reach for food or drink that is high in sugar and calories. This reaction to lack of sleep gives the brain the short-term energy it craves because it lacks the energy of a good night's rest.

A recent study by the National Institutes of Health showed sleep-deprived people consume 549 additional calories a day. Over a long period of time, these extra calories put people at risk of type 2 diabetes and early death. In addition to preventing type 2 diabetes and early death, sleeping eight hours per night has been shown to facilitate healthy weight loss (National Sleep Foundation, 2019; Schwartz, 2010).

Here is some research that might help those who struggle with sleep:

Turn off all electronics about an hour before trying to sleep. Unplugging includes phones, computers, tablets, and TV. The visual field holds the light from these devices for about an hour after viewing them. Also, things like social media and email excite many areas in the brain. This excitement is fun during the day, but can prevent one from relaxing, thus keeping you awake longer.

A cool, dark, and quiet environment promotes sleep. Try to control these variables as much as possible. Eye masks, earplugs, and white-noise machines might help if the bedroom does not allow for the creation of an ideal sleep environment.

Ever hear a teammate say, "I am going to go home and have a big glass of wine"? While alcohol helps bring sleep on, it reduces the quality of sleep dramatically. Drinking often leads to waking up in the middle of the night and limits the amount of deep restorative sleep. There is nothing inherently wrong with enjoying a drink or two; however, for a good night's sleep, the earlier in the evening that you enjoy that drink is better.

Blinking eyes quickly for several minutes (basically making them tired) signals to the brain that it is time to sleep. Reading can also help, but make sure the material is not something that is too emotionally or intellectually exciting. This excitement gets the mind racing and wanting to read on or ruminate about the material. Magazines are perfect for night reading. The articles are short, so even if they are interesting, they end relatively quickly without the yearning to read the next chapter (Graves, 2008).

Research shows that waking up and going to sleep at the same time every day trains the brain and helps promote getting to sleep faster, as well as increasing sleep quality. This strategy seems unappealing to many school staff, because of their normal early bedtime and wake-up routine during the school year. However, sleep consistency is one of the best strategies to help people who struggle with sleep.

We will cover mindfulness or meditation in more detail in a moment. Practicing mindfulness near bedtime releases many of the same neurobiological chemicals that also promote sleep. For those practicing yoga, a yoga instructor will help identify the right poses for before bed. There are specific poses that help to calm the nervous system, quiet the brain, and assist with sleep, particularly if they are consistently practiced each evening (Graves, 2008; Schwartz, 2010).

Exercise

Sleep refreshes the body's systems and sets the body and mind up for a great day. Exercise helps manage the chemical, physical, and psychological realities of working in one of the most stressful occupations in our society. To stay healthy under stress, movement is a must!

Visualize exercise as a release valve at the bottom of the cup. As the stress hormone cortisol fills the cup throughout the day, a good workout opens the release valve, and the stress flows out the bottom. If cortisol is not released, it just sits in the cup and accounts for many of the medical, occupational, and psychological effects of burnout and trauma explored in Chapter 11 (Rock, 2009; Stulberg & Magness, 2017).

Cortisol and stress prepare the body for physical action. Throughout human evolution, most stressful events required a physical response to help a person either run away from a predator or fight an enemy. Human evolution has not caught up with today's rapidly changing work environment, where stressful situations require an intellectual, not a physical, response.

Not exercising allows cortisol to remain in the body and become toxic. Over time this leads to long-term physical, mental, and social problems. Eventually, cortisol starts to kill off brain cells associated with memory and intellectual functioning. After a stressful day, exercising is probably the last thing anyone wants to do. However, fitting in a good workout can dramatically improve your mood for the rest of the day, let the body and mind fully recover from stress, and allow the person to bring their best self to school the next day (Rock, 2009).

While the physical benefits of exercise are well known, the effects on the brain are just as powerful. People who exercise have larger prefrontal cortexes. In addition to healthier and larger prefrontal cortexes, exercise helps create new neurons in the brain, a process called neurogenesis. Neurogenesis and the removal of cortisol helps improve learning and memory creation, as well as protect the brain from injury and aging (Kharrazain, 2013; University of Texas Southwestern Medical Center, 2010).

Exercise also delivers emotional benefits. Think for a moment about how it feels to run, walk in the park, or take a bike ride. Regular exercise has been shown to improve overall mental health. Since exercise lowers the level of stress and cortisol in the cup, you increase the ability to regulate emotions and engage cognitively in complex work (Fernandez, 2006).

Studies conducted with those suffering from depression clearly document the power of exercise. Getting 30-45 minutes of vigorous exercise six days a week can lower depression and anxiety as effectively as psychotropic medication. While this is not a suggestion to stop medications, it does show that exercise powerfully improves everyone's mental health. Exercising promotes overall happiness and provides the energy to live a fulfilled life, both at school and beyond (Rock, 2009).

For most people, the goal is to work up to exercising several times a week at an intensity that works up a good sweat. This consistency may seem like a far-off goal. However, start small and remember that the important thing is movement. For those who are not currently active, start by walking around the block at lunch, taking the stairs and not the elevator, or jogging for a bit and then walking briskly the rest of the way for a mile. The key is to do something active and try to build up more and more stamina. The positive effects will show in the body and brain almost immediately.

Diet

Due to individualized needs, allergies, and rapidly changing research on diet and nutrition, here we approach diet from a neurobiological standpoint. The challenge is to think about how diet impacts energy and mood during the school day.

Many people have a love/hate relationship with food. The human brain developed in a time when food was scarce and not always easy to get. People evolved to eat food whenever it was available. The more fat and sugar in the food, the happier the brain is, at least in the short term. This instinct to eat as much as possible when it's available was a great survival skill for our ancestors, who might have gone for days without a good meal. However, it doesn't work as well for people today when they walk by a box of donuts in their staff lounge!

Food is the fuel for the brain. Like a car or lawnmower, the better the fuel, the more efficient and effective the body and brain work. Putting too much, too little, or lousy fuel in the body impacts the functioning of the brain and has direct consequences for the quality of work (Kharrazain, 2013; Rock, 2009).

Mind Health

Mind health describes the ability to balance mental and emotional states, creating space for increased work productivity and effectiveness. Strategies to improve mind health are designed to counteract the negative psychological and emotional impacts of educational fatigue. In this section, we will cover how to maintain and maximize a healthy brain and serve as a model for well-being for students and families.

Mindfulness

Let's begin with mindfulness, which in addition to physical health, is one of the most potent ways to keep our brains healthy. Chapter 3 introduced the basics of mindfulness. This section will examine the research demonstrating how mindfulness practices keep people healthy in stressful jobs.

How much would people pay for a pill that had the following benefits? This pill improves medical health and immune functioning, and helps speed up the healing from injuries and illnesses. Also, the pill improves mental health, lowers stress levels, and improves work outcomes. This same magic pill also increases compassion and empathy, and even improves your marriage, friendships, and other relationships. Some studies are even showing that this pill increases the size of the prefrontal cortex and helps regulate the amygdala. The side effects of this pill are just 10 to 20 minutes out of your day (Davidson et. al., 2003; Davis & Hayes, 2012; Goleman & Davidson, 2017; Rock, 2009; Siegel, 2011; Seigel, 2016).

Of course, the pill is really a consistent mindfulness practice. The good news is that it is free! With all the amazing research on mindfulness and its integration into education, it is hard to come up with an excuse for school staff who don't pursue their own mindfulness practice.

As a self-care strategy for school staff, mindfulness has two key components. The first is a mindful practice. This practice requires a little time each day focusing attention on one specific object or on breathing, movement (such as a yoga pose or tai chi set), or a mantra, chant, or prayer that is repetitive in nature. This daily practice creates the ability to bring mindfulness into work and personal relationships.

Due to the high stress of education, it is ideal to practice mindfulness for ten minutes before school and ten minutes between the end of school and going to bed. What would this practice look like? Make it simple. Counting breaths, listening to a guided meditation, searching for specific strategies online, doing a short yoga practice, or taking a walk, where the only thing to focus on is taking the next step and your surroundings, are great forms of mindfulness practice.

The second component of mindfulness is presence at work. A mindful practice helps develop an easily accessible sense of calm and peace. When the cup starts to fill up at work, a sustained practice over time will allow the person to take a deep breath or repeat a mantra to bring the peace and calm from their practice into that stressful moment.

Mindfulness not only promotes greater overall emotional health, it also helps identify that the cup is filling up in the first place. People who practice mindfulness achieve greater awareness of their emotional states, especially when their cups are filling up. Mindfulness helps label feelings and catch them before they result in behaviors that are not helpful or healthy. While useful in the moment, mindfulness also helps identify when someone enters the stages of education fatigue. The earlier someone identifies that they are experiencing exhaustion, the sooner they will take action to prevent the harmful effects of later stages (Siegel, 2011).

Here are a few ideas that are easily researched online to find the best fit:

Mindful breathing:

- Pranayama
- 1 to 2 breathing
- Square breathing
- Counting breaths

Physical mindfulness:

- Yoga
- Tai Chi
- Walking meditation

Online or media-guided meditation:
- Loving Kindness Meditation
- Body scans
- Progressive relaxation
- Guided/directed practices

Purpose and Passion

For most, this work is much more than a job. It is a calling. A job is about a paycheck, whereas a calling is about fulfilling something ingrained deeply in one's personality. Most people went into education because of some of the fantastic teachers they were lucky enough to experience in their education. Others are drawn to fulfill a personal or spiritual calling to give back and reach students who might otherwise fall through the cracks.

"What ripens passion is the conviction that your work matters" (Duckworth, 2016). As school staff enter the guilt, doubt, and shame stage of education fatigue, it becomes harder to see the difference they are making in the lives of their students and families. When burnout, the stress of modern education, or problems with students overwhelm them, they lose sight of their purpose and passion, and risk moving even further down the stages of education fatigue.

Focusing on passion and purpose reduces the negative impact of stress. Passion and purpose put difficult interactions with families, student issues, and unsatisfying parts of a job in perspective. No self-care strategy will prevent hard days and stressful times throughout the school year. Focusing on passion and purpose keeps these hardships in perspective and prevents them from becoming all-encompassing.

Professionals who stay connected to their passion and purpose show improved well-being, endurance, energy levels, creativity, problem-solving, learning, and confidence. In other words, passion and purpose create resiliency in the face of stress and difficult work situations. Some more good news: those who live their purpose maintain better mental and physical health as they age (Duckworth, 2016; Duhigg, 2016).

The hard truth is that years of working in struggling communities and dysfunctional schools leave many school staff questioning their purpose and lacking passion for their jobs. Earlier in my own career, I noticed uncharacteristic thoughts entering my mind, such as, "It doesn't matter if I get a substitute today. This class will make the same progress with anyone teaching them." or berating myself for choosing to go into the field of education at all. I found myself envying friends who got to travel for their career or wishing that my graduate degree did not pigeonhole me into being a teacher. I am ashamed that I had these thoughts and feelings, but eventually, I was able to recognize that I was struggling with educator fatigue and I needed to make some drastic changes.

Working with students with trauma in modern education forces school staff to face a level of stress and trauma that other professions never confront. The one advantage they do possess is that they get to go to work each day and live their purpose. Not only does it feel good to do meaningful work and help children every day, but people who have a defined purpose and who fulfill that purpose also live healthier and more fulfilled lives (Duckworth, 2016).

Optimistic Mindset

The process of behavioral change, academic growth, and healing is a dance with positive steps forward that are accompanied by setbacks and frustration. It is easy to focus on the steps back and overlook the positive progress that students make over time.

The process of helping students and families is both frustrating and inspirational, traumatic and life-changing, depressing and exhilarating. Often these extremes happen all within one day or even within the same hour. One family finally agrees to start mental-health counseling for their child. The next minute, a student has a meltdown and threatens a classmate. Then a third student finally sees their hard work pay off when they get a perfect score on a spelling test.

Unfortunately, humans evolved to focus more on the negative than the positive. It is easy to miss the fantastic progress of students because the setbacks demand more time, energy, and attention. It is critical to take time to celebrate success with students and co-workers. Make a conscious effort to share success stories, recognize exceptional work in others, and always bring positive progress to the attention of students.

To maintain hope and a positive mindset, practice realistic optimism. Realistic optimism challenges people to exercise leniency in their evaluation of past events, actively appreciating the positive aspects of the current situation and routinely emphasizing possible opportunities for the future. The concept of realistic optimism pushes school staff to find the positive in the situation without being blind to some of the real challenges inherent in helping students in traumatic situations (Schneider, 2001).

School staff must apply an optimistic mindset to themselves and co-workers as well. Recognize the stress, trauma, challenges, and realities of education fatigue, while searching for the positive impact of the school's efforts on the social, emotional, and academic success of the students. At the same time, understand that many of the frustrating behaviors of co-workers do not result from inherent problems with them, but from the stress of the work. A positive and optimistic approach helps school staff find areas to support their co-workers without the judgment and harsh criticism that often lowers morale and team dynamics.

When people are in a positive and optimistic state, the amount of serotonin in the body increases. Serotonin impacts work performance by increasing learning capacity, improving thinking and problem-solving ability, increasing creativity, and undoing the adverse effects of stressful events. High-performing schools are positive places that foster optimism among staff and students (Achor, 2010).

Try to share three positive things that happened during the day with someone in your life. If teammates are interested, send each other emails with the three positives before leaving for the day. It is a great morale booster and puts everyone in a good mood to start the evening. If co-workers are not the right fit, find a family member or friends to partner with on the exercise.

The small act of sharing your positives does terrific things for health and wellness. Sharing gratitude and joy improves mental and physical health and enhances the quality of relationships. Those who practice gratitude get more satisfaction out of life, are more altruistic, and experience a greater degree of happiness. Taking just a few seconds to share positives between teammates over email builds morale and collaboration, and helps counteract the adverse events that happen throughout the typical week (Seppälä, 2013).

Therapy

A critical step in helping students heal from trauma is connecting them with mental-health services. Many professionals who fully understand the reasons behind referring students to mental-health treatment fail to view therapy as a tool that could also improve their own mental health and help them to recover from educator fatigue. Mental health plays a central role in trauma-sensitive schools for students, families, and staff.

Trauma-sensitive school staff realize that working with vulnerable children experiencing trauma puts their mental health at risk. Accessing therapy is not a sign of weakness. It is an opportunity to build resiliency and robustness. With the high levels of burnout and trauma inherent in education, it is hard to imagine a school staff who would not need mental-health services at some point in their career.

When should you or someone you know consider seeking mental-health services? Experiencing any stage of education fatigue beyond exhaustion is a clear sign that the work is starting to impact social and emotional health. A therapist will help resolve the root causes of guilt and doubt, as well as any resulting shame, and then help chart a path back to wellness. Also, being in the exhaustion stage for an extended period demonstrates that the person might not possess the ability to get out of this stage without help. The longer someone stays in exhaustion, the higher their risk to move on to the more detrimental stages of education fatigue.

Another way to assess if therapy could help is when a friend, family member, or partner identifies that things at work are impacting behavior, relationships, or enjoyment at home. Trauma and burnout will follow school staff home. When someone struggles in their role as parent, spouse, or friend, it is a good sign that they should seek support.

While outside the professional scope, the inverse is also true. So much happens in life outside work. It isn't always easy to keep trauma or stress in one's personal life from affecting professional performance. If someone finds it hard not to bring emotional issues from their personal life into work, it is a sign that the person could benefit from therapy. A therapist will help address these issues, keeping work performance as high as possible as the person works through personal trauma.

Too many people stigmatize mental-health services. Unfortunately, this stigma keeps thousands of people from getting the help they need to overcome their trauma. School staff in trauma-sensitive schools are role models for health and wellness. Don't let stigma keep you from living the healthy life you deserve.

Improving Cognitive Functioning

The final mind-health concept we'll cover here is how to increase our brainpower. While the workload of modern education will continue to challenge everyone to find the time to get everything done, certain work strategies profoundly impact productivity and whether someone will enter the stages of education fatigue. Let's discuss a few brain-friendly practices that have been proven to maximize brainpower at work.

First, take breaks whenever possible. Though the time for breaks is difficult to find in school settings, the brain only can operate at its best for 90 to 120 minutes before it experiences dramatic drops in productivity and effectiveness. Taking breaks periodically throughout the day allows school staff to maintain high levels of performance. Even spending five minutes to listen to a favorite song, do a couple of yoga poses, or take a quick walk around the school allows the brain to rest and continue its optimal functioning (Rock, 2009).

While most positions in a school require spending the majority of one's time with students, everyone grades assignments, checks email, fills out assessments, and expends significant time on administrative tasks. When something must get done, remember one critical piece of brain research: stop the madness of multitasking! The brain is terrific when it focuses on only one thing and suffers when distractions pull attention in multiple directions (Stulberg & Magness, 2017; Tracy, 2016).

Multitasking lowers productivity up to 90%, meaning the multitasker basically does not get anything done. Constant distractions from technology or people cost time, cognitive capacity, productivity, and quality. Studies show that when distracted by people or technology, it takes up to a half hour to get back to the task. They also demonstrate that every time people shift cognitive focus to a new task, it exhausts the brain and decreases IQ, making them less productive and increasing the number and severity of mistakes (Rock, 2009; Schwartz, 2010).

These are a few easy strategies to increase productivity and quality, and to get school staff home after a long day. Consider establishing open, honest communication within the school, allowing staff to communicate when they would like uninterrupted work time. Obviously, if something is incredibly urgent, a disruption is appropriate. However, if it is not urgent, send an email and check in with them later. This approach enables staff to focus, and when they do check in with teammates, they can give them their full attention.

When working on administrative tasks or grading papers, turn off the phone and email notifications if possible. Eliminating these distractions improves productivity and supports people in getting their work done, thus avoiding the stress of always feeling overwhelmed. Try to strategically schedule a time to return emails and other communication. Like other tasks, focusing just on communication with parents and others maximizes brainpower and lessens fatigue. Trauma-sensitive schools communicate that educating students is the number-one priority, so parents or other professionals should not expect emails or phone calls to be returned during the school day, on weekends, or over vacations (Rock 2009; Stulberg & Magness, 2017).

For most of us, the next strategy is the most important. School staff need to disconnect from work after school hours. Let's return to our cup analogy to demonstrate how checking emails and other messages throughout the evening pushes people into education fatigue.

During the day, stress builds in the body and fills the cup. This accumulation of stress is a natural part of any job, especially one in education. Leaving work shifts people from work mode to home, family, and personal mode. They relax, go to the gym, and connect with those they love. Hopefully, these activities decrease the amount of stress in their cup. After a good evening and a solid night's sleep, their cup is relatively empty, and they bring their best self to work the next day.

Alternatively, someone leaves work. They get home, relax a little, and then check their work email on their phone. What happens then is, instead of relaxing, they stop the recovery process. By nature, emails are stress-inducing because they require action. While many emails may require just a short response, others may trigger feelings of frustration, worry, or even anger, thus causing more stress.

Instead of disconnecting and getting the stress out of their cup, technology robs them of recovery time and adds additional stress into already full cups. The same is true for vacations and breaks. Due to the stressful nature of education, school staff need their time off to refresh and recover. Constantly checking emails brings the work stress into this critical recovery time, promoting further burnout. One important strategy to avoid education fatigue is working hard to disconnect from emails and other communication in the evenings and over breaks (Schwartz, 2010).

Social Health

Now let's look at social health. Social health speaks to the number of positive interactions, both personally and professionally, that a person has with supportive healthy individuals. These positive people and supportive interactions counteract the traumatic and frustrating situations faced when working with struggling students, education in general, and personal issues. The goal is to surround one's self with more positive social interactions than negative ones throughout the course of a day, a week, a month, and a year.

Personal Social Health

Just as school staff play a critical role in the lives of students by helping them decrease their level of stress, friends and family do the same for the staff. The quality of personal relationships is a significant influence on mental, emotional, and even cognitive health and well-being. Emotions and behaviors are highly contagious in nature, and many social sciences compare them to viruses that spread from person to person.

People will take on the behaviors and emotions of the people who surround them. If all their friends are running or playing tennis, they will likely engage in these healthy activities as well. The same is unfortunately true for smoking, overeating, and drug use. Social networks have both positive and negative influences on overall well-being. Education puts school staff in constant contact with students and families experiencing trauma and, as is too often the case, burnt-out co-workers. It's important to spend personal time with people who elicit feelings of joy and happiness, while promoting healthy behaviors (Christakis & Fowler, 2009).

Healthy social networks increase a person's long-term health, and they also play a role in regulating a person's more immediate stress and emotional states. Research shows that six hours a day of positive social time dramatically increases a person's well-being, while minimizing their stress and worry. The six-hour mark is also shown to correlate to people self-reporting that they had a great day. Anything less than six hours decreases these positive effects proportionally (Lieberman, 2014).

One last note on personal social networks. Just as others greatly influence us, our emotions, behaviors, and health will also impact our friends and family. People can either be a source of happiness and joy for their children, spouse or partner, and friends, or they can introduce negative emotions and unhealthy behaviors into the lives of those they love. Remember, behaviors and emotions are contagious. Pay attention to what you spread!

Professional Social Health

Of course, it's impossible to discuss social networks without mentioning the people we spend so much time with: our co-workers.

As members of each other's social network, the relationships between co-workers directly affect the physical and emotional health of all parties. It is nearly impossible to offset the stress experienced in dysfunctional teams or school cultures with personal self-care strategies. The staff could eat a perfect diet, run marathons, meditate on top of a mountain, and hang out with amazing friends, but if they walk into an unhealthy work environment every day, they will have trouble maintaining their health and motivation.

When co-workers support each other, great things happen both for the collective health of the organization and for the quality of education received by students. People working in healthy schools experience fewer mental- and emotional-health issues. They bring a greater sense of purpose to their work, perform better, get sick less, and recover faster from setbacks (Christakis & Fowler, 2009).

One additional benefit of healthy teams and schools is that everyone's intellectual capacity increases. There are a variety of experience levels and areas of expertise in any school. When everyone works well together and supports each other, they freely share this vast library of knowledge with co-workers, which makes everyone smarter and better problem solvers (Christakis & Fowler, 2009).

To keep out of the cycles of education fatigue, staff need to support each other. To thrive as a school, school staff need to share expertise and invest in the success and professional development of everyone in the school. Co-worker relationships are any school's greatest strength or most debilitating weakness.

An individual staff member possesses little control over the health of their co-workers outside the school environment. However, everyone must dedicate themselves to do everything possible to bring your best self to work every day. No one wants to become an additional source of burnout for their co-workers.

A Huge Step Forward

Mrs. Vaughn sat back and admired how the Trauma-Sensitive Transformation Team had grown into an unstoppable juggernaut. Each month, more district personnel, county staff, and parents showed up. Subgroups formed partly because of the amount of work the team took on, but mainly because the full team had expanded to over twenty people. More and more people from a variety of organizations saw the team's work as hope that the community could finally address some of its long-standing problems.

After her conversation with Dr. Rodriguez about the impact of trauma on the staff, Mrs. Vaughn asked if they could add a discussion about self-care to the agenda. While Dr. Rodriguez agreed to talk to the group about the high rates of burnout and trauma among primary educators, she asked Mrs. Vaughn to speak to why she thought the subject was important. Knowing that self-care would take up a good part of the meeting, Dr. Rodriguez put it at the top of the agenda.

Mrs. Vaughn started the meeting, "Hi, everyone! It is amazing to see our group continue to grow. While I'm so excited about our progress toward becoming a trauma-sensitive school, I believe we are missing an important issue that is going to become a roadblock sooner or later." Mrs. Vaughn had everyone's attention, including Dr. Griffin's.

"What's on your mind?" her principal asked, unaware of the discussion between Mrs. Vaughn and Dr. Rodriguez.

Mrs. Vaughn took a deep breath. "When I look at our student body, I see a group of kids greatly impacted by trauma. When I put the same lens on our staff, I am as worried about us as I am about our students. I know many of us come with our own histories of trauma. Besides, our exposure to the trauma of our students and families must impact us in ways we don't acknowledge or even recognize. How can those of us with ongoing or unresolved trauma effectively help others with trauma?"

Her question hung heavily on the group before Ms. Smith added, "In addition, teachers, principals, and social workers are among the top five occupations for burnout. It's like we get hit twice: once with the intense stress of modern education and again with the exposure to our students' trauma."

Dr. Rodriguez came forward to provide the group with a shared language. She introduced the concepts of empathetic intensity and the effects of the stages of education fatigue. Many in the group shared that schools weren't the only ones struggling with these issues, as they were also rampant among social-service, mental-health, and medical organizations.

"Okay," Dr. Griffin wanted the floor, but needed a second to get her thoughts organized. She began with a sense of resignation. "In our initial planning meetings, we identified self-care as an important part of our journey. It's hard to admit in front of you all, but I was hoping we would get to summer break without bringing it up. Of course, I care about my staff and their health, but there is so much work to get done that I'm not really sure where to start."

"I think just admitting that is a great start," Mrs. Vaughn said, with a tone of support and understanding. "I know that personally, I have certainly struggled with burnout and trauma over the years, and I know that my own performance steadily declined as a result." Despite speaking only about her own experience, Mrs. Vaughn also had Mr. Anderson at the forefront of her mind.

"Then I look at this new teacher next to me. She reminds me of myself so many years ago." Mrs. Vaughn nudged Ms. Smith in a manner that was half joking and half a sign of affection. "We are a mess. Teachers in particular are so burned out. I hurt because I don't know how to help my fellow teachers and our staff. If I'm sincere, I'm afraid what doing more self-reflection would reveal about myself. I'm no role model for wellness or health, especially this late in the year."

A few other members from different professional backgrounds shared similar concerns about the well-being of their teammates and their personal battles against burnout and trauma. One of the nurses who did terrific work in the mobile medical unit added that, even though teachers and principals were high on the burnout list, nurses and physicians were second and first on that list, respectively.

"Wow, the race no one wants to win!" Dr. Rodriguez added.

"I think it is a pretty powerful realization." Ms. Smith paused a second, aware that sometimes her youth and enthusiasm could rub some folks the wrong way. However, it rarely stopped her from saying what was on her mind. "Here we are in a room full of educators, leaders, and healers, and we rarely take the time to address our own health."

The room sat silent for several painful moments.

Dr. Griffin sheepishly broke the silence, not liking the words coming out of her mouth. "Should we stop the process and shift our focus to the self-care of our staff? With what Dr. Rodriguez taught us, how could any change process succeed when we are not addressing the well-being of the staff?"

Dr. Rodriguez was about to speak, but made eye contact with Ms. Smith and nodded, knowing the message would be best coming from a teacher in the school.

Ms. Smith said, "Dr. Griffin, I don't see self-care as separate from our trauma-sensitive transformation work. It's part of the journey. There is no way to know for sure, but I would guess all our efforts so far might end up saving a life or possibly keeping a child out of jail. I know we stopped several incidents of abuse just by asking the right questions. I refuse to lose this momentum."

Dr. Griffin smiled, giving Ms. Smith silent permission to continue challenging her, as she wanted to be wrong.

Ms. Smith continued, "Our initiatives with students are rolling right along. It is a great time to create a structure and strategy for self-care. Summer is almost here, so we could implement the new structure beginning in the next school year, when everyone is fresh."

Dr. Griffin nodded, "That makes sense. What would this structure look like?"

Ms. Smith looked back at Dr. Rodriguez, who readily took the floor, beaming with pride for her former student.

Dr. Rodriguez said, "I always like to start out with obtaining some data."

"We just took our school-safety and staff-satisfaction surveys and should get the feedback by our next transformation meeting," Mrs. Vaughn said. Only afterward did she wonder whether Dr. Griffin would want to share the information with the entire group.

Moving forward, Dr. Rodriguez continued, "Great. It's always good to have a baseline to track progress. Another step we could take is to create a self-care plan for each of the staff. I have some plan templates, and it would be great to get them completed this school year so people can reflect on how to improve wellness over the summer break."

Dr. Griffin said, "Assuming it isn't too intensive, we could have staff fill out their plans at the next staff meeting. Dr. Rodriguez, could you attend the meeting and present on burnout and trauma? I think creating a shared language with all our staff is important to help emphasize the importance of creating self-care plans." Dr. Griffin felt relief in moving to the problem-solving stage. However, she was a little worried about sharing the staff survey data with the group. It hadn't always been positive over the last couple of years.

"I would love to come to the next staff meeting. It's just an idea, but I know Ms. Smith did a larger research paper on teacher wellness. I would love it if she took the lead, and maybe a few of the experts around the table could also present strategies to improve physical, mental, and social health." Dr. Rodriguez felt Ms. Smith had earned the respect of her school at this point and was ready for a more significant challenge.

Everyone at the table agreed to the plan, including Dr. Griffin. However, she thought something seemed unresolved. "Okay, we agree that everyone will complete a self-care plan. However, I can't see how a simple self-care plan is going to help burned-out teachers recover and stay healthy during the entire school year. It seems like a great start, but not quite enough."

This time, Ms. Smith shot Dr. Rodriguez a glance. Dr. Rodriguez had presented some powerful lectures about the need for trauma-sensitive coaching and more robust teacher support. She had commented on how the current structure of teacher supervision and school leadership was inadequate to address the stress and trauma of teaching. It was one thing to bash the existing educational structure to a roomful of college students who were easily excited about her vision for a better future. It was another to present her innovative model in a room with district leadership and Dr. Griffin.

Dr. Rodriguez smiled reassuringly at Ms. Smith. "I agree 100%, Dr. Griffin. I have some thoughts, but since they are so school-specific and we have a few more agenda items to cover, I wonder if we might huddle with some of the district leadership after the meeting and find a time to discuss details."

Dr. Griffin got the hint, "I love working with people who not only point out problems, but have solutions before you even ask."

Everyone chuckled.

CHAPTER 13
Trauma-Sensitive School Culture and Climate

The culture plus the climate of a school create an intangible feeling that students, families, and professionals experience when they walk into a school building. According to the Association for Supervision and Curriculum Development (2019),

> School climate refers to the school's effects on students, including teaching practices; diversity; and the relationships among administrators, teachers, parents, and students.
>
> School culture refers to the way teachers and other staff members work together and the set of beliefs, values, and assumptions they share.

Take a moment to reflect on your feelings about your district and school. Do you feel a sense of pride? Consider your relationships with your co-workers, principal, or supervisor. Think about the atmosphere on your team and staff meetings. What feelings fill your body? Now think about how you feel when students show up in the morning and leave in the afternoon. Does this put a smile on your face?

The collective feelings of the staff about the district, school, and co-workers make up a school's culture. The health of schools is a crucial determinant to their effectiveness and the quality of education delivered to students. High-performing schools create cultures where school staff love to come to work each day and support each other personally and professionally.

MacNeil, Prater, and Busch (2009) found that "the culture of a school has far-reaching impacts on every aspect of the organization. Student achievement, teacher effectiveness, teacher retention, community support and student enrollment are all affected by the explicit and implicit cultural aspects of a school."

A healthy culture combined with the approaches and strategies in this book creates a trauma-sensitive school climate. When staff treat each other with respect and compassion, families and students feel welcomed, safe, and a part of the school community. For families and students who have experienced trauma, a healthy school climate is an essential component for academic success.

Creating and maintaining a trauma-sensitive school culture is difficult work that requires constant focus, dedication, and accountability from every member of the school staff. The goal is to establish and nurture a healthy environment where families feel like partners in their children's education, students heal from trauma and are encouraged to reach their social and academic potential, and school staff feel respected and safe.

Toxic Cycles

In every school culture, there are two competing cycles of emotional energy operating at any given time. The toxic cycle contains the negative thoughts, feelings, and actions of the school staff toward co-workers, students, and families. There is also an inverse cycle reinforcing positive thoughts, feelings, and actions about co-workers, students, and families.

Lewis, 2006

Toxic emotions are associated with dishonesty, lack of trust and safety, social cliques that exclude specific individuals, and talking behind another staff member's back. At times, toxic emotions are short-term, such as those caused by a particularly tough day, a trauma that occurred in the school community, a staff member struggling with personal trauma, a fight among students, or negative interactions with a family. These short-term events all introduce negative emotions into the school environment. The goal is to address these issues by supporting co-workers, so these momentary struggles and the resulting stress doesn't escalate and start to destroy the emotional health and motivation of everyone in the school.

Toxic emotions destroy the morale of individual staff. If you have ever worked in a toxic environment or experienced a dysfunctional relationship, you know how hard it is to maintain your health. As the health and morale of certain school staff start to crash, so does productivity, effectiveness, empathy, compassion, and motivation (Bloom, 2006).

Obviously, if an individual staff member's performance starts to decline, the overall effectiveness of the school suffers. However, underperforming staff are much more detrimental to overall school success than one might think. One underperformer in a group of average-to-high performers pulls everyone's performance down significantly over time. Lack of morale and motivation are highly contagious within a group culture. As time passes, one unmotivated low-performing school staff member threatens to pull down the performance of their team and then the entire school (Schwartz, 2010).

Toxicity destroys many schools' ability to provide adequate educational services to their students. Burnout, trauma, and dysfunction define the school's culture. Staff members form cliques and develop a "them versus us" mentality against the leadership or other staff members. Everyone's tolerance and metaphorical cups start to overflow with unhealthy emotions. If allowed to persist, this toxicity creates a school climate where staff begin to loathe everything about their school, co-workers, families, and students.

Healthy Cycles

Integrity is the dedication to the moral principle of always acting in the best interests of co-workers, students, and families. If integrity does not exist, toxicity fills the vacuum. The reality is that both cycles are operating within every school, influencing the strength or weakness of the other.

If the toxicity cycle gains momentum, it threatens to destroy integrity. The stronger the healthy cycle, the better it contains toxicity. Containing toxicity occurs when staff identify and address an adverse event before it evolves into a broader issue. Staff members face a critical choice. Their behaviors and emotions reinforce either the toxic or the healthy aspects of their school. Each person needs to take both individual and collective responsibility for how they impact others.

How do individuals and schools increase healthy cycles and contain toxicity? It must occur through a relentless dedication to integrity. Integrity emerges from a commitment to honesty, trust, safety, universal expectations, accountability, and recognition. Schools possessing these characteristics create educational environments where everyone thrives and supports each other through the inevitable difficult times.

Honesty

Honesty is the foundation of a trauma-sensitive school culture. Without honesty, integrity is impossible to maintain. People don't trust or feel psychologically safe around those they believe are dishonest. Holding each other accountable for operating within universal expectations requires a strong dedication to honest and open communication. When people all believe everyone is genuinely and honestly acting in the best interest of the school, the committees and teams function better, promoting effective collaborative decision making.

The challenge of honesty goes far beyond not lying to another person. It requires people to abstain from saying things behind another's back that they lack the courage to say to them directly. A staff member who puts down or gossips about fellow staff members and lacks the integrity to talk to their co-workers directly is intensifying toxicity in the school culture.

Honesty challenges school staff to confront behaviors such as gossip and passive-aggressive behaviors, and to hold everyone accountable to the universal expectations. As people work together and hold themselves and each other accountable to the universal expectations, trust and safety increase. Honest schools confront difficult issues and toxicity in their culture head-on, while maintaining mutual respect and empathy for all involved (Kouzes & Posner, 2007).

Trust

In Chapter 4, we discussed the crucial role of trust and safety in helping students and families who are working through trauma. We defined trust as an assured reliance on the character, ability, and strength of the school staff. When speaking about trust in the context of school culture, we include the staff's ability to predict the quality and consistency of their co-worker's behavior. Trust is both about who you are as a person, your ability to meet other's expectations, and doing what you say you will do. Particularly in co-teaching models, trust is essential to the team's ability to effectively plan trauma-sensitive instruction, modify teaching practices, and communicate openly and honestly.

Trust is fluid and ever-changing. It takes years to build high levels of trust in schools and, regrettably, just a few negative interactions to destroy it. Trauma-sensitive schools purposefully focus on improving trust when things are going well. Trust will help everyone overcome trauma, challenges, and painful events. Building trust during good times helps create a capacity for collective resiliency when problems occur.

When trust is high, good things happen. Research demonstrates trust's positive impact on everything from turnover, applicants for employment, productivity, ability to learn, and the reduction of stress-based aggressive responses. Honesty sets the stage for trusting relationships. Trust helps promote physical, moral, and psychological safety (Bloom & Farragher, 2013; Wagner & Harter, 2006).

Safety

Three levels of safety exist in trauma-sensitive school cultures. In this context, safety is the freedom from hurt, injury, or loss. The first level of safety is freedom from physical harm. Physical safety provides reassurance that the school and staff work hard to prevent and respond effectively to any violence occurring at the school.

Physical safety is an issue for many people who work with students who live with trauma and have intense emotional outbursts. Part of physical safety involves the school's structure and security. Just as important to staff is the ability to trust that the principal and their co-workers support them and react effectively when potentially dangerous situations do occur.

The next level of safety in a trauma-sensitive school is psychological safety. Psychological safety refers to having confidence that staff will respect each other's feelings and psychological well-being. Psychological safety leads to innovation, as people trust that when they put forth new ideas, challenge the status quo, and speak out, they will not face ridicule. Just as with the students, without psychological safety, the brain will classify certain co-workers as a threat and become triggered, limiting staff members' intellectual capacity and creativity.

Finally, the third level of safety is moral safety. Moral safety occurs when people develop faith that their district and school leaders do not operate in hypocrisy, they value staff, and they always act in the best interest of students and families. Few things destroy morale faster than feeling your school's policies and procedures are hurting people. Lack of moral safety quickly evolves into a "them versus us" battle between leadership and staff.

When you feel safe, all your energy goes into your work. If you feel unsafe, your energy redirects to establishing as much safety as possible. This energy is most often focused on the self and takes focus away from actions that improve the academic performance of the students (Bloom & Farragher, 2011).

Universal Expectations and Accountability

As mentioned in Chapter 6, universal expectations are for everyone: students, educators, administrators, and families. Part of the dedication to universal expectations is holding everyone accountable for abiding by them every day. In a trauma-sensitive culture, accountability is a supportive process that helps everyone stay focused on the norms that drive a healthy culture and climate.

When a school staff believes someone's behavior falls outside the universal expectations, they should avoid jumping to the conclusion that the person is intentionally breaking expectations. Maybe they did not sleep last night because of a sick child. Is something going on at home that filled their cup up last night? Did they experience empathetic intensity due to an intense situation with a student or family?

Accountability in a trauma-sensitive school is about support more than confrontation. If a co-worker's behavior is not putting a student at risk, or something else that might require more formal action, check in to make sure they are alright. Make statements such as, "Hey, that seemed like a tough student interaction. Are you doing okay? How can I support you?" This approach shows support and the desire to help if possible.

A high accountability culture is more productive and creative, and achieves better results for students. Accountability also fosters the mindset that everyone is in this together, and if one member of the team is struggling, everyone will pitch in to help them out as much as possible. Accountability to teammates also improves staff's ability to hold themselves accountable when necessary. Ideally, staff would self-identify when they fall short of meeting universal expectations and would then self-correct or ask for help (Wagner & Harter, 2006).

Recognition

High-performance cultures recognize the great work done by their staff members. High-recognition cultures far outperform those that do not appreciate and honor the fantastic work of others in their school community. These cultures promote happy staff, loyalty among staff members, more engaged students, and staff dedicated to academic excellence. Recognizing the fantastic work done in the school doesn't just feel good; it improves the culture (Gostick & Elton, 2009).

Recognition boosts the mood of the person getting recognized and the person acknowledging their actions. Recognition keeps staff members healthy, as they are focusing on the positives of their school and co-workers. Remember, people thrive when they get 5.6 times more positive feedback than negative. High-recognition cultures achieve 39% higher staff satisfaction, 73% higher morale, 45% more loyalty (measured in turnover), 20% increase in productivity, and better economic health (Connors & Smith, 2009).

Recognition does not include merely telling someone they did a great job. To fully realize the positive outcomes associated with recognition, staff can formalize the process. Here are some best practices for recognition programs:

- Recognize people for effort, supporting the growth mindset. What did the person do to embody universal expectations, help a struggling family, help a student find their island of competency, or further the school on its trauma-sensitive journey?
- Make it timely. The closer the recognition is to the behavior, the more the compliment is appreciated.
- Make it formal. Consider a formal process where staff go to the office, have a place to write down who they are recognizing and why, and get something (even if it is just a cut-out of a star or other symbol) to hand to the person they are recognizing. This approach also provides leadership with an ongoing record of the great work done at the school.
- Go big when appropriate. When someone does something fantastic, invite district leaders and others. It gives everyone a chance to brag about the person and their accomplishments.

Trauma-Sensitive Coaching

Traditional models of education provided minimal coaching to help staff improve professional performance or maintain wellness. Many teachers are lucky to get one or two observations per year. These limited interactions create a great deal of stress for the teacher and often offer little valuable feedback to improve teacher performance. This frustratingly illogical and ineffective approach to effective coaching does not fit into a trauma-sensitive framework.

What distinguishes the way a trauma-sensitive school supports staff is how it intentionally separates formal evaluations from ongoing coaching. Formal observations and evaluations are an inherent part of working in education. However, coaching focuses on helping the school staff develop as professionals, as well as supporting their mental and emotional health and well-being (Achor, 2010; Fernandez, 2006; Hoopes & Kelly, 2004; Maslach & Leiter, 1997; Siebert, 2005).

What is trauma-sensitive coaching? We use Bob and Megan Tschannen-Morgan's (2010) five concerns of effective coaching to structure our definition, as explained below.

Concern for Connection

The first goal of a trauma-sensitive coach concerns building a trusting and psychologically safe relationship with the educator. Coaches need training in effective and supportive communication strategies, such as those presented in Chapter 4. Mental-health professionals might fill the role of a coach, but will only give limited feedback on instructional effectiveness. A teacher well trained in supportive communication and trauma, and with a basic understanding of wellness and mental health, will bring both classroom expertise and relationship skills to the role. The stronger the trust and sense of psychological safety, the more effective the coach and the school staff they support.

Concern for Consciousness

The trauma-sensitive coach helps the school staff gain self-awareness and insight with a nonjudgmental approach. Coaches do not evaluate performance. The trauma-sensitive coach works with the school staff on developing self-care strategies like those we discussed in Chapter 12. The coach then meets with the staff regularly to spend time checking in on health and wellness.

Coaches serve as a reflective sounding board for the school staff to help them assess and improve wellness over time. The coach provides an objective perspective on whether any staff are in the stages of educator fatigue. They are positioned to support the staff in maintaining their physical and emotional health.

Concern for Competence

A coach provides leadership in the trauma-sensitive transformation process. Coaches serve as trauma trainers and subject-matter experts as they build knowledge within the school community. They also help administration review policies and procedures to ensure alignment with trauma-sensitive principles. Finally, they also provide coaching to teachers to help evolve their academic and behavioral-management approaches for students dealing with the effects of trauma.

Concern for Contribution

Working with students every day makes it sometimes tricky to identify progress, especially when it comes to gains in the social and emotional health of students experiencing trauma. The coach provides an objective perspective on the progress of specific students. Coaches will get to know the caseload of students struggling with trauma in the school building. They work with their teachers and other school staff to find the right approaches for those students. Improvements in relational skills, frustration tolerance, or self-calming techniques would typically not show up on standardized tests or other measures. This role allows the coach to become a partner in the emotional healing and post-traumatic growth of students.

Concern for Creativity

Successfully transforming classrooms and schools requires a great deal of innovation and creativity. School staff under stress naturally fall back on old habits, routines, and what they think worked well in the past. The coach invites them to think creatively and supports them in implementing new strategies and approaches. In a trusting and safe relationship with the coach, the staff is encouraged and supported when stepping outside their comfort zone to find new ways to help students thrive.

Let's address the apparent problem staring us in the face. How would a school or district justify the full implementation costs associated with this type of coaching? Here is our rationale:

- 8% of teachers leave the profession every year. Why? Top reasons include burnout, not enough respect, and lack of support. The inability to retain teachers is costing the educational system up to an estimated $2.2 billion a year (Carver-Thomas & Darling-Hammond, 2017; Schaffhauser, 2014).
- Replacing teachers is expensive: $9,000 for a rural teacher, $11,000 for a suburban teacher, and $21,000 for an urban teacher. Reducing turnover alone is a strong justification for trauma-sensitive coaching (Carver-Thomas & Darling-Hammond, 2017).

Creating a position and training a trauma-sensitive coach is an investment that pays off financially, improves the wellness and performance of staff, and supports the trauma-sensitive transformation process. The research clearly demonstrates that current educational approaches are failing both students with trauma and school staff. A trauma-sensitive coach is positioned to address these deficits and improve the performance of the school.

Trauma-Sensitive Leadership

In our narrative, how much progress would Mrs. Vaughn and Ms. Smith have achieved without the support of their principal, Dr. Griffin? Now that we are approaching the end of our exploration of trauma-sensitive schools, we land on an important and, for some, uncomfortable place. Without strong leadership from principals, vice or assistant principals, and those at the district level, schools will stay stuck in the traditional models of education that fail too many students with trauma.

Terrible leadership is epidemic in our society. Three out of every four people report their leader is the most stressful part of their day and that the worst part of their day is time spent with their boss. Even darker, over a quarter of people report being bullied by their leader. Poor leadership is killing us, as research demonstrates that a lousy leader increases the risk of a severe heart problem by 39%. Also, if the principal is the most stressful and worst part of a staff's day, that boss is filling up the staff member's cup, putting them at considerable risk of cancer, diabetes, addiction, stroke, mental illness, and cognitive decline (Rock, 2009; Schwartz, 2010; Sutton, 2010).

A trauma-sensitive school needs a trauma-sensitive leader. A trauma-sensitive leader holds two focuses: affective leadership and intellectual leadership. The leader understands that both are necessary for academic excellence. Affective refers to the experience of an emotion or feeling. In other words, leaders have an affective focus on how staff and students feel when they walk through the doors of the school and interact with each other.

Affective leadership works to create a school environment that maximizes well-being, quality, and motivation. The leader works to establish relationships based on integrity, safety, and a positive approach to student success. They serve as the role model for integrity, mindfulness, self-care, and resiliency. When trauma occurs in the school community, the leader creates a calm and safe environment for their students and staff to process the subsequent emotions and pain.

Leaders play an outsized role when it comes to the health of the school's climate and culture. The leader's emotional state is the most contagious in the school. If the leader's cup is spilling over, it inevitably overwhelms everyone else. A trauma-sensitive leader understands that their emotional and mental health has a tremendous influence on everyone at the school.

Besides serving as the role model for strength, health, and resiliency, the trauma-sensitive leader understands that the quality of relationships between the leader and their staff sets the standard for how staff treat each other, students, and families. The relationship between leadership and staff sends a powerful message. It communicates to all the staff, "Here is how we treat people at this school." A strong leader understands that trust and safety are highly predictive of staff health and their ability to give their best selves to servicing the students.

The second focus of a trauma-informed leader is a relentless dedication to excellence, which we term intellectual leadership. Without emotional health, most leadership and district change initiatives will fail to realize their desired results. Once the school establishes a stable, healthy climate and culture, the leader helps focus the collective energy to achieving great things for the school's students and families.

In one survey, 77% of leaders believed their staff weren't giving 100% at work. The same survey showed 73% of employees admitted they were not giving their best each day (Murphy, 2010). Unfortunately, when leaders get frustrated, they fall into what Connors and Smith (2009) term the accountability fallacy.

> Accountability Fallacy captures a common mistake people make when they assume that others fail to follow through because there is something wrong with them…When leaders fall prey to the Accountability Fallacy, they not only assume that their people are flawed, but that they themselves can do little or nothing to change those flaws except punish people for having them. Real accountability always requires us to begin by looking at ourselves for anything that might be missing.

The leader becomes frustrated with staff performance and finds it challenging to work through their frustration while maintaining their own integrity. The leader's lack of integrity is contagious and leads to a general sense of frustration among staff. Surveys powerfully demonstrate this reality. One out of every two people felt their well-being didn't matter at all to their leader, and only 10% felt like a vital asset to the success of their organization (Schwartz, 2010).

Trauma-sensitive leaders celebrate the fact that the staff at the school are the most significant factor in achieving academic success. Part of this focus requires them to work relentlessly to ensure the health of all staff. Just as importantly, the leader must work hard to ensure that the school has the best staff possible in positions where they thrive.

Fit is ensuring that the right people are in the right places to promote student success at the school. Hiring is an essential aspect of fit. Interview questions such as "Why do you think children struggle academically?" and "Why do you think some children cannot manage their behaviors?" help assess an applicant's philosophy. Even if they have not learned about trauma's impact on behavior and academic success, trauma-sensitive leaders remain cautious of staff who believe that students are bad because they choose not to try or misbehave.

The harder aspect of fit is the action needed to address the reality that someone is in a position where they cannot meet the universal expectations and challenges of a trauma-sensitive school. Any change process will meet resistance from certain people. The leader's job is to assess the reasons behind the resistance (Collins, 2001).

In many cases, resistance is a sign of burnout and trauma. Other times, specific staff will struggle to adjust to a new teaching philosophy that is contrary to one they previously held. Through honest and compassionate conversations, the leader needs to do everything possible to help the staff recover or work through their hesitation.

Unfortunately, some staff will not live up to the demands of a trauma-sensitive school or its universal expectations. It does not mean that something is inherently wrong with the person. Not everyone fits into a specific school's culture and climate. Too often in education, a person with a poor fit remains in a position where they cannot experience success.

When fit is missing, the person struggles every day and accelerates their journey down the stages of education fatigue. Not only does the staff member experience burnout, but their students also get a subpar education. The person who doesn't fit in that position will fail to provide the empathy and compassion needed to adequately implement the critical aspects of a trauma-sensitive classroom or support the school in their transformational journey.

Once the school gets the right people in the right places, creating a healthy and motivated culture becomes much more manageable. Next, the leader works with the trauma-sensitive transformation team to establish a vision for the future. Creating a shared understanding of what the school is working toward will increase motivation and dedication to realizing the benefits of a trauma-sensitive school.

Leaders choose their level of involvement in the transformation process. Some lead it from beginning to end. Other play a supportive role, ensuring that the team has the required time and resources, while delegating the leadership of the process to another qualified staff member. Regardless of the level of involvement, the leader helps maintain focus through honest conversations and accountability to universal expectations. The leader supports behaviors that further the journey toward the shared vision of a trauma-sensitive school.

The Last Meeting of a Transformative Year

As the last few minutes of the school year slipped away, tears came to Mrs. Vaughn's eyes. While she was more than ready for summer vacation, her mind filled with pride and worry. The mix of emotions was too much to hold in.

Caleb continued to make incredible strides throughout the school year. He started to take pride in his behavioral improvements and academic progress. At times his striving for perfection set him up for huge disappointments. He would beat himself up when his behaviors slipped or when he didn't do as well as he wanted to on an assignment. Mrs. Vaughn's year went from trying to keep everyone safe from Caleb to helping him learn how to handle small failures and treat himself with kindness.

His mom's situation was a little chaotic at first. She took advantage of the substance-abuse treatment offered by one of the school's community partners. Relapses plagued her attempts to maintain sobriety and her ability to get Caleb back into her home full time. Even through the ups and down, she regularly attended Caleb's team meetings. As she walked into the classroom for the final day of the school goodbye celebration, she handed Mrs. Vaughn a small coin.

"Well, it is about time parents started tipping teachers," Mrs. Vaughn joked before looking at the coin. Upon examining it, she saw the words "Narcotics Anonymous" and "8 Weeks Sobriety." Now Mrs. Vaughn couldn't hold back her emotions.

As tears flowed down her face, Caleb's mom reached for her hand. "Thank you for everything you and the school did for Caleb and me. Another month of sobriety and I'll get full custody back."

The two women, whose history went back decades, hugged.

Caleb, busy working on a final project with Malik and Emilia, noticed his mom and realized both she and Mrs. Vaughn were crying. He ran over and joined the hug, which gave Mrs. Vaughn a chance to chuckle and regain her composure.

"Why don't you show your mom the project your group is finishing up?" Mrs. Vaughn said, as several other parents walked through the door.

Emilia's mom shyly approached her. "Hi, Maria. It's been such a pleasure to have Emilia in my class this year," said Mrs. Vaughn.

If Caleb and his mom were examples of how the school could bridge mental-health and substance-abuse services to help families, Maria and Emilia demonstrated the impact of the resource-rich family center. After Mrs. Vaughn's discussion with the county social-service administrator, Maria signed a release of information document and a team formed to help the family. Since their immigration status made it difficult to get community mental-health services, the district stepped up and provided these services through one of their mental-health professionals newly trained in trauma-treatment best practices. Both Maria and Emilia were making significant progress in treatment.

The family-center interns took the family on as one of their "proof of concept" projects. "Proof of concept" was a label they came up with as part of their mission to demonstrate that every school would benefit from a center like theirs. They connected Maria with an immigration lawyer who was working to help her obtain a green card and get Emilia's dad released from ICE custody. Maria also began attending free adult English classes in the evenings.

Emilia started to come out of her shell. Mrs. Vaughn witnessed her shed her freeze response gradually, as her home life stabilized and she progressed in treatment. Her transformation was just as powerful as Caleb's growth.

Maria said in her growing yet still broken English, "Mrs. Vaughn, thank you. Thank you for my family." She was holding back tears.

The two enjoyed a moment talking about Emilia's fantastic progress and things to work on over the summer. No one realized Emilia had come over. She still maintained her ability to go unnoticed.

"Emilia, I was just talking to your mom about your amazing progress this year," Mrs. Vaughn said.

Emilia blushed and turned her head downward as her mom gave her a side hug. Peeking out from behind her mom's leg, Emilia asked quietly, "Mrs. Vaughn, I want you as my teacher next year too. Can I stay in your class?"

Mrs. Vaughn smiled. She was not worried about Emilia. However, she wondered how Caleb and some other students in second grade would fare next year. A teacher from the third grade was involved in the Trauma-Sensitive Transformation Team. However, not all the teachers were entirely on board. She worried about how fragile the progress was for many of the students with trauma and hoped that they could continue getting teachers with trauma-sensitive training, no matter where they landed in future grades.

"Emilia, I taught you everything I know. You worked so hard this year. If you keep working this hard, you'll learn so much more next year. Just promise to come back and teach me a little of what you learn in the third grade." Mrs. Vaughn smiled, deep down, hoping that Emilia would continue to feel connected to her as she moved forward.

Mrs. Vaughn enjoyed the end-of-the-year celebration. As everyone was hugging her on their way to summer vacation, Malik's mom and dad hung back. The three of them were the only ones left, as Malik quickly ran out with Caleb to get some final fun in on the playground.

Malik's recovery from his physical trauma and the altercation with Caleb was no less powerful than the healing of his peers, Emilia and Caleb. Most children would develop a fear for taking risks after such a debilitating injury, but Malik showed no such hesitancy. His parents' love seemed to give him an unlimited pool of resiliency to pull from as he recovered both from his physical injuries and the altercation with Caleb.

After hugging her, Malik's mom broke the powerful silence that fills a classroom at the end of a school year. "We just wanted you to know that, after the incident with Caleb earlier this year, we really considered pulling Malik from the school." She paused and looked at her husband.

He continued. "We are so glad we decided against it. It is amazing how you transformed your classroom this school year."

"I'm sure it took a lot of hard work, but it seemed effortless from our perspective. We appreciate your taking Malik's safety seriously. However, what you did with Caleb is astounding. I can't begin to imagine how his life changed because he was lucky enough to have you as his teacher," Malik's mom added.

"Thank you. That is great feedback to end my year. You have an amazing kid, and I thank you so much for all the hours you volunteered," Mrs. Vaughn said, feeling herself choke up again.

They exchanged hugs. Mrs. Vaughn was left alone in her classroom with the silence of its emptiness. She reflected on her personal transformation and that of her classroom this school year. The thought, "Next year, I'll really be ready" entered her mind.

At that moment, Ms. Smith popped her head in the door. "You heading to the LAST staff meeting of the year?"

"Welcome to your first summer vacation as a teacher! Boy, did you earn it." Mrs. Vaughn smiled as she grabbed her things and headed to the library.

Entering a room full of teachers who had just finished their last school day of the year was a wonderful feeling. The energy was palpable, and the joy was contagious.

Dr. Griffin was running a little late. A few weeks earlier, at their last in-service day, Dr. Rodriguez presented on self-care and the dangers of empathetic intensity and burnout. She was strategically meeting with specific staff who she thought were further along in the stages of education fatigue.

A few teachers were defensive. Most appreciated that a principal showed concern for their health and well-being. More than a few tears fell when people shared the adverse effects that work stress had on their personal lives and health. Dr. Griffin was surprised by how many people were open to referrals to therapy through their employee assistance program. She chuckled to herself with pride that her staff and school probably had more teachers in therapy than any school in the country.

The meeting that stood out most for Dr. Griffin was the one with Mr. Anderson. She tried hard to use OARS to show empathy and help him explore some of his recent behavioral changes and emotional outbursts. Quickly his anger turned to sadness.

"I feel so guilty. The abuse was going on for months. I could have stopped it. I failed," Mr. Anderson said, with tears running down his face.

"Kevin, please don't take this all on yourself. Think of what you stopped by asking the right questions." Dr. Griffin tried to console him with an affirmation.

"So much trauma! Do these kids even stand a chance?" He was asking himself more than Dr. Griffin.

"Kevin, I know you have dealt with terrible things in the past. This one seems to hit especially close to home." Dr. Griffin used a complex reflection.

Silence fell for nearly a minute. "When Dr. Rodriguez talked about how sometimes the trauma of our students' retriggers memories of our own trauma…" His statement trailed off.

"Yes, how we are at risk of retraumatization." Dr. Griffin reflected.

"I need help. I know that I have not been the same at home, at school, or with my basketball team since the abuse revelation. Part of it is guilt. I think it goes deeper than that." Mr. Anderson sounded defeated, like he had failed somehow by coming to this conclusion.

"You are a human being. I hope you understand what Dr. Rodriguez said, that experiencing retraumatization is not a sign of weakness. It is a sign that we are human. You are such a great teacher. I want the old Mr. Anderson back. I laugh so much less without him." She affirmed his value to the school. "I wonder what you would tell one of your players who is struggling. Would you encourage him to give up, or would you challenge him to face the challenge and come back stronger and more resilient?"

Mr. Anderson chuckled. "I need a summer vacation. Give me some information on that free therapy the district offers. But I really need a vacation from you, Ms. Smith, and Mrs. Vaughn OARSing me all the time."

They both smiled. Dr. Griffin gave him the information on the employee assistance program. She had talked with the folks there to identify a few therapists with trauma experience and encouraged Mr. Anderson to contact one of them directly. "Summer vacation or not, I'm here for you if you need anything."

As Dr. Griffin ran into the library, she felt the intensity of the school year follow her into the room. "All right people, I'm not going to take too much of your time."

At that, the room exploded in applause.

"Funny. So, I'd like you all to know that all our school families received an email letting them know that staff are not permitted to check emails over vacation. If I have an emergency or something critical, I'll call you. Otherwise, you are to disconnect after this meeting."

Even louder applause came from her staff.

"Your only task over the summer is to recover and work on self-care strategies. When we come back as a staff, I will meet with each of you individually and talk about how the school and I will support your staying healthy next year." Dr. Griffin's voice relayed a sense of seriousness to her words.

"And…" Mrs. Vaughn added.

"And, I will share my self-care goals with you all. I expect us all to hold each other accountable next year. That includes your helping me to bring my best self to work each day." Dr. Griffin paused as surprised looks stared back at her.

"One more thing before we get the heck out of here." She took a deep breath, knowing the power of her next words. "This year, we started and made great progress toward becoming a trauma-sensitive school. Next year, we will integrate trauma-sensitive principles into the DNA of our culture and climate. This transformation is incredibly hard work and may be a journey that you are unable to commit to fully at this point in your career. Please seek me out this summer if you would like to discuss how I can support you. Please know that if you feel this may not be the right fit for you, I am happy to support any decision you may make."

Her audience's faces were a mix of huge smiles, astonished looks, and a few frustrated scowls. "If you choose to walk into this school next August, it means you are 100% invested in our efforts to create a trauma-sensitive school. If you feel any hesitation, please contact me. Have a great summer, everyone." Dr. Griffin walked out quickly.

Mrs. Vaughn shot a smile at Ms. Smith, who winked back at her.

Conclusion

To conclude our examination of trauma-sensitive schools, we want to tie together all the research presented in this book to answer a Miracle Question (Metcalf, 2007). The question goes like this: "You wake up tomorrow and a miracle has happened, where your dream became a reality. How would that reality differ from the present?" If a billionaire showed up tomorrow and wrote us a blank check to create a trauma-sensitive primary school, what would we create to help implement the concepts and approaches presented in this book?

Educational Assistants

In creating our trauma-sensitive school, we would begin with making classrooms the right size. Teachers are experts at academic instruction. Our dream is to give them the time and opportunity to utilize their expertise. The most consequential change necessary in the creation of a trauma-sensitive school is additional support in the classroom. In our school, every classroom would consist of a teacher, a paraprofessional, and additional support based on the student needs outlined in Individualized Education Plans. While support is essential during academic instruction, extra help is also critical for recesses, lunchtimes, and transitions to help students with trauma regulate emotions and behaviors.

We don't love the job title "paraprofessional," because we believe it fails to recognize the true worth of the people in these positions. We prefer the term "educational assistant." Our educational assistants would receive training in trauma-sensitive instructional strategies and behavioral management. They would also get trained in de-escalation, conflict resolution, restorative justice, and mental-health first aid. In our school, we would ensure that our educational assistants got paid more than just a livable wage. They would receive a salary and benefits designed to retain them, honor their importance, and invest resources into building their expertise.

With an educational assistant in every classroom, they could establish a true working partnership with the teacher. The educational assistant, trained in a variety of behavioral-management strategies, would support the students' emotional regulation and readiness to learn. If a child needs to visit a sensory room before a lesson, needs to participate in a quick mindfulness activity, or needs a walk around the school building to de-escalate, the educational assistant would be available to make these accommodations.

The additional staff presence would drastically increase opportunities to differentiate instruction. The educational assistant could pull out small groups to help students who are behind the rest of the class or to challenge students who are ready to advance. They could also work one-on-one with specific students to introduce and assist with differentiated activities and lessons.

In my experience as a teacher and Matt's as a school administrator, we find nothing improves the quality of teacher effectiveness as much as adding support in the classroom. Districts pay hundreds of thousands of dollars for new technology, curriculum, and pet projects. We see a massive payoff for a relatively small investment in staffing. Teachers could deliver instruction, instead of investing most of their time in behavior management.

Students would get the support needed for emotional regulation, which would decrease behavior issues and reduce suspensions. The additional support would alleviate many of the most significant reasons teachers leave the profession. Just imagine the difference in Mrs. Vaughn's classroom if she had this level of support.

Trauma-Sensitive Coach and Mental-Health Professional Support

After we hired our educational assistants, we would then work to train trauma-sensitive coaches and hire trauma-trained mental-health professionals. These professionals would be assigned to grade-level teams.

Depending on the size of the school and the caseload of students with trauma, it may be necessary to hire several individuals to take on these crucial roles. Our goal would be to hire and train enough coaches to support teachers and enough mental-health professionals to meet the social, emotional, and mental-health needs of the students.

The services provided by mental-health professionals would allow the coaches to focus their support on the health and wellness of the teachers and educational assistants. It would enable the coach to become part of the classroom team. Partnered with a mental-health professional, the coach could also help the teacher and educational assistant find students' islands of competency. The coach could create and implement strategies to assist students with trauma in achieving academic success. The coach would spend meaningful time in the classroom, getting to observe and partner with the classroom staff to find creative educational approaches.

We want our school to integrate mental health into classrooms. While the traditional model of pulling individual students out of class to receive services would still exist, our school would also position the mental-health professional as an additional classroom support for the students, teachers, and educational assistants. With expertise in behavioral management, the mental-health professional should spend at least as much time in the classrooms as outside them.

Currently, most mental-health professionals in schools see a student individually or in a small group. In trauma-sensitive schools, the mental-health professional needs the time to help integrate the progress made outside the classroom into the student's daily activities. The complexity of trauma and the intensity of behaviors associated with it requires that mental-health expertise inform classroom behavioral management.

As we rethink mental health, we cannot forget the families. We understand that the level of therapeutic support that families often need requires extensive time outside the scope of our in-school mental-health support. Our ideal school would partner with community providers to adequately address the mental-health needs of families at no or low cost.

The Fuel for the Brain

We mentioned the importance of diet in Chapter 12. What you put in your mouth becomes the fuel for your brain. This fact is especially true for the rapidly developing brains of primary students.

Our school cafeteria would look more like a health-food store than a fast-food restaurant, including salad bars, healthy meals, and nutritious drinks. We would not offer options that did not promote physical and emotional health. Any child could get three meals a day and regular access to healthy snacks at our school to ensure that every child had food security. If a family had financial issues, we would send a healthy meal home with the student. For us, food security is a human right, and schools are ideally positioned to end hunger in our communities.

Going into the connection between diet, behaviors, and cognitive performance is beyond the scope of this book and our expertise. Knowing that there is a link is enough motivation for every school to partner with a dietitian or nutritionist to strategically create healthy meals for students. If we expect our students' brains to perform well in the classroom and on standardized tests, we must ensure that they get the best fuel possible.

Specialize Specials

Specials such as gym, art, and music play a crucial role in supplementing the students' educational experience. We believe they also play a central role in a trauma-sensitive school. Let's start with gym. Our school would provide physical education every day for every student. We want to provide opportunities at recess and lunch for unstructured play outdoors. However, structured physical activities and sports are too important to get only once or twice a week. Learning cooperation and teamwork is just as important as releasing energy and exercising.

According to the Trauma Institute and Child Trauma Institute (2018):

Trauma-focused therapy plus as few as three half-hour exercise sessions per week, plus some walking, has been found to lead to greater symptom reduction than trauma-focused therapy alone. Many types of exercise, including sports, aerobic movement, resistance training, yoga, and dance, have been found to be effective in numerous cases, in supplementing treatment as well as maintaining and/or extending the benefits of the primary treatment. (Levine & Land, 2015; Ley, Barrio, & Koch, 2017; Neukirch, Reid, & Shires, 2018; Rosenbaum, Vancampfort, Steel, Newby, Ward, & Stubbs, 2015; West, Liang, & Spinazzola, 2017).

Being dedicated to helping our students find their island of competency makes all specials a crucial part of a trauma-sensitive school. The arts provide a variety of valuable learning experiences and help build skills and confidence. Music and art also offer an opportunity for personal expression.

There are now certifications for trauma-informed music and art therapy. In our ideal school, we would hire full-time, trauma-certified art and music therapists. These professionals would work as a team with the art and music teachers. They would also facilitate special groups for classes, small groups, and individuals.

Physical Space

A trauma-sensitive space is soothing, culturally representative of its students, and welcoming. It balances the energy of a vibrant and engaging environment with one that does not overstimulate students, especially those with trauma or disorders that make them especially sensitive to lighting, noise, and overstimulation. As the trauma movement evolves, architectural agencies are starting to specialize in trauma-informed design and buildings.

Our school would work with one of these companies to create the most trauma-sensitive environment possible. While architecture is not one of our areas of expertise, we know the questions we would ask when advocating for our students with trauma:

- What paint colors are soothing and support emotional regulation?
- What is the best lighting for ideal brain functioning?
- How do we minimize noise and other distractions outside the classroom?
- How do we provide a variety of furniture options that meet the sensory needs of all students?
- How do we create quiet areas within the classroom and school, so

teachers, educational assistants, coaches, and therapists all have space to meet individually with students to help them regulate?
- How do we plan for the flow of traffic to make it less congested during times of transition?
- How do we make a naturally stimulating environment like the lunchroom more sensory sensitive?

Leadership and Teams

With coaches, educational assistants, mental-health professionals, and art and music therapists servicing students throughout the school building, the school requires effective leadership to manage, supervise, and coordinate the work of all these professionals. One person is not enough to adequately fill this role. In our ideal school, a dedicated assistant principal, or maybe even two assistant principals, depending on the enrollment at the school, would help provide oversight and support to classrooms.

The leader would provide administrative, performance, and wellness support to the professionals on their team. Having training in trauma-sensitive approaches and self-care, they would support the team in working with students to provide their educational, behavioral, and community-resource expertise. Their knowledge of the students would allow them to help coordinate teams of school staff and community organizations for students and families struggling with trauma and other issues.

Back to Reality

Now let's assume that a billionaire does not show up with a blank check. How could we begin to justify the cost of our dream trauma-sensitive school?

We need to stop viewing education as merely a cost, and instead start seeing our children as an investment in our future. Trauma-sensitive schools will not eliminate criminal behavior, homelessness, addiction, violence, and preventable chronic disease. Other issues such as systematic racism, lack of upward mobility, and poverty exacerbate these problems. However, we hope this book makes a strong argument that identifying and healing trauma in childhood would significantly lower the cost of these societal problems on our government, communities, and families.

Trauma is not the fault of the child. Treatment for trauma is a human right. Trauma-sensitive schools help ensure that no child carries the pain and suffering from trauma into adulthood. If every school in the country were trauma-sensitive, how many tens, if not hundreds of thousands, of young people would avoid the later symptoms of trauma and instead fulfill their unlimited potential? Instead of carrying the pain, suffering, and symptoms of trauma into adulthood, they would bring resiliency, robustness, and wisdom into all their future endeavors.

Yes, it would take a financial investment to implement the model presented in this book. However, think about how many times over that this investment would repay itself in reduced costs in the criminal-justice system, homelessness, preventable chronic diseases, and addiction. While it might take a decade or two to realize all the benefits, imagine a society where no child carried the pain and suffering of their trauma into adulthood.

Now that we understand the lifelong impact of childhood trauma, how can we not make this investment?

A New Year

Over the summer, a few staff decided not to return to their teaching positions the following fall. Dr. Griffin worked with the district to identify motivated veteran teachers who desired a transfer into her school. She also hired a few recent graduates from Dr. Rodriguez's program. Mrs. Vaughn felt the energy as she walked into the first staff meeting of the new school year.

"Welcome. Everyone ready for this?" Dr. Griffin opened the meeting, hardly able to maintain her enthusiasm.

"Yes!" came a collective roar from the staff.

"Why don't we start by going around the room, introducing ourselves, and sharing why you decided to join us on this journey."

Ms. Smith's hand shot up, and before anyone acknowledged her, she started "I'm here because I dreamed of working in a trauma-sensitive school. I'm here to change education and show the world what a trauma-sensitive school can do for students and the community."

As they went around the room, answers varied. The teachers who transferred from other schools discussed how they had heard about the school's vision and wanted to participate in redefining education. The new teachers spoke of their respect for Dr. Rodriguez and of being motivated by Ms. Smith speaking to their college class about how trauma principles were transforming her school.

"I'm here because my boss cared enough about me to ask how I was doing personally." Mr. Anderson spoke with a strength that Mrs. Vaughn had only previously heard when he got excited about the basketball season. Gone were the anger and sadness. "I'm here because no one recognized when trauma impacted me as a child. After years of struggling, I'm finally getting the help I need. I'm ready to be the person for our students that Dr. Griffin was for me."

Applause rose from the group.

Mrs. Vaughn was the last to speak, wiping a tear from her eye that had fallen as Mr. Anderson spoke. "I'm Mrs. Vaughn, and I'm the Trauma-Sensitive Coach at our school."

As she finished, all in attendance clapped their hands and cheered.

As they quieted down after a minute, Mrs. Vaughn continued. "A year ago, a first-year teacher gave me a new, research-based, and more compassionate way to teach. I hope that I am half the mentor to you as she was for me," Mrs. Vaughn said, looking directly at Ms. Smith.

Once Dr. Griffin had secured the funding for the coach position, the three of them had had a long conversation about who should fill the role. Mrs. Vaughn thought Ms. Smith was the obvious choice. With insight well beyond her age, she countered back that Mrs. Vaughn was the right choice because of her decades of classroom experience. Ms. Smith argued that she still had so much to learn about being a classroom teacher.

Dr. Griffin let the Mrs. Vaughn's announcement hang in the air for a moment before continuing, "Okay. I know you are all anxious to get to work in your classrooms. As you go, please sign up for a time to review your self-care goals with Coach Vaughn and me. Next week, Dr. Rodriguez will conduct two days of training for new staff and a full day for all of us. She'll work with grade-level teams to create plans for trauma-sensitive integration. Let's have an amazing year and show the rest of the district and the world what we can do!"

As her staff filtered out, Dr. Griffin was excited to connect with Mrs. Vaughn for the first time as their trauma-sensitive coach. As they got comfortable in Dr. Griffin's office, Mrs. Vaughn demanded, "Let me see it."

Dr. Griffin opened a drawer on her desk and pulled out a piece of paper with the title "My Self-Care Plan." Mrs. Vaughn took her time reading through it and offered a few suggestions.

"You know, I thought being a principal was hard. I think all that responsibility is pretty easy compared to being the role model for wellness!" Dr. Griffin said with sincere concern in her voice.

"Tell me about it. Everyone will look to us each day to see if we are prioritizing self-care. I'm amazed by how much my life changed over the summer just by implementing the very basics of self-care."

They discussed the initial plan for how to start the school year and the first meeting of the new Trauma-Sensitive Transformation Team. There were so many opportunities. It was hard to prioritize and find the best place to start. Luckily, all the work done the previous year provided a rough road map.

Their excitement was mixed in with a great deal of worry. The primary concern was funding and sustainability. The district and a local foundation worked together to fund Mrs. Vaughn's position for two years. All parties hoped to continue the position, but needed to see tangible results in reducing the number of suspensions, retaining staff, and, most importantly, increasing academic achievement.

The district was also implementing a new curriculum in several grade levels, which would take up a great deal of training time and capacity for staff. While Mrs. Vaughn's position helped provide time to focus the effort, the amount of work to support the transformation demanded a great deal of work from everyone. Not to mention, the new staff would need time to integrate into the school's climate and culture.

Dr. Griffin joked, "Mrs. Vaughn, I feel like we are the first people on the moon. Most everyone wanted it to happen, yet no one really knew how to turn such a colossal dream into a reality. A few brave, or maybe crazy, souls stepped forward to say, 'We'll do it.'"

"It does feel like we are at the beginning of something special." Mrs. Vaughn paused to let her nerves and excitement settle before meeting with her third-grade team for the first time. As she walked out of Dr. Griffin's office, she hesitated, "Do you think others have the passion and courage to do what we are attempting?"

Acknowledgments

We want to thank Jerry and Lauren Yager. Jerry hired Matt in 2003 at a residential childcare facility. He introduced him to the research and science on trauma. Matt could not have asked for a better mentor, teacher, and friend. Sarah and Lauren met shortly after and connected through their shared passion for education. Thank you both for all your work and for serving as our role models.

Two experts volunteered their time to help us develop this book. Carey Purkey and Elandriel Lewis provided great insight and expertise. Thank you both for your time, work, and passion for trauma-sensitive early education.

We would also like to thank our editors. Our first editor, Robin Leist, played a central role in the development of the book. She took a rough first draft and helped us polish it into a cohesive book. Learn more about Robin and her great Ittybag games and tools at www.ittybags.com.

Matt worked with Kathy Nida on his first two books. Kathy's expertise in education knowledge and trauma-sensitive education made her the perfect partner for this project. We feel so fortunate to work with such a fantastic editor on this book.

Several school districts and professionals that Matt worked with throughout the years gave him a laboratory to collaboratively develop the concepts in this book. Matt would like to thank Lisa Zimprish, Carey Purkey, Joe Fabey, and all the great staff from Fountain-Fort Carson School District in Colorado. Thanks for all the amazing opportunities and the incredible innovation and dedication to trauma-sensitive schools. Also, thank you for providing excellent educational services to our military families.

Matt also wants to recognize the great folks at Young and Healthy and at Pasadena Unified School District in California. Mary Putman, Whitney Harrison, Liz Arnold, and all the great staff at Young and Healthy serve as role models for how a relatively small organization utilizing trauma research can change an entire community. Matt also wants to acknowledge the great work of Julianne Reynoso and those at Pasadena Unified School District who are working to integrate trauma-sensitive approaches.

Matt would also like to thank Dr. Marcia G. Zashin and the Cleveland Metropolitan School District for years of collaboration. Matt always loves his trips to and trainings in Cleveland. He would also like to thank Danny Henley and the terrific folks at the El Monte City School District in California.

Matt wants to give thanks to additional training partners: Colorado Department of Education, Galileo School of Math and Science in Colorado Springs, New America School in the Denver, Colorado area, and Colorado Family Resource Center Association and its member organizations around Colorado. Thank you to all those organizations that allow Matt to share his passion.

Finally, we want to thank all our friends and family, who served as constant support throughout the process of writing this book. People thrive in healthy and supportive relationships. We are so lucky to live a life surrounded by those who love and support us!

Bibliography

Achor, S. (2010). *The happiness advantage*. New York: Crown Business.

Ainsworth, M. D., Blehar, M. C., Waters, E., & Wall, S. N. (2015). *Patterns of attachment: A psychological study of the strange situation (Classic edition)*. New York: Psychology Press.

The American Institute of Stress. (2012). www.stress.org.

Association for Supervision and Curriculum Development (2019). http://www.ascd.org/research-a-topic/school-culture-and-climate-resources.aspx.

Australian Society for Evidence Based Teaching (2019). https://www.evidencebasedteaching.org.au/crash-course-evidence-based-teaching/teacher-student-relationships/.

Baer, R. A., Smith, G. T., Hopkins, J., Krietemeyer, J., & Toney, L. (2006). Using self-report assessment methods to explore facets of mindfulness. *Assessment*, 13(1), 27¬¬¬–45.

Bailey, B. (2015). *Conscious discipline building resilient classrooms*. Oviedo, FL: Loving Guidance, Inc.

Bennett, M. S. (2017). *Connecting paradigms: A trauma-informed and neurobiological framework for Motivational Interviewing implementation*. Denver, Colorado: Bennett Innovation Group.

Bennett, M. S. (2018). *Talking about trauma & change. A connecting paradigms' supplement*. Denver, Colorado: Bennett Innovation Group.

Biffle, C. (2013). *Whole brain teaching for challenging kids*. Yucaipa, CA: Whole Brain Teaching LLC.

Biffle, C. (2018). *Whole brain teaching for challenging kids: Fast track: Seven steps to teaching heaven*. Yucaipa, CA: Whole Brain Teaching LLC.

Blackwell, L. S., Trzesniewski, K. H., & Dweck, C. S. (2007). Implicit theories of intelligence predict achievement across an adolescent transition: A longitudinal study and an intervention. *Child Development*, 78(1), 246–263.

Bloom, S. L. (2000). Creating sanctuary: Healing from systematic abuses of power. *Therapeutic Communities: The International Journal for Therapeutic and Supportive Organizations* 21(2), 67–91.

Bloom, S. L. (2006). Organizational stress as a barrier to trauma-sensitive change and system transformation. A white paper for National Technical Assistance Center for State Mental Health Planning (NTAC).

Bloom, S. L., & Farragher, B. (2011). *Destroying sanctuary: The crisis in human service delivery systems.* New York: Oxford University Press.

Bloom, S, L., & Farragher, B. (2013). *Restoring sanctuary: A new operating system for trauma-informed systems of care.* New York: Oxford University Press.

Bridgeland, J., & Raikes, T. (2018). Opinion: 1.3 million students are homeless. Here's how we can help them. PBS News Hour.

Bronson, P., & Merryman, A. (2009). *NurtureShock: New thinking about children.* New York: Twelve.

Brooks, R., & Goldstein, S. (2012). *Training resilient children with autism spectrum disorder: Strategies for helping them maximize their strengths, cope with adversity, and develop a social mindset.* New York: McGraw-Hill.

Bruns, E. J., Walrath, C., Glass-Siegel, M., & Weist, M. D. (2004). School-based mental health services in Baltimore: Association with school climate and special education referrals. *Behavioral Modification*. 28(4): 491–512.

Burdick, D. (2013). *Mindfulness skills workbook for clinicians & clients: 111 tools, techniques, activities, & worksheets.* Eau Claire, WI: PESI Publishing and Media.

Carver-Thomas, D., & Darling-Hammond, L. (2017). *Teacher turnover: Why it matters and what we can do about it.* Palo Alto, CA: Learning Policy Institute.

Casanueva, C., Wilson, E., Smith, K., Dolan, M., Ringeisen, H., & Horne, B. (2012). *NSCAW II wave 2 report: Child well-being. OPRE Report*

#2012-38, Washington, DC: Office of Planning, Research and Evaluation, Administration for Children and Families, U.S. Department of Health and Human Services.

Centers for Disease Control and Prevention (2016, April 1). Adverse Childhood Experiences (ACEs). http://www.cdc.gov/violenceprevention/acestudy/.

Christakis, N. A., & Fowler, J. H. (2009). *Connected: The surprising power of our social networks and how they shape our lives*. New York: Little, Brown and Company.

Cole, S. F., Greenwald O'Brien, J., Gadd, M. G., Ristuccia, J., Wallace, D. L., & Gregory, M. (2009). *Helping traumatized children learn*. Boston: Massachusetts Advocates for Children.

Collins, J. (2001). Good to great: *Why some companies make the leap…and others don't*. New York: HarperCollins.

Connors, R., & Smith, T. (2009). *How did that happen*. New York: Portfolio/Penguin.

Courtois, C. A., & Ford, J. D. (Eds.) (2009). *Treating complex traumatic stress disorder: An evidence-based guide*. New York: Guilford Press.

Cozolino, L. (2006). The neuroscience of human relationship: Attachment and the developing social brain. New York: W.W. Norton & Company, Inc.

Cozolino, L. (2010). *The neuroscience of psychotherapy: Healing the social brain*. New York: W.W. Norton & Company, Inc.

Craig, S. E. (2016). *Trauma-sensitive schools: Learning communities transforming children's lives*, K-5. New York: Teachers College Press.

David, D. S. (2009). *Mindful teaching and teaching mindfulness: A guide for anyone who teaches anything*. Somerville, MA: Wisdom Publications.

Davidson, R. J., Kabat-Zinn, J., Schumacher, J., Rosenkranz, M., Muller, D., Santorelli, S. F., Urbanowski, F., Harrington, A., Bonus, K., & Sheridan, J. F. (2003). Alterations in brain and immune function produced by mindfulness meditation. *Psychosomatic Medicine*, 65(4), 564–570.

Davis, D. M., & Hayes, J. A. (2012). What are the benefits of mindfulness. *Monitor on Psychology*, 43(7), 64.

Duckworth, A. (2016). *Grit: The power of passion and perseverance.* New York: Scribner.

Duhigg, C. (2016). *Smarter, faster, better.* New York: Penguin Random House.

Dweck, D. S. (2006). *Mindset: The new psychology of success.* New York: Ballantine Books.

Ellis, E., Gable, R. A., Gregg, M., & Rock, M. L. (2008). REACH: A framework for differentiating classroom instruction. *Preventing School Failure,* 52(2), 31–47.

Ferlazzo, L. (2011). Involvement or engagement? *Schools, Families, Communities,* 68(8), 10-14.

Fernandez, A. (2006). Physical fitness and brain fitness. [Wed log comment]. Retrieved October 15, 2010, from http://sharpbrains.wordpress.com/2006/08/13/role-of-physical-fitness.

Foa, E. B., Keane, T. M., Friedman, M. J., & Cohen, J. A. (2009). *Effective treatments for PTSD: Practice guidelines from the International Society for Traumatic Stress Studies* (2nd ed.). New York: Guilford Press.

Forbes, H. T. (2012). *Help for Billy: A beyond consequences approach to helping challenging children in the classroom.* Boulder, Colorado: Beyond Consequences Institute.

Hamel, G., & Breen, B. (2007). *The Future of management.* Boston: Harvard Business Press.

Henderson, A. T., Mapp, K. L., Johnson, V. R., & Davies, K. (2007). *Beyond the bake sale: The essential guide to family/school partnerships.* New York: The New Press.

Herman, J. L. (1997). *Trauma & recovery.* New York: Basic Books.

Human Rights Watch (2008). *A violent education: Corporal punishment of children in US public schools.* New York: Human Rights Watch.

Human Rights Watch and American Civil Liberties Union Statement (2010). *Corporal punishment in schools and its effect on academic success: For the hearing before the House Education and Labor Subcommittee on Healthy Families and Communities.* https://www.hrw.org/news/2010/04/15/

corporal-punishment-schools-and-its-effect-academic-success-joint-hrw/aclu-statement.

Geisinger Health System (2008). Counseling trauma victims causes secondary trauma, study shows. *ScienceDaily*. Retrieved May 19, 2010, from http://www.sciencedaily.com¬ /releases/2008/04/080421170211.htm.

Geller, J. A., & Madsen, L. H. (2004) *Secondary trauma: A team approach*. New York: Springer Science Business Media, Inc.

Gladwell, M. (2005). *Blink: The power of thinking without thinking*. New York: Little, Brown and Company.

Goleman, D. (2006). *Social intelligence: The new science of human relationships*. New York: Bantam Books.

Goleman, D., & Davidson, R. J. (2017). *Altered traits: Science reveals how meditation changes your mind, brain, and body*. New York: Avery.

Gostick, A., & Elton, C. (2009). *The Carrot Principle*. New York: Free Press.

Graves, G. (2008). *10 strategies for a more restful night's sleep*. http://www.msnbc.msn.com.

Greene, R. W. (2008). *Lost at school: Why our kids with behavioral challenges are falling through the cracks and how we can help them*. New York: Scribner.

Harris, M., & Fallot, R. D. (Eds.) (2001). *Using trauma theory to design service systems*. San Francisco: Jossey-Bass.

Harris, N. B. (2018). *The deepest well: Healing the long-term effect of childhood adversity*. New York: Houghton Mifflin Harcourt.

Harvard National Scientific Council for the Developing Child (2018). https://developingchild.harvard.edu/resources/serve-return-interaction-shapes-brain-circuitry/.

Hattie, J. (2009). *Visible learning: A synthesis of 800 meta-analyses relating to achievement*. New York: Routledge.

Hebb, D. O. (1949). *Organization of behavior: A neuropsychological theory*. New York: Psychology Press.

Henderson, A. T., & Mapp, K. L. (2002). *A new wave of evidence: The impact *of school, family, and community connections on student achievement*. Austin, Texas: National Center for Family and Community Connections with Schools.

Herman, J. L. (1997). *Trauma and recovery*. New York: Basic Books.

Hickmon, M. (2008). *Paddling vs. ACT scores and civil immunity legislation*. http:// www.stophitting.com/index.php?page=paddlingvsact.

Hodge, T. (2014). *Transgenerational trauma*. Huntington, West Virginia: Marshall University.

Hoopes, L., & Kelly, M. (2004). *Managing change with personal resilience: Keys for bouncing back & staying on top in turbulent organizations*. Raleigh, NC: MK Books.

Hughes, D. A. (2017). *Building the bonds of attachment: Awakening love in deeply traumatized children* (3rd ed.). Lanham, Maryland: Rowman & Littlefield Publishers.

Kharrazain, D. (2013). *Why isn't my brain working? A revolutionary understanding of brain decline and effective strategies to recover your brain's health*. Carlsbad, CA: Elephant Press.

Kouzes, J. M., & Posner, B. Z. (2007). *The leadership challenge*. San Francisco: Jossey-Bass.

Kuypers, L. (2011). *Zones of regulation*. Think Social Publishing. San Jose, CA.

Langer, E. J. (2009). *Counterclockwise: Mindful health and the power of possibility*. New York: Random House.

Lesley Institute for Trauma Sensitivity (2019). https://lesley.edu/professional-development-and-continuing-education/center-for-inclusive-and-special-education/lesley.

Levine, B., & Land, H. M. (2015). A meta-synthesis of qualitative findings about dance/movement therapy for individuals with trauma. *Qualitative Health Research*, 26, 330–344. http://dx.doi.org/10.1177/1049732315589920.

Lewis, G. (2006). *Organizational crisis management: The human factor*. Boca Raton, FL: Auerbach Publications.

Ley, C., Barrio, M. R., & Koch, A. (2017). "In the Sport I Am Here": Therapeutic processes and health effects of sport and exercise on PTSD. *Qualitative Health Research*, 28,491–507. http://dx.doi.org/10.1177/1049732317744533.

Lieberman, M. D. (2014). *Social: Why our brains are wired to connect.* New York: Broadway Books.

Lipsky, L. V. D. & Burk, C. (2009). *Trauma stewardship: An everyday guide to caring for self while caring for others.* San Francisco: Berrett-Koehler Publishers, Inc.

Lipton, B. H. (2006). *The wisdom of your cells: How your beliefs control your biology.* Louisville, CO: Sounds True, Inc.

MacNeil, A. J., Prater, D. L., & Busch, S. (2009). The effects of school culture and climate on student achievement. *International Journal of Leadership in Education*, 12:1, 73–84. https://doi.org/10.1080/13603120701576241

Maslach, C., & Leiter, M. P. (1997). *The truth about burnout: How organizations cause personal stress.* San Francisco: Jossey-Bass.

Mate, G., & Levine, P. A. (2010). *In the realm of hungry ghost: Close encounters with addiction.* Lyons, CO: The Ergos Institute.

McLaughlin, K. (2018). Teachers are seeing their colleagues leave the profession at an alarming rate, and this might be why. https://www.insider.com/teachers-are-seeing-their-colleagues-leave-at-an-alarming-rate-2018-11.

Merriam-Webster (2014). *The Merriam-Webster Dictionary.* Martinsburg, WV: Merriam-Webster, Incorporated.

Metcalf, L. (2007). *The miracle question: Answer it and change your life.* Bethel, CT: Crown House Publishing.

Miller, W. R., & Rollnick, S. (2012). *Motivational interviewing: Helping people change* (3rd ed.). New York: Guilford Press.

Mischel, W., Ayduk, O., Berman, M. G., Casey, B. J., Gotlib, I. H., Jonides, J., Kross, E., Teslovich, T., et al. (2010). 'Willpower' over the life span: Decomposing self-regulation. Social Cognitive and Affective Neuroscience. 6(2), 252–256.

Murphy, J. J. (2008). *Solution-focused counseling in schools* (2nd ed.). Alexandria, VA: American Counseling Association. http://counselingoutfitters.com/vistas/vistas08/Murphy.htm.

Murphy, M. (2010). *Hundred percenters: Challenge your employees to give it their all and they'll give you even more.* New York: McGraw Hill.

Nakazawa, D. J. (2016). *Childhood disrupted: How your biography becomes your biology, and how you can heal.* New York: Atria Books.

National Sleep Foundation (2019). *Lack of sleep may increase calorie consumption.* https://www.sleepfoundation.org/articles/lack-sleep-may-increase-calorie-consumption.

Neukirch, N., Reid, S., & Shires, A. (2018). Yoga for PTSD and the role of interoceptive awareness: A preliminary mixed-methods case series study. *European Journal of Trauma & Dissociation,* https://doi.org/10.1016/j.ejtd.2018.10.003.

Ogden, P., Minton, K., & Pain, C. (2006). *Trauma and the body.* New York: W. W. Norton and Company, Inc.

Parnell, L. (2008). *Tapping in: A step-by-step guide to activating your healing resources through bilateral stimulation.* Boulder, CO: Sounds True, Inc.

Prochaska, J. O., DiClemente, C. C., & Norcross, J. C. (1992). In search of how people change: Applications to addictive behaviors. *American Psychology* 47,1102.

Professional Quality of Life Elements Theory and Measurement (2017). http://www.proqol.org.

Rath, T., & Harter, J. (2010). *Wellbeing: The five essential elements.* New York: Gallup Press.

Restak, R. (2007). *The naked brain: How the emerging neurosociety is changing how we live, work, and love.* New York: Broadway Books.

Roche, M. K., & Strobach, K. V. (2016). *Nine elements of effective school community partnerships to address student mental health, physical health, and overall wellness.* http://www.nasponline.org/documents/Research%20and%20Policy/Advocacy%20Resources/Community%20Schools%20White%20Paper_Jan_2016.pdf.

Rock, D. (2009). *Your brain at work: Strategies for overcoming distraction, regaining focus, and working smarter all day long.* New York: HarperCollins.

Rosenbaum, S., Vancampfort, D., Steel, Z., Newby, J., Ward, P., & Stubbs, B. (2015). Physical activity in the treatment of post-traumatic stress disorder: A systematic review and meta-analysis. *Psychiatry Research*, 230, 130-136. http://dx.doi.org/10.1016/j.psychres.2015.10.017.

Saxe, G. N., Ellis, B. H., & Kaplow, J. B. (2007). *Collaborative treatment of traumatized children and teens.* New York: Guilford Press.

Schaffhauser, D. (2014). *The problem isn't teacher recruiting; It's retention.* https://thejournal.com/articles/2014/07/17/the-problem-isnt-teacher-recruiting-its-retention.asp.

Schneider, S. (2001). In search of realistic optimism: Meaning, knowledge, and warm fuzziness. *American Psychologist* 56(3), 250–263.

Schwartz, J. D., & Begley, S. (2002). The mind and the brain: Neuroplasticity and the power of mental force. New York: HarperCollins.

Schwartz, T. (2010). *The way we are working isn't working.* New York: Free Press.

Seaton, J. (2017). *More than 13 million kids in this country go to school hungry.* Washington Post.

Seppälä, E. M. (2013). *The science behind the joy of sharing joy.* Psychology Today. https://www.psychologytoday.com/us/blog/feeling-it/201307/the-science-behind-the-joy-sharing-joy.

Shenk, D. (2010). *The Genius in all of us.* New York: Doubleday.

Siebert, A. (2005). *The resiliency advantage.* San Francisco: Berrett-Koehler Publishers Inc.

Siegel, D. J. (2007). *The mindful brain.* New York: W. W. Norton & Company, Inc.

Siegel, D. J. (2011). *Mindsight: The new science of personal transformation.* New York: Bantam Books.

Siegel, D. J. (2016). *Mind: A journey to the heart of being human.* New York: W. W. Norton & Company, Inc.

Stamm, B. H. (2010). *The concise ProQOL manual.* Pocatello, ID: ProQOL.org.

Streibel, B. J. (2002). *The manager's guide to effective meetings.* New York: Briefcase Books.

Stulberg, B., & Magness, S. (2017). *Peak performance: Elevate your game, avoid burnout, and thrive with the new science of success.* New York: Random House, LLC.

Sutton, R. (2010). *Good boss, bad boss.* New York: Business Plus.

Tomlinson, C. A. (2001). *How to differentiate instruction in mixed-ability differentiated instructions provides access for all students to the general education curriculum. The method of assessment may look different for each child, however the skill or concepts taught is the same. Classrooms* (2 ed.). Alexandria, VA: Association for Supervision and Curriculum Development.

Tomlinson, C. A. (2003). *Fulfilling the promise of the differentiated classroom: Strategies and tools for responsive teaching.* Alexandria, VA: Association for Supervision and Curriculum Development.

Tracy, B. (2016). *Get smart!: How to think and act like the most successful and highest-paid people in every field.* New York: TarcherPerigee.

Trauma Institute and Child Trauma Institute (2018). Exercise to support trauma healing. http://www.childtrauma.com/blog/exercise/.

Treleaven, D. A. (2018). *Trauma-sensitive mindfulness: Practices for safe and transformative healing.* New York: W. W. Norton & Company.

Tschannen-Morgan, B., & Tschannen, M. (2010). *Evocative coaching: Transforming schools one conversation at a time.* San Francisco: Jossey-Bass.

United States Department of Education, Office of the Deputy Secretary, Planning and Evaluation Service (2001). The longitudinal evaluation of school change and performance in Title I schools (Executive Summary), 1.

United States Department of Health and Human Services and U.S. Department of Education (2014, Dec. 10). Policy statement on expulsion and suspension policies in early childhood settings.

University of Texas Southwestern Medical Center (2010, April 1). New brain nerve cells key to stress resilience. *ScienceDaily.* http://www.sciencedaily.com/releases/2010/03/100331080859.htm

Van der Kolk, B. (2014). T*he body keeps score: Brain, mind, and the body in healing trauma*. New York: Penguin Books.

Wagner, R., & Harter, J. K. (2006). 12: *The elements of great managing*. New York: Gallup Press.

West, J., Liang, B., & Spinazzola, J. (2017). Trauma sensitive yoga as a complementary treatment for posttraumatic stress disorder: A qualitative descriptive analysis. *International Journal of Stress Management*, 24, 173–195. http://dx.doi.org/10.1037/str0000040

White, M. G. (2019). *Which professionals are prone to burnout?* Love to Know: https://stress.lovetoknow.com/Which_Professionals_are_Prone_to_Burnout.

Wilson, J. P., & Lindy, J. D. (Ed.) (1994). *Countertransference in the treatment of PTSD*. New York: Guilford Press.

Wisconsin Department of Public Instruction (2019). *School mental health project*. https://dpi.wi.gov/sspw/mental-health/trauma.

Wolynn, M. (2016). *It didn't start with you: How inherited family trauma shapes who we are and how to end the cycle*. New York: Viking.

Yehuda, R., Engel, S. M., Brand, S. R., Seckl, J., Marcus, S. M., & Berkowitz, G. S. (2005). Transgenerational effects of posttraumatic stress disorder in babies of mothers exposed to the world trade center attacks during pregnancy, *Journal of Clinical Endocrinology & Metabolism* 90(7) (July 2005), 4115–4118.

Index

A

acceptance 99, 100, 108, 170
accountability 216, 222, 278, 280, 282, 283, 288, 290
Accountability Fallacy 288
ADHD 18, 79, 103
adrenal glands 41
adrenaline 41
Adverse Childhood Experience Study 22
affirmations 100, 102, 103
amygdala 41, 42, 43, 54, 72, 77, 79, 158, 234, 262
anger 43, 76, 77, 88, 110, 113, 114, 118, 130, 133, 134, 149, 172, 190, 191, 225, 227, 269, 294, 304
anxiety 29, 35, 36, 58, 76, 77, 79, 83, 84, 86, 106, 149, 196, 239, 240, 244, 245, 260
anxious relational template 36
art therapy 202, 301
Assessment of Lagging Skills and Unsolved Problems 120
attachment 34, 35, 36, 37, 181, 187, 194, 202, 309, 314
attention grabbers 159
avoidant relational templates 35
awareness 79, 202, 247, 248, 263, 285, 316

B

background check 183
back-to-school nights 185
behavioral-management systems 97, 118, 119, 142, 144, 148
behavior-management skills 157
belly breathing 80, 91, 130, 158, 173
brain 12, 14, 15, 33, 34, 35, 37, 38, 39, 40, 43, 44, 49, 50, 51, 53, 54, 55, 56, 57, 61, 66, 72, 77, 79, 80, 81, 85, 86, 91, 94, 95, 96, 108, 114, 121, 137, 142, 145, 146, 154, 157, 159, 160, 161, 162, 164, 166, 190, 203, 234, 248, 258, 259, 260, 261, 262, 268, 282, 300, 301, 309, 311, 312, 313, 314, 316, 317, 318
breaks 73, 83, 91, 232, 268, 270
Broca's area 54, 55, 76
bully 47, 54, 59, 96
bullying 23, 59, 82, 108, 110, 112
burnout 232, 233, 234, 237, 240, 241, 242, 256, 260, 264, 267, 270, 272, 273, 274, 275, 286, 289, 290, 294, 315, 318, 319

C

callousness 248, 249, 250
cause and effect 44, 51, 57, 119, 123, 137, 140, 142, 143, 145
Centers for Disease Control and Prevention 22, 311
chaos 28, 29, 47, 105, 109, 142, 150, 172, 177, 208, 235
check-ins 77, 91, 92, 109, 171
closed questions 103
cognitive-behavioral therapy 97
cognitive dissonance 123

Come If We Call Schools 181, 182, 189
community agencies 189, 199, 200, 206, 210, 218
community meetings 108
community partners 199, 200, 206, 221, 223, 291
compassion 99, 100, 108, 111, 116, 118, 151, 249, 253, 262, 278, 279, 290
complex reflections 101, 105, 236
consequences 12, 17, 27, 35, 38, 40, 44, 48, 51, 55, 58, 61, 72, 97, 98, 107, 110, 113, 114, 115, 117, 120, 121, 138, 140, 142, 150, 232, 241, 245, 246, 257, 261, 312
cortex 40, 42, 44, 45, 50, 55, 56, 60, 77, 79, 82, 107, 154, 158, 160, 161, 234, 262
cortisol 38, 41, 54, 79, 105, 106, 259, 260
crisis 50, 217, 250, 251, 310, 314
curiosity 54, 60, 95, 127, 147, 179, 192
cynicism 248, 249, 250

D

depression 76, 79, 84, 118, 245, 260
DHT 105, 106, 107
diet 16, 261, 271, 300
differentiated instruction 154, 155
digestion 41
dihydrotestosterone 105
disconnecting 248, 270
disorganized behaviors 36
disorganized relationship templates 58
distractions 268, 269, 301
DNA 34, 296
doubt 9, 244, 247
dysregulation 72

E

educational assistants 10, 297
education fatigue 8, 244
emotional regulation 34, 39, 40, 53, 71, 73, 75, 77, 79, 80, 81, 83, 85, 87, 89, 91, 105, 107, 119, 144, 154, 157, 158, 179, 190, 202, 203, 205, 234, 298, 301
emotions 35, 36, 41, 42, 43, 45, 49, 50, 55, 67, 72, 75, 76, 86, 89, 91, 96, 107, 118, 123, 133, 135, 136, 142, 145, 148, 149, 150, 157, 158, 168, 202, 203, 208, 209, 217, 226, 239, 260, 270, 271, 279, 280, 288, 291, 297
empathetic intensity 238
empathy 35, 50, 99, 101, 103, 113, 116, 119, 121, 123, 188, 238, 249, 262, 279, 281, 290, 294
employee assistance program 221
epigenetics 34, 72
episodic memory 56, 57
executive functioning 40, 41, 42
exercise 9, 259, 260, 318
exhaustion 9, 244, 245, 250
expectations 12, 13, 45, 49, 50, 51, 78, 79, 98, 106, 119, 120, 137, 138, 139, 140, 141, 142, 144, 145, 146, 147, 148, 149, 151, 152, 153, 156, 158, 164, 165, 167, 168, 171, 173, 219, 220, 222, 247, 280, 281, 282, 283, 284, 289, 290
expressive language 54, 55, 76, 95, 160
expulsions 12, 98, 117

F

family center 197, 198, 199, 200, 206, 208, 209, 210, 212, 225, 235, 251, 292
fear 19, 22, 35, 36, 43, 76, 77, 90, 108, 118, 196, 197, 207, 208, 227, 239, 293
fight 25, 41, 42, 43, 44, 54, 57, 62, 63, 80, 109, 202, 209, 235, 249, 260, 279
fit 289
fixed mindset 82, 83, 84, 85, 118, 204
flight 16, 42, 43, 44, 54, 57, 62, 63, 80, 202, 235, 249
food security 198, 300
Fortress Schools 181, 182, 189
freeze 42, 43, 44, 57, 63, 202, 211, 235, 292

G

gratification 58
growth mindset 83, 84, 85, 103, 155, 156, 166, 201, 204, 205, 284
Guilt 9, 242, 244, 247

H

hippocampus 41, 43, 56, 160, 161, 162
homeless 198, 247, 310
honesty 9, 280, 281
hope 25, 45, 52, 59, 66, 67, 83, 84, 85, 86, 102, 108, 116, 118, 165, 170, 188, 191, 193, 197, 205, 206, 210, 215, 240, 266, 272, 295, 302, 304
HPA axis 41, 42
hypothalamus 41

I

I message 95
integration 203, 204, 205, 262, 305
intergenerational trauma 37, 38
island of competence 155, 156

L

labeling 55, 76, 145, 148
language 54, 55, 56, 76, 84, 89, 91, 95, 103, 109, 139, 160, 162, 185, 186, 199, 207, 237, 273, 275
lesson planning 27, 157, 164, 233

M

memory 40, 43, 56, 57, 137, 138, 139, 145, 160, 161, 162, 203, 258, 260
mental health 23, 50, 117, 195, 206, 233, 246, 253, 255, 260, 261, 262, 267, 285, 288, 299, 310, 316, 319
mind 25, 33, 47, 48, 52, 54, 67, 72, 78, 82, 105, 112, 130, 135, 156, 159, 209, 210, 219, 236, 245, 246, 257, 259, 260, 262, 265, 268, 273, 274, 291, 294, 313, 317, 319
mindfulness 6, 9, 74, 78, 79, 262, 263, 310
mind health 262
mirror 7, 161, 162
moral action 123
Motivational Interviewing 101, 309
multitasking 268
music therapists 301, 302

N

nervous system 72, 80, 106, 146, 259
neurogenesis 38, 39, 260
neurons 38
neuroplasticity 66
neuroscience 56, 66, 72, 154, 159, 311
noncoding DNA 34
nonverbal students 76
norepinephrine 41

O

OARS 6, 100, 101, 102, 103, 104, 105, 106, 107, 119, 126, 176, 191, 238, 294
occupational therapists 185
Open-Door Schools 181, 182, 189
open-ended questions 104
oxytocin 106, 107

P

paddlings 117
partnerships 100, 177, 178, 182, 199, 200, 201, 218, 312, 316
Partnership Schools 181, 182, 183, 189
passion 19, 25, 64, 70, 86, 93, 95, 228, 249, 264, 265, 306, 307, 308, 312
perfectionistic 54
personal narrative 204
physical health 256
physical safety 107, 108, 282
pituitary gland 41
play therapy 202

policymaker 15
post-traumatic growth 61, 62, 84, 203, 205, 286
prefrontal cortex 40, 42, 44, 45, 50, 55, 56, 60, 77, 79, 82, 107, 154, 158, 160, 161, 234, 262
Professional Quality of Life Measure 244
pruning 39
psychological safety 108, 202, 281, 282, 285
PTA/PTO 187
PTSD 18, 41, 79, 238, 252, 312, 315, 316, 319
punishments 97, 121, 142, 143, 144, 145, 149, 166
purpose 41, 204, 264, 265, 271

R

rainbow breathing 80, 90
rattlesnake 71
realistic optimism 266
receptive language 54, 55, 95
recognition 149, 280, 283, 284
reflections 6, 101
reframing 84
regulate 35, 36, 50, 61, 72, 75, 77, 78, 86, 107, 123, 135, 136, 138, 141, 145, 146, 148, 149, 157, 158, 171, 203, 260, 262, 297, 302
relate 7, 146
repressed memories 203
resilience 79, 84, 314, 318
restorative justice 121
retraumatized 41, 163, 253
rewards 12, 44, 51, 58, 95, 100, 142, 143, 144, 145, 148, 149
rigid 51, 158, 234
RNA 34
robustness 233, 234, 267, 303

S

safety 6, 9, 59, 107, 281

school climate 277
school culture 277
secure attachment 34, 35, 36, 194, 202
self-regulation 55, 75, 78, 94, 315
sensory strategies 72, 75
sequential memories 56
serve-and-return 94, 96, 101, 107, 113, 126, 132, 159, 160, 164, 168, 172, 187
shame 48, 82, 99, 145, 149, 186, 197, 247, 248, 249, 250, 264, 267
simple reflections 101
skill building 119
sleep 16, 52, 175, 196, 239, 243, 245, 256, 257, 258, 259, 269, 283, 313, 316
social health 270
social networks 270
special education 19, 57, 75, 76, 78, 116, 310
speech-language support 56
speech-language therapists 185
square breathing 81, 263
standardized testing 53
statements 6, 103, 104, 196
states 5, 6, 28, 43, 75, 117, 198, 318
Stop, Start, Continue, Change 218, 223
summaries 100, 104, 105
suspensions 12, 48, 98, 117, 224, 298, 305
sympathetic nervous system 80
synapses 38, 39

T

task-specific expectations 140
thalamus 40, 41
therapy 9, 202, 267
toxic cycle 278
traits 5, 43, 57
transitions 24, 50, 77, 78, 81, 82, 124, 141, 142, 158, 184, 216, 297
trauma assessments 194
trauma-sensitive classrooms 72, 83, 102, 156
trauma-sensitive coaching 10, 284
trauma-sensitive environment 149, 301

trauma-sensitive leader 287, 288
Trauma-Sensitive School Checklist 215, 218, 223
trauma-sensitive schools 11, 14, 106, 118, 170, 171, 182, 189, 197, 198, 201, 269, 281, 302, 303, 311
trauma-sensitive transformation team 8, 205, 206, 211, 219, 220, 221, 222, 223, 224, 225, 228, 230, 251, 252, 255, 272, 293, 305
trauma treatment 195, 201, 202, 221
triggers 55, 122, 162, 163, 164, 203, 245, 246, 248, 253
trust 36, 45, 79, 102, 105, 106, 107, 108, 168, 170, 175, 183, 184, 188, 189, 198, 201, 202, 209, 279, 280, 281, 282, 285, 288
turn and talk 160, 161
two-generation approach 179

U

universal expectations 138, 139
unworthiness 118, 149, 163

V

vagus nerve 42
values 122, 123, 185, 277

W

wait time 96, 111
Wernicke's area 54

Y

yoga 74, 82, 263, 316

Z

zone 76, 77, 78, 88, 89, 90, 91, 109, 124, 138, 146, 168, 173, 286